COMMUNITY ANALYSIS
AND PLANNING TECHNIQUES

COMMUNITY ANALYSIS AND PLANNING TECHNIQUES

Richard E. Klosterman

ROWMAN & LITTLEFIELD PUBLISHERS, INC.
Lanham • Boulder • New York • Toronto • Plymouth, UK

ROWMAN & LITTLEFIELD PUBLISHERS, INC.

Published in the United States of America
by Rowman & Littlefield Publishers, Inc.
A wholly owned subsidary of The Rowman & Littlefield Publishing Group, Inc.
4501 Forbes Boulevard, Suite 200, Lanham, Maryland 20706
www.rowmanlittlefield.com

PO Box 317
Oxford
OX2 9RU, UK

British Library Cataloguing in Publication Information Available

Library of Congress Cataloging-in-Publication Data

Klosterman, Richard E.
Community analysis and planning techniques/Richard E.
Klosterman.
p.   cm.
Includes bibliographical references.
1. City planning—Statistical methods.   2. City
planning—Data processing.   3. Urban economics—
Statistical methods.   I. Title.
HT166.K5845   1990
307.1'2'015195—dc20   89-70193

ISBN 0-8476-3951-7 (alk. paper)
ISBN 0-8476-7651-X (pbk. alk. paper)

Printed in the United States of America

 ^{TM} The paper used in this publication meets the minimum requirements of
American National Standard for Information Sciences—Permanence of
Paper for Printed Library Materials, ANSI Z39.48–1984.

To Kathie, Michelle, and Kimberly,
my parents, and friends,
who make it all worthwhile.

Contents

Illustrations

FIGURES

TABLES

Preface

Computers first entered city and regional planning in the early 1960s on the crest of a general belief that scientific methods and computer-assisted analytic techniques could solve society's most pressing problems. The unparalleled accuracy and apparently unlimited computational power of computers seemed to foreshadow the birth of a new urban planning based on the scientific understanding and guidance of the urban development process. Computerized models of the city promised to increase planners' understanding of the urban development process, to improve their ability to identify the effects of public and private actions, and to allow them to forecast accurately future states of the metropolis. This obvious appeal and the availability of large federal research grants led to the development of ambitious and well-financed metropolitan simulation efforts in Pittsburgh, San Francisco, and several other American cities.

Urban planning's first computer revolution had ended, largely in defeat, by the mid-1970s. Experience revealed that the large-scale urban development models were overly comprehensive and complex, inadequately grounded in theory and data, and poorly adapted to the needs of policymakers. Computers were still used by transportation planners to model traffic behavior, by economists to build sophisticated econometric and input-output models, and by some large planning agencies. However, most planning agencies had no access to computers, and the majority of planners continued to employ manual computational procedures that had changed little since the 1950s. Computer use in planning schools was similarly limited primarily to the use of social science–oriented statistical packages and specialized packages for computer mapping and transportation planning.

This book introduces and describes four techniques, which are at the core of professional practice and education: The first technique, curve-fitting/extrapolation, projects an area's population, employment, or other characteristics by identifying and extending historical trends. The second technique, the cohort-component technique, projects an area's population by dividing it into a uniform set of population subgroups or cohorts and applying the three components of population change—mortality, fertility, and migration—to each cohort. The third technique, the economic base technique, projects local economic change by dividing a local economy into basic and nonbasic sectors and by focusing analytic attention on the basic sector. The fourth technique, the shift-share technique, projects an area's economic activity by relating it to the activity of the state or nation in which it is located.

This book provides (1) examples of each technique; (2) thorough discussions of their underlying assumptions, advantages, and limitations; (3) decision criteria for selecting the most acceptable projection (or projections); and (4) extensive reference lists. The text can be used in graduate or advanced undergraduate methods courses and by practitioners and others seeking a detailed introduction to each technique.

The three chapters in Part One of this text examine the curve-fitting/extrapolation technique. Chapter 1 offers a brief introductory view of the technique. Chapter 2 describes six curves that can be used to describe and extend past trends: linear, geometric, parabolic, modified exponential, Gompertz, and logistic. Chapter 3 describes the criteria for evaluating alternative projections for a particular data set and assesses the extrapolation technique. Appendix A provides computational examples using data from a real community to illustrate the required procedures for fitting and extrapolating each curve.

Part Two describes the cohort-component technique. Chapter 4 introduces the technique, and Chapters 5, 6, and 7 examine the three components of population change—mortality, fertility, and migration—and use data from an actual community to illustrate the computational procedures for projecting each component. Chapter 8 integrates the three components into a complete projection model, describes criteria for evaluating alternative projections, and assesses the cohort-component technique.

Part Three considers the economic base and shift-share projection techniques. Chapter 9 introduces these techniques, and Chapters 10 and 11 use data from an actual community to describe and evaluate three procedures for estimating the basic and nonbasic sectors of a local economy. Chapter 12 examines and assesses the constant-share and shift-share projection techniques. Chapter 13 reviews procedures for converting basic sector projections into other projections of interest and evaluates the economic base technique.

Note

The following materials are also available from the author:

The Community Analysis and Planning Programs (CAPP), an integrated set of menu-driven programs for the IBM Personal Computer and compatible equipment, that implement the computational techniques described in the *Community Analysis and Planning Techniques* textbook. CAPP works with data from readily available published sources and includes help screens, data-entry prompts, error checks, and on-screen and hard copy graphics output for most printers and plotters. The *CAPP Users Guide* (Klosterman 1989) provides: detailed guidance on CAPP installation and use; sample program input and output; complete information on sources for all required data; and extensive lists of federal and state agencies providing these data at little or no cost.

The *Community Analysis and Planning Techniques Workbook* containing a collection of worksheets that duplicate the computational examples in the *Community Analysis and Planning Techniques* textbook. The worksheets allow hand computational methods to be used in applying the analysis techniques described in the textbook to readily available information for a real community. They can also be used with the examples in the textbook to prepare electronic spreadsheets for conducting the desired analyses. An instructor's package is also available providing sample homework and examination questions, class assignments, and transparencies for all of the tables and figures in *Community Analysis and Planning Techniques*.

The *Community Analysis and Planning Techniques* text, Community Analysis and Planning Programs, and *CAPP Users Guide* provide an integrated package designed to meet the analytic needs of practitioners and the instructional needs of educators. Together, they make sophisticated computer-assisted analytic techniques available to practitioners, students, and private citizens with limited technical skills, limited computer experience, and minimal computer equipment.

For further information contact:

Richard E. Klosterman
Center for Urban Studies
University of Akron
Akron, Ohio 44325-7903

Acknowledgments

I would first like to acknowledge the assistance of the numerous students and research assistants who suffered through and helped improve several earlier versions of the textbook. Their eagerness to help me complete and improve the book made its preparation more enjoyable and the result immeasurably better.

I would also like to acknowledge the assistance of Andrew Isserman of the West Virginia University, who took time from his busy schedule to read the entire text and offer many extremely helpful suggestions. Charlie Hoch of the University of Illinois at Chicago, Richard K. Brail of Rutgers University, and many other colleagues also provided greatly appreciated assistance and support.

Most important, I would like to thank my family for the understanding and support they provided as I struggled with "Daddy's boring old book."

Part One

The Extrapolation Technique

The curve-fitting/extrapolation techniques described in Chapters 1 to 3 are more formal, explicit, and reproducible versions of graphical techniques in which the analyst plots the data for the past, visually fits a curve to the data, and extends the curve by hand to project future values. The underlying procedure is identical: A curve is selected that "best fits" the past data. This curve is then extended to project future values. However, mathematical extrapolation techniques replace the intuitive process of visually fitting a curve with explicit quantitative criteria for identifying the best-fitting curve. They also replace the judgmental extension of the best-fitting curve with formal computational procedures for continuing past trends.

Chapters 2 and 3 describe six different curves that can be used to project a given set of observation data. Chapter 2 describes the six curves: linear, geometric, parabolic, modified exponential, Gompertz, and logistic. Computational procedures for fitting and extrapolating these six curves are described in detail in Appendix A and illustrated with fully worked-out computational examples. Chapter 3 examines a number of criteria for evaluating alternative projections and assesses the extrapolation technique.

Chapter 1

Extrapolation Technique: An Introduction

Since its beginning at the turn of the century, urban and regional planning has been largely justified as an institutional mechanism for providing information about the future to guide current decision making (Klosterman 1985). As experts on future trends, local planners are faced with a particularly difficult task—preparing reliable long-term (20- to 30-year) projections for small areas such as counties, cities, and neighborhoods. Reliable short-term projections for these areas are relatively easy to prepare because 2- or 3-year demographic and economic changes are generally small. Reliable long-term projections for large areas such as countries are not difficult because growth or decline in some subregions is generally offset by countervailing changes in others. Long-term changes for small areas can be large, making reliable forecasts difficult to prepare.[1]

The forecasting task confronting planners is further complicated by a lack of reliable, timely, and consistent information at the proper level of spatial and sectoral aggregation and by an inadequate understanding of the complex relationships that shape society. Predictions in the natural sciences are based on well-developed bodies of theory and carefully controlled experiments. Such assurance is impossible in the social sphere. Private sector forecasts are based on large quantities of reliable current and historical data that are unavailable in the public sector. As a result, forecasters in these areas can rely on sophisticated projection techniques that are inappropriate for most public sector applications.[2]

3

Planners' attempts to project the future are frustrated by the fact that they are no more able to see the future than the public they serve. As a result, their projection techniques are only quantitative procedures for using limited information about the past and simplifying assumptions about the future to predict the unknowable future. The planners' task is to combine the most reliable information about the past with the most appropriate assumptions about the future to prepare the best possible forecast. To ask for more is to require the impossible.

Paradoxically, attempts to predict the future may inhibit good planning by helping create conditions that are neither inevitable nor desirable. Areas forecasted to grow will often do so because people and firms are attracted to them by the prospect of jobs and markets and because public infrastructure has been provided in the anticipation of the predicted growth. Declining regions are often handicapped because private firms are reluctant to invest in areas predicted to recede. Planning assumes that individuals and regions can control their fate and take action to forestall undesirable futures. To the extent that effective planning is able to create a better future, planning "success" may mean forecasting "failure" (Isserman and Fisher 1984, 36–37).

ESTIMATES, PROJECTIONS, AND FORECASTS

Population projections and forecasts are among the most important studies prepared by local, state, and national planners. Local comprehensive plans for future residential, commercial, and related land requirements are derived from forecasted population levels and projected space needs per capita. Federal, state, and local funding decisions for capital facilities such as transportation systems, sewage treatment facilities, and schools are based on the projected number of people who will be served by them.

Although the terms are often used interchangeably, it is important to distinguish between *estimates, projections,* and *forecasts.*[3] An *estimate* is an indirect measure of a present or past condition that can be directly measured. For example, the current population of a county could be estimated from systematic data such as voter registration records when a complete population census is impractical.[4]

A *projection* or prediction is a conditional ("if, then") statement about the future. Projections are calculations of future conditions that would exist (the "then") as a result of adopting a set of underlying assumptions (the "if"). For example, an analyst may state, "If current birth, death, and migration rates continue, the county's population will exceed 250,000 in the year 2000." In making this projection, the analyst is not claiming that current rates will continue or that the county's population will exceed 250,000 in 2000. She is not predicting what *will* happen, only stating what would happen *if* other events occur.

As a result, projections can only be wrong if computational errors are made or if faulty data are used. Otherwise, if the projected population levels are not reached, it is because the assumptions did not hold, that is, the "if" did not occur. Since the analyst did not claim that the assumptions would occur, she has made no error.

A *forecast* is a judgmental statement of what the analyst believes to be the most likely future. Unlike analysts who merely state what would happen if a set of assumptions are satisfied, forecasters accept the responsibility for evaluating alternative "ifs" and selecting those that are most likely to occur. On this basis they can proceed to state what they believe the future to be.

The distinction between projections and forecasts is important because planners and public officials often use projections when they should be using (or preparing) forecasts. That is, they base their decisions and recommendations on projections prepared by others without understanding the conditional nature of the projections or determining whether the assumptions underlying the projections are reasonable. Even worse, analysts may prepare projections that they know will be accepted as forecasts without evaluating the assumptions implicit in their analytic results.

EXTRAPOLATION PROCEDURE

The curve-fitting/extrapolation technique described in this part is unique in using aggregate data from the past to project the future. Extrapolation data are aggregated in two ways. First, they consider only the total population or employment of an area without identifying its racial or occupational makeup or other subcomponents of the local population or economy. Second, they deal only with aggregate trends from the past without attempting to identify or account for the underlying demographic and economic processes that caused these trends.

Curve-fitting/extrapolation procedures are theoretically less appealing than the projection techniques examined in Parts Two and Three, which divide an area's population and economy into subcomponents and attempt to identify the underlying causes for past and future trends. Nevertheless, the aggregated analysis provided by extrapolation techniques is perfectly appropriate for many uses. Aggregated data are generally easier to obtain and analyze, which makes extrapolation projections particularly useful when time, resources, and data are limited. Since disaggregated population and employment data are often unavailable for small areas, only aggregated analyses can be prepared. Underlying causal processes may be unknown or too complex to permit detailed modeling. More sophisticated analyses may also be unwarranted if population and employment projections are only minor elements in a more complex projection model (Pittenger 1976, 29–30).

All extrapolations are based on a simple two-stage process. The first stage, curve fitting, analyzes past data to identify an overall trend of growth or decline. The second stage, curve extrapolation, extends this trend to project the future. This process is revealed most clearly in graphical or "judgmental" extrapolations in which the analyst plots the historical data, visually fits a curve to the data, and extends the curve by hand to project future values.

For example, in Figure 1.1 observed population totals for 1930 through 1980 have been plotted, and a solid curve has been drawn to

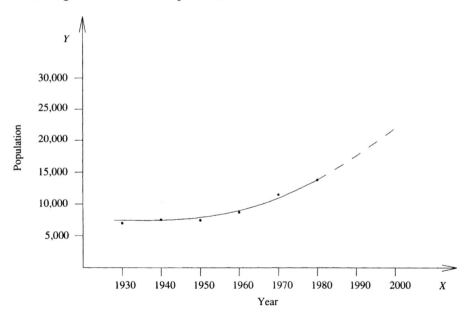

Figure 1.1   Judgmental Trending Example

fit these data. The dotted line extends this curve to project the population in 1990 and 2000.

Graphic conventions assume that the "independent" or "causal" variable is plotted on the horizontal (or X) axis and the "dependent" variable is plotted on the vertical (or Y) axis. This suggests in Figure 1.1 that the area's population is dependent on (or "caused by") time. Clearly this is not the case. Population change reflects the aggregate effect of three other factors—births, deaths, and migration. These three factors are time-related and caused, in turn, by other time-related factors such as health levels and economic conditions. As a result, the time dimension serves as a composite variable reflecting the net effect of a large number of unmeasured events and causal processes.[5]

It is important to recognize that the extrapolation technique should never be used to blindly assume that past trends of growth or decline will continue into the future. Past trends are observed not because they will always continue without change but because they generally provide the best available information about the future. As a result, past trends must be carefully analyzed to determine whether they can be expected to continue. If their continuation seems unlikely, alternative forecasts must be considered.

ENDNOTES

1. These general observations are supported by empirical tests of forecast accuracy. See, for example, Smith (1987b).

2. See Armstrong (1978) for a comprehensive, nontechnical introduction to these more sophisticated forecasting techniques.

3. The following discussion draws heavily on Isserman (1984) and Pittenger (1976, 3–4).

4. Population and economic estimation procedures are not discussed in this book. For excellent reviews of current small-area population estimation techniques, see National Research Council (1980) and Lee and Goldsmith (1982).

5. See Pittenger (1976, 30–44) for a further discussion of the judgmental extrapolation technique.

Chapter 2

Alternative Extrapolation Curves

LINEAR CURVE

The simplest and most widely used extrapolation curve is the linear or first-degree curve, which has the general form

$$Y_C = a + bX \qquad (2.1)$$

As shown in Figure 2.1, the curve is linear because it plots as a straight line; it is a first-degree curve because the highest exponent on the X variable is one. Y_C is the calculated value for the dependent variable (e.g., population or employment) when the independent variable (e.g., time) is equal to X. Y designates the observed values for the dependent variable. For example, for the solid line in Figure 2.1 (curve A) when the observation period, X, is 3, the observed population, Y, is 24,000, and the estimated population, Y_C, is 24,500.

The a and b terms are *parameters* that remain fixed for a given curve and assume different values for different curves. For example, the solid line in Figure 2.1 (curve A) has an a parameter of 20,000 and a b parameter of 1,500; the dashed line (curve B) has an a parameter of 23,000 and a b parameter of 300. X and Y_C are *variables* that assume different values for a particular curve. For example, all of the X and Y_C values on the solid line in Figure 2.1 are related by the linear relationship $Y_C = 20,000 + 1,500X$. Substituting different values for the X variable into this equation yields Y_C values that lie on this line. For example, when $X = 2$, $Y_C = 20,000 + 1,500(2)$, or 23,000, and when $X = 6$, $Y_C = 20,000 + 1,500(6)$, or 29,000.

The X and Y_C values on the dashed line define a second linear curve,

9

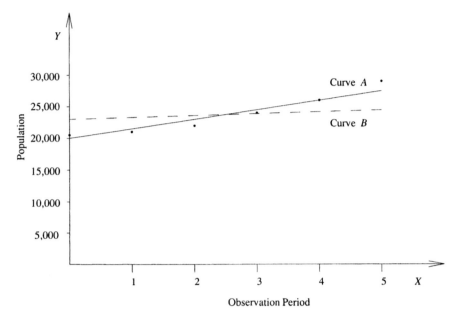

Figure 2.1   Sample Linear Curves

Y_C = 23,000 + 300X. Substituting X values into this equation yields Y_C values that differ from those for the first linear curve. For example, when X = 2, Y_C = 23,000 + 300(2), or 23,600, and when X = 6, Y_C = 23,000 + 300(6), or 24,800.

The a parameter for the linear curve is equal to the Y intercept or the value of Y_C when X is equal to zero. For example, for the solid line in Figure 2.1, the a parameter is equal to 20,000—the value of Y_C when X equals zero.[1] The b parameter is the slope of the line or the change in the dependent variable Y_C for a unit change in the independent variable X. For example, for the solid line in Figure 2.1, the b parameter of 1,500 indicates that each unit increase in observation period is accompanied by a 1,500 increase in the population.

As Figure 2.2 illustrates, the linear curve plots as a straight line because all unit changes in the X variable are accompanied by a constant change in the dependent variable Y_C equal to the b parameter. The linear curve increases without limit if the b parameter is greater than zero and decreases without limit if the b parameter is less than zero. If the b parameter is equal to zero, the curve is a horizontal line.[2]

It is worth noting that the constant incremental growth assumed by the linear curve is rarely appropriate for demographic and economic

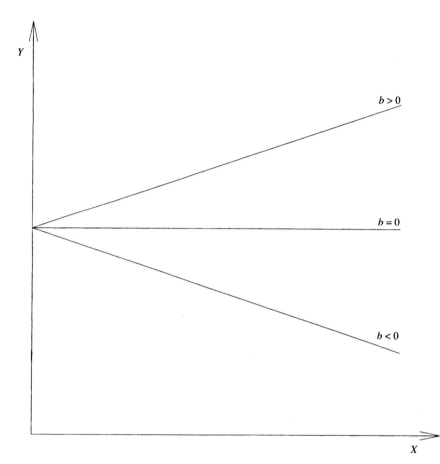

Figure 2.2   Alternate Forms of the Linear Curve

phenomena. Newly developing regions generally experience rapid
growth rates and increasing incremental changes. Growth eventually
levels off as the region matures, leading to declining incremental
changes. As a result, Pittenger (1976, 47) suggests that the linear curve
be used only when data limitations prohibit the use of all other
extrapolation curves. On the other hand, Isserman (1977a) finds that
the linear curve provides the most accurate projections for small, slow-
growing regions in Illinois and Indiana. In any case, analysts cannot
merely assume that the linear curve is the most appropriate model
without considering the other curves described in this chapter.

Least Squares Criterion

A region's population or employment rarely grow in a perfectly linear pattern. As a result, a decision rule must be used to identify the parameters for the linear curve that best fits a particular data set. The most widely used decision rule is the *least squares criterion*, which minimizes the sum of squared deviations (or vertical distances) between the observed values and computed estimates.

Squared deviations are used because the deviations between the observed and estimated values are positive in some cases and negative in others. Adding these positive and negative values may result in cancellations that mask the extent of the actual deviations. For example, Figure 2.1 illustrates two possible linear curves for six population observations. While curve *A* clearly provides the better fit, the sum of the deviations for both curves reported in Table 2.1 is zero, suggesting that the two curves are equally appropriate.

Squared deviations eliminate all negative numbers. As a result, minimizing the sum of these values ensures that the overall error or total distance between the observed and estimated values is as small as possible. For example, in Table 2.1 the sum of squared deviations for curve *A* is dramatically smaller than the sum for curve *B*, indicating that it is clearly the better curve, as visual inspection suggests.

Procedures for identifying the parameters, estimates, and projections for the linear curve that minimizes the sum of squared deviations are a standard feature of statistical packages and elementary textbooks. Particularly convenient procedures fitting and projecting a linear curve by hand or with an electronic spreadsheet are described in detail in Appendix A.

GEOMETRIC CURVE

The second widely used extrapolation curve is the exponential or geometric curve. Exponential curves have the general form

$$Y_C = ae^{bx}$$

where e is a natural number equal to 2.71828.[3] Exponential curves describe the instantaneous rate of compound growth that many natural processes approach as the intervals between the X variables become increasingly smaller. Geometric curves have the general equation

$$Y_C = ab^x \qquad (2.2)$$

Table 2.1

Error of Estimates for Sample Linear Curves

Curve *A* Equation: $Y_C = 20,000 + 1,500X$

Period (1)	Observed (Y) (2)	Estimate (Y_C) (3)	Deviation (Y − Y_C) (4)	Squared Deviation [(Y − Y_C)²] (5)
0	20,500	20,000	500	250,000
1	21,000	21,500	−500	250,000
2	22,000	23,000	−1,000	1,000,000
3	24,000	24,500	−500	250,000
4	26,000	26,000	0	0
5	29,000	27,500	1,500	2,250,000
Sum	...	...	0	4,000,000

Curve *B* Equation: $Y_C = 23,000 + 300X$

Period (1)	Observed (Y) (2)	Estimate (Y_C) (3)	Deviation (Y − Y_C) (4)	Squared Deviation [(Y − Y_C)²] (5)
0	20,500	23,000	−2,500	6,250,000
1	21,000	23,300	−2,300	5,290,000
2	22,000	23,600	−1,600	2,560,000
3	24,000	23,900	100	10,000
4	26,000	24,200	1,800	3,240,000
5	29,000	24,500	4,500	20,250,000
Sum	...	...	0	37,600,000

and describe the compound growth of phenomena measured in discrete time intervals. Because economic and population data are measured at discrete points in time (e.g., by year or by month), the discussion here deals only with geometric curves.

Geometric curves are unique in describing phenomena that grow by a constant growth rate, *r*. The *growth rate* is defined as the change in the dependent variable, *Y*, for a time period divided by the *Y* value at the beginning of the period. That is, the growth rate, *r*, for any period from time *t* to time *t* + 1 is equal to the incremental growth for the period, $Y_{t+1} - Y_t$, divided by the initial value, Y_t, or

$$r = \frac{Y_{t+1} - Y_t}{Y_t} \tag{2.3}$$

Table 2.2 illustrates the difference between the *constant incremental*

Table 2.2

Comparison of Linear and Geometric Curves

Linear Curve Equation: $Y_t = 20{,}000 + 1{,}500X$

Observation Period (X_t)	Linear Value (Y_t)	Growth Increment $(Y_t - Y_{t-1})$	Growth Rate $\left[\dfrac{(Y_t - Y_{t-1})}{Y_t}\right]$
(1)	(2)	(3)	(4)
0	20,000	...	...
1	21,500	1,500	0.075
2	23,000	1,500	0.070
3	24,500	1,500	0.065
4	26,000	1,500	0.061
5	27,500	1,500	0.058

Geometric Curve Equation: $Y_t = 20{,}000(1.5)^X$

Observation Period (X_t)	Geometric Value (Y_t)	Growth Increment $(Y_t - Y_{t-1})$	Growth Rate $\left[\dfrac{(Y_t - Y_{t-1})}{Y_t}\right]$
(1)	(2)	(3)	(4)
0	20,000	...	...
1	30,000	10,000	0.50
2	45,000	15,000	0.50
3	67,500	22,500	0.50
4	101,250	33,750	0.50
5	151,875	50,625	0.50

growth of the linear curve and the *constant growth rate* of the geometric curve. The two curves have the same a parameter and similar b parameters. However, the linear curve has equal growth increments for all values of X and decreasing growth rates. The geometric curve has a constant growth rate, which means that the growth increments increase as X increases.

Examples of geometric growth include money deposited in a savings account yielding a constant interest rate and biological populations whose growth is not limited by resource constraints. For example, the current value of $100 deposited in a savings account yielding 6 percent interest per year can be expressed as a geometric equation by substituting the initial value ($100) for the a parameter and 1.0 plus the interest rate expressed as a decimal for the b parameter. That is,

$$Y_C = \$100(1.00 + 0.06)^x$$

or

$$Y_C = \$100(1.06)^x$$

The current value at any point in time can be computed by substituting the appropriate X value into this equation. For the initial deposit,

$$X = 0$$
$$Y_C = \$100(1.06)^0 = \$100.00$$

After the first year,

$$X = 1$$
$$Y_C = \$100(1.06)^1 = \$106.00$$

After the second year,

$$X = 2$$
$$Y_C = \$100(1.06)^2 = \$112.36$$

and so on. The growth rate r for the first year is equal to

$$r = \frac{\$106.00 - \$100.00}{\$100.00} = \frac{\$6.00}{\$100.00} = 0.06$$

and the growth rate for the second year is

$$r = \frac{\$112.36 - \$106.00}{\$106.00} = \frac{\$6.36}{\$106.00} = 0.06$$

That is, the money is growing at a constant growth of 6 percent equal to the interest rate.

As Figure 2.3 indicates, the a parameter for the geometric curve is equal to the Y intercept or the value of the dependent variable Y when the independent variable X is zero.[4] The b parameter is equal to one plus the growth rate, r. If b is greater than one, the geometric curve increases without limit. If b is between zero and one, the geometric curve approaches zero as X increases. And if b equals one, the geometric curve is equal to a for all values of X.[5]

Extrapolations based on the geometric curve implicitly assume that population or economic growth will continue at a constant rate.[6] As Pittenger points out (1976, 47–53), this assumption is often reasonable because demographic processes generally tend to approach a fixed or intrinsic growth rate. However, because geometric growth continues by increasingly larger increments (if b is greater than one), the geomet-

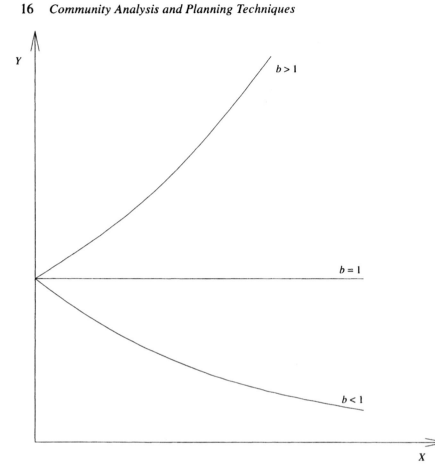

Figure 2.3   Alternate Forms of the Geometric Curve

ric curve may not account for the fact that growth will eventually be restricted by congestion and resource constraints. Thus while possibly appropriate for short-term projections for rapidly growing regions, the geometric curve often produces unrealistically high projections for the long term.

Linear Transformation of Geometric Curve

The geometric curve parameters can be computed by transforming the geometric curve equation, $Y_c = ab^x$, into an equation with the linear form, $Y_C = a + bX$. This allows the relatively straightforward linear curve–fitting equations to be used to fit the geometric curve. This transformation requires the application of the laws of logarithms, which are reviewed in Appendix B. The procedure is as follows:

1. The geometric curve equation is
$$Y_C = ab^X$$
2. Taking the logarithm of both sides of the equation yields
$$\log Y_C = \log (ab^X)$$
3. Applying the law for the logarithm of the product of two numbers yields
$$\log Y_C = \log a + \log (b^X)$$
4. Applying the law for the logarithm of a number raised to a power yields
$$\log Y_C = \log a + \log b(X) \qquad (2.4)$$

Equation (2.4) has the same form as the linear curve $Y_C = a + bX$, except that the Y_C term has been replaced by $\log Y_C$, the a term has been replaced by $\log a$, and the b term has been replaced by $\log b$. As a result, the computational procedures for fitting a linear curve can be used to fit and project the geometric curve. Appendix A illustrates a convenient procedure for fitting and projecting a geometric curve for a set of observation data.

PARABOLIC CURVE

The third extrapolation curve, the *parabolic* or *second-degree* curve, has the following form:

$$Y_C = a + bX + cX^2 \qquad (2.5)$$

Like the linear or first-degree curve, the parabolic curve is a member of a larger family of *polynomial* curves that share the general form

$$Y_C = a + bX + cX^2 + dX^3 + \ldots + mX^n$$

The third-degree (or cubic) curve has the general formula $Y_C = a + bX + cX^2 + dX^3$; the fourth-degree (or quartic) curve has the general formula $Y_C = a + bX + cX^2 + dX^3 + eX^4$; and so on. The degree of these curves is equal to the highest exponent on the independent variable, X, and the number of parameters is equal to the degree of the curve plus one.

As Figure 2.4 indicates, the parabolic curve generally has a con-stantly changing slope and one bend. Given a sufficient range of X values, the parabolic curve is positively inclined (or upward sloping) in one section and negatively inclined (or downward sloping) in another section.

The a parameter is equal to the Y intercept or the value of Y_c when X is equal to zero.[7] The b parameter is equal to the slope (change in Y_c per unit change in X) at the Y intercept. When c is positive, the curve is concave upward. When c is negative, the curve is concave down-ward. And when c is zero, the parabolic curve becomes a linear curve with a Y intercept of a and a slope of b.

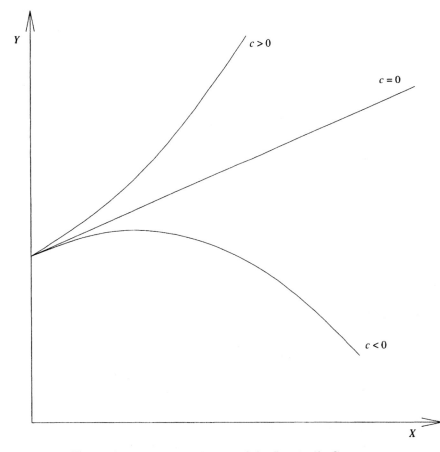

Figure 2.4   Alternate Forms of the Parabolic Curve

As Figure 2.4 indicates, growth increments for the parabolic curve increase or decrease as X increases. While this type of growth may be reasonable for rapidly growing (or declining) areas, extended projections may soon become exceedingly large (or small). As a result, extreme caution should be exercised in using the parabolic curve for long-range projections. Appendix A describes a convenient procedure for fitting and projecting a parabolic curve for a particular set of observation data.[8]

MODIFIED EXPONENTIAL CURVE

Linear, geometric, and parabolic projections generally assume that growth or decline will continue without limit. While these trends may continue for some time, it is extremely unlikely that they will continue forever. At some point a region's growth will be impeded by a lack of adequate resources, public facilities, and other amenities. Declining communities rarely disappear entirely; rather, they decline only until they reach population and employment levels appropriate to their current position in the regional or national economy. In both cases it seems reasonable to assume that long-term growth or decline will continue at a decreasing rate until the region's population or employment approaches an upper or lower limit.

The modified exponential curve is one of a number of *asymptotic growth curves* that recognize that a region's population or employment will eventually approach an upper or lower growth limit or asymptote.[9] The general equation for the modified exponential curve is

$$Y_c = c + ab^x \tag{2.6}$$

which is equivalent to the geometric curve, $Y_c = ab^x$, with an additional parameter, c.

As shown in Figure 2.5, the modified exponential curve assumes four different shapes depending on the values of the a and b parameters. The most interesting version, graph (a), has a negative a parameter and a b parameter between zero and one. In this situation the c parameter is an upper asymptote, which Y_c approaches as X increases. That is, as X increases, the value of Y_c gets closer and closer to—but never equals—the asymptotic value c.

This form of modified exponential curve is illustrated in Figure 2.6, which plots the curve $Y_c = 114 - 64(0.75)^x$. The c parameter, 114, is the upper limit that Y_c approaches as X increases. The Y intercept, 50,

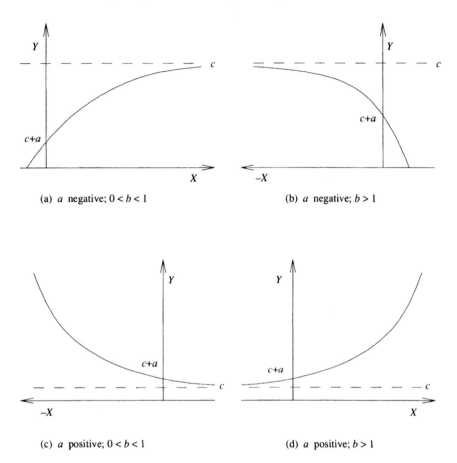

(a) *a* negative; $0 < b < 1$ (b) *a* negative; $b > 1$

(c) *a* positive; $0 < b < 1$ (d) *a* positive; $b > 1$

Figure 2.5   Alternate Forms of the Modified Exponential Curve

Source: Croxton, Cowden, and Klein (1967, 264). Reprinted with modified labels by permission.

is equal to the upper limit, 114, plus the *a* parameter, -64.[10] The *b* parameter, 0.75, is equal to the ratio of successive growth increments. For example, when $X = 0$, $Y_C = 114 - 64(0.75)^0$, or 50.0. When $X = 1$, $Y_C = 114 - 64(0.75)^1$, or 66. And when $X = 2$, $Y_C = 114 - 64(0.75)^2$, or 78. The growth increment for the first interval is $66 - 50$, or 16; the growth increment for the second interval is $78 - 66$, or 12.

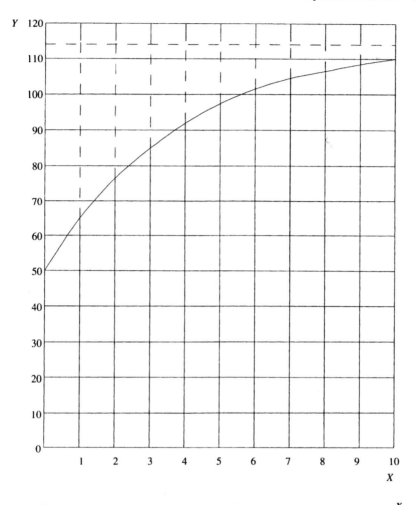

Figure 2.6   Modified Exponential Curve for $Y_C = 114 - 64(0.75)^X$

Source: Croxton, Cowden, and Klein (1967, 265). Reprinted by permission.

The ratio of these increments, 12/16, or 0.75 is equal to the *b* parameter.

The difference between the upper limit, *c,* and the modified exponential curve, Y_C is equal to ab^x. If *b* is less than one, b^x decreases as X increases, and the difference becomes increasingly smaller. However, no matter how large X gets, b^x is never equal to zero, which means that Y_C is never equal to *c.*

The modified exponential curve has obvious theoretical appeal in recognizing that growth or decline must eventually taper off. It also allows the analyst to assume an upper or lower growth limit or to derive the limit implicit in past trends (given appropriate values of the *a* and *b* parameters). If this limit is reasonable given past information on the analysis region and regions with similar growth histories, the modified exponential projections are supported. If the limit is unreasonable, the modified exponential estimates and projections curve are also questioned.

Linear Transformation for Assumed Growth Limits

As already noted, logarithms can be used to convert the geometric curve, $Y_C = ab^x$, to the linear form, $\log Y_C = \log a + \log b(X)$. This allows the linear curve–fitting procedures to be used to fit the geometric curve. Similar procedures can be used to convert the modified exponential curve with an assumed upper or lower growth limit to the linear form.

The procedure for projections with an assumed upper limit, *c*, that is, for the situation shown in graph (a) of Figure 2.5, is the following:

1. The *a* parameter for curves with an upper growth limit is negative; as a result the modified exponential curve equation can be expressed as follows:
$$Y_C = c - ab^x$$
2. Rearranging terms yields
$$c - Y_C = ab^x$$
3. Taking the logarithms of both sides yields
$$\log (c - Y_C) = \log (ab^x)$$
4. Applying the laws for the logarithms of products and powers yields
$$\log (c - Y_C) = \log a + \log b(X) \tag{2.7}$$

Similarly, the *a* parameter for modified exponential curves with a lower growth limit is positive. As a result, the modified exponential curve equation can be expressed
$$Y_C = c + ab^x$$

Rearranging terms and applying logarithms yields the following formula for modified exponential curve for an assumed lower limit, c, that is, for the situation shown in graph (c) of Figure 2.5:

$$\log (Y_C - c) = \log a + \log b(X) \tag{2.8}$$

Equations (2.7) and (2.8) have the same form as the linear curve, $Y_C = a + bX$, except that the Y_C term is replaced by $\log (c - Y_C)$ or $\log (Y_C - c)$, the a term is replaced by $\log a$, and the b term is replaced by $\log b$. As a result, the procedures for fitting a linear curve can be used to fit and project a modified exponential curve for a particular data set and assumed growth limit. Appendix A illustrates a convenient procedure for doing this. It also describes a method for computing the growth limit and the other curve parameters and for using these values to project the modified exponential curve that best fits a particular data set.

GOMPERTZ CURVE

The fifth extrapolation curve is the Gompertz curve developed by Benjamin Gompertz (1779–1865), an English actuary and mathematician.[11] The general equation for the Gompertz curve is

$$Y_C = ca \exp (b^x) \tag{2.9}$$

that is, the dependent variable, Y_C, is equal to the c parameter multiplied by the a parameter raised to the b^x power.

Applying logarithms to the Gompertz curve demonstrates that it is very similar to the modified exponential curve. Taking the logarithm of both sides of Eq. (2.9) yields

$$\log Y_C = \log [ca \exp (b^x)]$$

Applying the law for the logarithm of products yields

$$\log Y_C = \log c + \log [a \exp (b^x)]$$

Applying the law for the logarithm of powers yields

$$\log Y_C = \log c + \log a(b^x) \tag{2.10}$$

Expressed as Eq. (2.10), the Gompertz curve equation is identical to the modified exponential equation, $Y_C = c + ab^x$, except that $\log Y_C$, $\log c$, and $\log a$ replace the Y_C, c, and a terms. As a result, the Gompertz curve grows by a constant ratio of the increments in the *logarithms* of the observations comparable to the constant ratio of the *growth increments* for the modified exponential curve.[12]

As shown in Figure 2.7, the Gompertz curve is similar to the modified exponential curve in assuming different shapes depending on the values of the *a* and *b* parameters. The most interesting version is graph (a), in which the logarithm of the *a* parameter is negative and the *b* parameter is between zero and one. In this case the Gompertz curve is "S"-shaped with an upper limit of *c* for large positive values

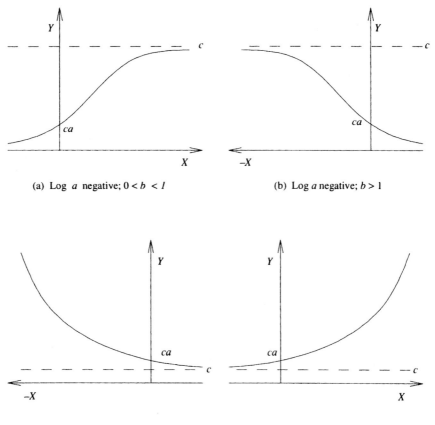

(a) Log *a* negative; $0 < b < 1$ (b) Log *a* negative; $b > 1$

(c) Log *a* positive; $0 < b < 1$ (d) Log *a* positive; $b > 1$

Figure 2.7   Alternate Forms of the Gompertz Curve

Source: Croxton, Cowden, and Klein (1967, 264). Reprinted with the modified labels by permission.

of X and a lower limit of zero for large negative values of X. That is, if b is less than one, b^x approaches zero as X increases. As a result, the Gompertz curve approaches ca^0, or the upper limit of c for large positive values of X. And if b is less than one, b^x grows rapidly for increasingly large negative values of X. As a result, the curve approaches zero for large negative values of X.

For these parameter values, the Gompertz curve describes a growth pattern that is initially quite slow, increases for a period, and then tapers off so that the dependent variable approaches an upper limit or asymptote. This upper limit can either be assumed or derived from the observation data to provide an independent check on the Gompertz projections.

Linear Transformation for Assumed Growth Limits

As is true for the modified exponential curve, logarithms can be used to convert the transformed Gompertz curve, $\log Y_C = \log c + \log a(b^x)$, into the linear form, $Y_C = a + bX$. This allows the linear curve–fitting procedures to be used to fit a Gompertz curve to a set of observation data with assumed upper or lower growth limits. The procedure is identical to that for the modified exponential curve except that $\log c$ replaces the c term, $\log Y_C$ replaces the Y_C term, and $\log a$ replaces the a term.

As a result, the transformed Gompertz curve for an assumed upper limit, c, that is, for the situation in graph (a) of Figure 2.7, is the following:

$$\log (\log c - \log Y_C) = \log (\log a) + \log b(X) \qquad (2.11)$$

The transformed Gompertz curve for an assumed lower limit, c, that is, for the situation shown in graph (c) of Figure 2.7, is the following:

$$\log (\log Y_C - \log c) = \log (\log a) + \log b(X) \qquad (2.12)$$

Appendix A illustrates the use of these equations to derive the Gompertz curve parameters, estimates, and projections that best fit a given data set and assumed growth limit c. It also describes a procedure for computing the growth limit and other curve parameters and using these values to calculate the Gompertz estimates and projections that best fit a set of observation data.

LOGISTIC CURVE

Perhaps the most popular equation for describing population growth is the logistic curve discovered in the 1830s by the Belgian mathematician P. F. Verhurst.[13] The curve was subsequently forgotten and rediscovered in the 1920s by Raymond Pearl and Lowell J. Reed and is thus frequently referred to as the *Pearl-Reed curve* or *Pearl curve*.

The equation for the logistic curve is

$$\frac{1}{Y_C} = c + ab^x$$

that is,

$$Y_C^{-1} = c + ab^x \qquad (2.13)$$

or

$$Y_C = \frac{1}{c + ab^x}$$

that is,

$$Y_C = (c + ab^x)^{-1} \qquad (2.14)$$

The logistic curve is identical to the modified exponential and Gompertz curves except that the observed values of the modified exponential curve and the logarithms of observed values of the Gompertz curves have been replaced by *reciprocals* of the observed values. As a result, the ratio of successive growth increments for the reciprocals of the Y_C values for the logistic curve are equal to a constant.[14]

As shown in Figure 2.8, the logistic curve is similar to the modified exponential and Gompertz curves in adopting different shapes depending on the values of the curve parameters. Of particular interest is the

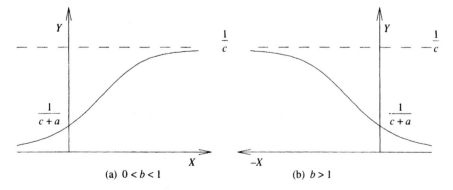

(a) $0 < b < 1$ (b) $b > 1$

Figure 2.8   Alternate Forms of the Logistic Curve

logistic curve for a *b* parameter between zero and one.[15] In this situation, the logistic curve assumes an "S" shape similar to the Gompertz curve when log *a* is negative and *b* is between zero and one. For these values, the logistic curve approaches an upper limit of $1/c$ for large positive values of *X* and a lower limit of zero for large negative values of *X*.[16] When *X* is equal to zero, the *Y* intercept is equal to $1/(c + ab^0)$ or $1/(c + a)$.

This form of the logistic curve has a great deal of theoretical appeal for describing phenomena that have small initial growth increments followed by rapid growth and then increasingly slower growth that continues until the curve approaches an upward limit. Studies by Pearl and Reed and others demonstrate that this curve accurately describes a wide range of phenomena including the growth of albino rats and the tails of tadpoles and the number of fruit flies in a bottle with a limited food supply.

Pearl and Reed used the logistic curve to project the population of the United States just before the release of the 1920 population census. A logistic curve was fit to population data from the 1790 through 1910 national censuses. This provided remarkably accurate projections through the year 1950. Projection errors ranged from less than 0.4 percent for 1930 to 3.5 percent for 1940. However, the 1960 projection was 159.2 million, whereas the actual population—including the new states of Alaska and Hawaii—was 179.3 million. The curve's upper asymptote was 197.3 million, which is less than the 1970 census count of 203.2 million (Pittenger 1976, 62–63).[17]

Linear Transformation for Assumed Growth Limits

As is true for the modified exponential and Gompertz curves, logarithms can be used to transform the logistic curve, $Y_C^{-1} = c + ab^X$, into the linear form, $Y_C = a + bX$. The procedure is identical to that for the modified exponential curve, except that Y_C^{-1} replaces the Y_C term and only one equation is required for an assumed upper or lower growth limit.[18] As a result, the transformed logistic curve equation for an assumed upper or lower growth limit, $1/c$, is the following:

$$\log (Y_C^{-1} - c) = \log a + \log b(X) \qquad (2.15)$$

Equation (2.15) has the same form as the linear curve, $Y_C = a + bX$, except that $\log (Y_C^{-1} - c)$ replaces the Y_C term, $\log a$ replaces the *a* term, and $\log b$ replaces the *b* term. As a result, the linear curve–fitting/extrapolation procedures can be used to fit and project the

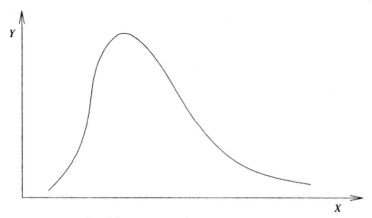

(a) First differences for the Gompertz curve

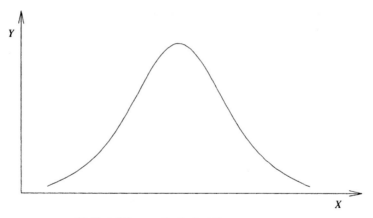

(b) First differences for the logistic curve

Figure 2.9   First Differences for the Gompertz and Logistic Curves

Source: Croxton, Cowden, and Klein (1976, 268). Reprinted by permission.

logistic curve for an assumed growth limit $1/c$. Appendix A illustrates the use of these procedures for fitting and projecting the logistic curve for an assumed growth limit, $1/c$. It also describes a procedure for computing the growth limit and other curve parameters and using these values to project the logistic curve that best fits a set of observation data.

Comparison of Logistic and Gompertz Curves

The logistic and Gompertz curves both describe time series that grow or decline by a decreasing percentage. However, they differ in that the Gompertz curve has a constant ratio of increments for the *logarithms* of the Y_C values and the logistic curve has a constant ratio of increments for the *reciprocals* of the Y_C values. In addition, the first differences for the Gompertz curve have a skewed frequency distribution, as shown in graph (a) of Figure 2.9. The first differences for a logistic curve have a normal frequency distribution as shown in graph (b) of Figure 2.9.

ENDNOTES

1. This can be demonstrated by substituting an X value of zero into the linear curve equation, that is, $Y_c = a + b(0)$ or a for all values of a and b.

2. This can be demonstrated by substituting a b value of zero into the linear curve equation: $Y_c = a + 0X$, or a for all values of X.

3. The number e is equal to the limit as m approaches infinity of the expression $(1 + 1/m)^m$. This expression can be shown to approach 2.71828 by substituting increasingly large values for m into this expression. When m equals 1, the expression is equal to $(2.00)^1$, or 2.000; when m equals 10, it is equal to $(1.10)^{10}$, or 2.594; when m equals 100, it is equal to $(1.01)^{100}$, or 2.705; when m equals 1,000, it is equal to $(1.001)^{1000}$, or 2.71692; and when m equals 10,000, it is equal to $(1.0001)^{10000}$, or 2.71815.

4. This can be shown by substituting a value of zero into the geometric curve $Y_c = ab^x$ to yield $Y_c = ab^0$. Since any number raised to the zero power is equal to one, b^0 is equal to one for any value of the b parameter and Y_c is equal to a.

5. The geometric curve is undefined for negative values of the b parameter because the curve is not continuous in this case. If b is negative, odd X values yield negative geometric values because negative numbers raised to an odd power are negative; for example, $(-1)^3$ equals -1. Even values of X yield positive geometric values because negative numbers raised to an even power

are even; for example, $(-1)^2$ equals one. As a result, the values of the geometric curve flip-flop around the X axis if the b parameter is negative.

6. As Isard et al. (1960, 11, n. 11) point out, the geometric curve was the basis for Malthus's theory of population growth and was widely used in the early twentieth century to project the population of both closed and open areas.

7. This can be demonstrated by substituting $X = 0$ into the parabolic curve equation to yield $Y_c = a + b0 + c0^2$, or a for all values of the a, b, and c parameters.

8. As Isard et al. (1960, 10, n. 10) indicate, the parabolic curve was widely used in the early twentieth century to project the population of closed and open areas.

9. The following discussion of the modified exponential curve is adopted from Croxton, Cowden, and Klein (1967, 262–67).

10. This can be demonstrated by setting the X value in the modified exponential curve equation equal to zero. That is, $Y_c = c + ab^0$. Since b^0 is equal to one, the Y intercept is equal to $c + a$.

11. The following discussion of the Gompertz curve is adapted from Croxton, Cowden, and Klein (1967, 267–74) and Dickey and Watts (1978, 138–39).

12. The Gompertz curve grows at a growth rate of $Y_c \log (c/Y_c)$. For increasingly large values of X, c/Y_c becomes increasingly smaller. As a result, $\log (c/Y_c)$ approaches zero and the growth rate declines. The Y intercept is equal to $ca \exp (b^0)$, that is, ca^1 or ca.

13. The following discussion of the logistic curve is adopted from Croxton, Cowden, and Klein (1967, 274–82); Pittenger (1976, 62–67); and Dickey and Watts (1978, 137–38). Isard et al. (1960, 14–15, n. 21) cite numerous studies that have used the logistic curve to project the population of closed and open areas.

14. The logistic curve is often written

$$Y_c = \frac{c}{1 + e^{a + bX}}$$

Depending on the value of the b parameter, it will look like either graph (a) or graph (b) of Figure 2.8. The parameters for this formulation of the logistic curve are identified using three equidistant observation years. See Croxton, Cowden, and Klein (1967, 274–79) and Pittenger (1976, 63–66).

15. The logistic curve is not continuous for negative values of the a parameter. For negative X values, the curve approaches zero for a lower limit and negative infinity as it approaches the point at which c is equal to the absolute value of ab^x. For positive X values, the curve approaches $1/c$ for an upper limit and positive infinity as it approaches the point at which c is equal to the absolute value of ab^x.

16. Note that the upper limit for the logistic curve is equal to the *reciprocal* of the c parameter. For the modified exponential and Gompertz curves it is *equal to* the c parameter.

17. For other applications of the logistic curve to project the population of closed and open areas, see Isard et al. (1960, 14–15, n. 21).

18. Only one equation is required because the a parameter is positive in all cases.

Chapter 3

Selecting Appropriate Extrapolation Projections

Chapter 2 describes six curves that can be used to fit and project a given set of observation data. The examples in Appendix A fit and project these curves for a common data set—the observed population for Leon County, Florida, for 1940 through 1980. Table 3.1 lists six sets of estimates and projections, each providing the "best fit" for a particular curve. However, because each curve incorporates different assumptions about past and future growth, the population projections for the year 2000 range from 117,600 for the linear curve to 211,100 for the geometric curve—a difference of almost 80 percent.

Given automated computational procedures such as those in the Community Analysis and Planning Programs, additional projections can easily be generated by selecting different observation periods, assuming different limits for the growth curves, and deleting or adjusting questionable observation values. As a result, analysts must often select the best set of estimates and projections from dozens of extrapolations, each of which is computationally correct and provides the best fit for a particular curve.

It is the job of planners to identify the projection (or projections) that provide the most reasonable forecast for the future. It is unreasonable to demand that they will know the future. Nevertheless, they can be expected to base their forecasts on more than mere whim, wishful thinking, or arbitrary choice. As professionals, planners can be expected to defend and justify their projections on the basis of generally acknowledged and justifiable decision criteria.

Table 3.1

Alternate Estimates and Projections

Year	Linear[a]	Geometric[b]	Parabolic[c]	Modified Exponential[d]	Gompertz[e]	Logistic[f]
(1)	(2)	(3)	(4)	(5)	(6)	(7)
1940	12,200	18,500	17,600	17,800	17,100	17,800
1945	21,000	22,600	22,300	22,700	21,600	22,400
1950	29,800	27,700	28,200	28,400	27,100	28,000
1955	38,600	33,900	35,300	35,000	33,600	34,900
1960	47,300	41,600	43,500	42,800	41,400	43,000
1965	56,100	50,900	52,800	51,900	50,400	52,500
1970	64,900	62,400	63,300	62,400	60,800	63,300
1975	73,700	76,400	75,000	74,800	72,800	75,400
1980	82,400	93,600	87,900	89,200	86,500	88,600
1985	91,200	114,700	101,900	106,000	102,000	102,400
1990	100,000	140,600	117,100	125,600	119,300	116,500
1995	108,800	172,300	133,400	148,500	138,600	130,500
2000	117,600	211,100	150,900	175,200	160,000	143,900

[a] These data are from Appendix A, Table A.2.
[b] These data are from Appendix A, Table A.6.
[c] These data are from Appendix A, Table A.8.
[d] These data are from Appendix A, Table A.12.
[e] These data are from Appendix A, Table A.16.
[f] These data are from Appendix A, Table A.20.

Fortunately, a number of criteria can be used to identify and defend the most appropriate set of estimates and projections. None of these criteria provides a clear-cut test that unequivocally identifies the single best projection. The criteria consider different factors, examine different information, and often identify different projections as the most appropriate. However, the criteria do help guide the selection process and provide the basis for informed and defensible decision making about the unknowable future, which is all one can expect.

The first, most important, and simplest procedure for evaluating any quantitative analysis is to plot the data. Graphs quickly and easily reveal trends and anomalies that can be extremely difficult to identify in tables of numbers. The observation data should be plotted and examined prior to the curve-fitting/extrapolation process. These plots are very useful for identifying erroneous data values that should be revised or eliminated. They are also helpful for uncovering discontinuities in past trends and for identifying observation periods that are most appropriate for projecting the future.

Plots of the observed and estimated values are also extremely helpful for identifying curves that are inappropriate for a given data set. For example, Figure A.1 in Appendix A suggests that the linear curve is inadequate for projecting the population of Leon County, which clearly does not follow a straight line. Plots of the observed and projected values are also useful for determining whether a curve reasonably extends past trends.

The rather subjective procedures of plotting and visually evaluating alternative extrapolation curves can be supplemented by more precise and replicable evaluative procedures. The first procedure identifies the extrapolation curve that most closely corresponds to the underlying pattern in the observation data. The second identifies the curve that best fits the observation data. These procedures are described in the next two sections and applied to the data in Table 3.1 in the third section. The last section reviews other, nonquantitative evaluation procedures and evaluates the curve-fitting/extrapolation procedure.

INPUT EVALUATION PROCEDURES

The first evaluation procedure examines the observation data to identify the extrapolation curve that corresponds most closely to these data.[1] The procedure assumes that growth patterns that corresponded to a given curve in the past will continue to do so in the future. This assumption does not always hold true, of course. However, given a fundamental inability to foresee the future, it provides a reasonable basis for evaluating alternative extrapolation curves.

The input evaluation procedure begins by recognizing that the extrapolation curves considered in Chapter 2 incorporate different growth assumptions. The procedure compares the underlying patterns in the observation data to the assumed pattern for each curve. The curve whose growth assumptions correspond most closely to the observation data is assumed to be the most appropriate extrapolation curve. Because the observation data rarely match any of the curves exactly, a statistical test of the relative dispersion in the test values is used to identify the most appropriate curve. The assumptions and input evaluation tests for each curve are described below, followed by procedures for applying the test statistics.

Curve Assumptions and Input Evaluation Tests

Linear Curve. As pointed out in Chapter 2, the linear curve is characterized by constant growth increments, that is, by a constant change in the dependent variable for each unit change in the independent variable. As a result, if the growth increments, or first differences, for the observation data are approximately equal, the linear curve can be assumed to provide the best estimates and projections.

As shown in Table 3.2, this test computes the first differences between the observed values (column 3) and determines whether they are approximately equal. As shown in Figure A.1 in Appendix A, the observed values can also be plotted as a function of the observation period. If the trend approximates a straight line, the linear curve can be considered.

Geometric Curve. As shown in Chapter 2, logarithms can be used to transform the geometric curve, $Y_C = ab^x$, to the linear form, log $Y_C =$ log a + log $b(X)$. This implies that the growth increments for the logarithms of the geometric curve are equal to a constant. As a result, if the first differences between the logarithms of the observed values are approximately equal, the geometric curve can be assumed to be the most appropriate extrapolation curve.

As shown in columns 5 and 6 of Table 3.2, this test computes the logarithms of the observed values and determines whether the first differences between the logarithms are approximately equal. The logarithms of the observation data can also be plotted. If the overall trend approximates a straight line, the geometric curve should be considered.

Parabolic Curve. The parabolic curve is characterized by constant second differences, that is, the differences between the first differences, for the dependent variable. As a result, if the second differences

Table 3.2

Input Evaluation Tests for Linear, Parabolic, and Geometric Curves

Year	Observed Value[a]	First Difference (Linear)	Second Difference (Parabolic)	Logarithm of Observed Value	Difference of Logarithms (Geometric)
(1)	(2)	(3)	(4)	(5)	(6)
1940	17,000	...	...	4.2304	...
1945	23,000	6,000	...	4.3617	0.1313
1950	29,000	6,000	0	4.4624	0.1007
1955	35,000	6,000	0	4.5441	0.0817
1960	43,000	8,000	2,000	4.6335	0.0894
1965	52,000	9,000	1,000	4.7160	0.0825
1970	63,000	11,000	2,000	4.7993	0.0833
1975	77,000	14,000	3,000	4.8865	0.0872
1980	87,000	10,000	−4,000	4.9395	0.0530

[a] These data are from Table A.1, column 2.

between the observed values are approximately equal, the parabolic curve can be assumed to provide the best projections.

As shown in columns 3 and 4 of Table 3.2, the second differences are determined by computing the first difference between the observations and then calculating the differences between these values. For example, the first difference for the 1940 to 1945 period is 23,000 − 17,000, or 6,000; the first difference for the 1945 to 1950 period is 29,000 − 23,000, or 6,000. The second difference for these periods is the difference between these differences, that is, 6,000 − 6,000, or 0.

Modified Exponential Curve. The modified exponential curve is characterized by first differences that decline or increase by a constant percentage. As a result, if the ratios of successive first differences between the observation values are approximately equal, the modified exponential curve is assumed to be most appropriate.

As shown in Table 3.3, this test computes the difference between the observed values and examines the ratios between these differences. For example, the difference between the observed values for 1940 and 1945 is 23,000 − 17,000, or 6,000; the difference for the 1945 to 1950 period is 29,000 − 23,000, or 6,000. The ratio of these differences shown in column 4 is 6,000/6,000, or 1.

Gompertz Curve. As shown in Chapter 2, logarithms can be used to transform the Gompertz curve, $Y_C = ca \exp (b^x)$, to the modified exponential curve, $\log Y_C = \log c + (\log a)b^x$. As a result, the Gompertz curve is characterized by first differences in the *logarithms* of the dependent variable that decline by a constant percentage.

Table 3.3

Input Evaluation Test for Modified Exponential Curve

Year (1)	Observed Value[a] (2)	First Difference (3)	Ratio of First Differences (4)
1940	17,000	...	...
1945	23,000	6,000	...
1950	29,000	6,000	1.000
1955	35,000	6,000	1.000
1960	43,000	8,000	1.333
1965	52,000	9,000	1.125
1970	63,000	11,000	1.222
1975	77,000	14,000	1.272
1980	87,000	10,000	0.714

[a] These data are from Table 3.2, column 2.

Therefore, if the ratios of successive first differences between the logarithms of the observation values are approximately equal, the Gompertz curve should be considered.

As shown in Table 3.4, this test computes the logarithms of the observed values (column 3), calculates the differences between these logarithms (column 4), and determines the ratio between successive logarithm differences (column 5). If these ratios are approximately equal, the Gompertz curve should be considered. The first differences between observations can also be plotted. If the plot resembles the skewed distribution in graph (a) of Figure 2.9, the Gompertz curve is supported.

Logistic Curve. The logistic curve is characterized by first differences in the *reciprocals* of the observation values that decline by a constant percentage. As a result, if the ratios of successive first differences between the reciprocals of the observation values are approximately equal, the logistic curve should be considered.

As shown in Table 3.5, this test computes the reciprocals of the observed values (column 3), calculates the differences between these reciprocals (column 4), and determines the ratios between the reciprocal differences (column 5). If these ratios are approximately equal, the logistic curve should be considered. The first differences between observations can also be plotted. If the plot resembles the "normal" distribution shown in graph (b) in Figure 2.9, the logistic curve is supported.

Table 3.4

Input Evaluation Test for Gompertz Curves

Year (1)	Observed Value[a] (2)	Logarithm (3)	Difference of Logarithms (4)	Ratio of Logarithm Differences (5)
1940	17,000	4.2304	...	...
1945	23,000	4.3617	0.1313	...
1950	29,000	4.4624	0.1007	0.767
1955	35,000	4.5441	0.0817	0.811
1960	43,000	4.6335	0.0894	1.094
1965	52,000	4.7160	0.0825	0.923
1970	63,000	4.7993	0.0833	1.010
1975	77,000	4.8865	0.0872	1.047
1980	87,000	4.9395	0.0530	0.608

[a] These data are from Table 3.2, column 2.

Table 3.5

Input Evaluation Test for Logistic Curve

Year	Observed Value[a]	Reciprocal	Difference of Reciprocals	Ratio of Reciprocal Differences
(1)	(2)	(3)	(4)	(5)
1940	17,000	588×10^{-7}	...	...
1945	23,000	435×10^{-7}	-153×10^{-7}	...
1950	29,000	345×10^{-7}	-90×10^{-7}	0.588
1955	35,000	286×10^{-7}	-59×10^{-7}	0.655
1960	43,000	233×10^{-7}	-53×10^{-7}	0.898
1965	52,000	192×10^{-7}	-41×10^{-7}	0.773
1970	63,000	159×10^{-7}	-33×10^{-7}	0.805
1975	77,000	130×10^{-7}	-29×10^{-7}	0.879
1980	87,000	115×10^{-7}	-15×10^{-7}	0.517

[a] These data are from Table 3.2, column 2.

Input Evaluation Statistics

As Tables 3.2 through 3.5 suggest, observation data rarely correspond clearly to the assumptions underlying any of the extrapolation curves, making the input evaluation tests inconclusive. As a result, it is useful to compute a test statistic that measures the relative dispersion in the input evaluation values. The curve with the least dispersion as measured by the test statistic can then be easily identified as corresponding most closely to the observation data.

An obvious dispersion measure is the *standard deviation* defined as follows:

$$s = \left[\frac{\Sigma(Z_i - \mathbf{Z})^2}{M - 1} \right]^{1/2} \tag{3.1}$$

where

Z_i = input evaluation values for a curve

M = number of input evaluation values

The mean of the input evaluation values, $\mathbf{Z}$, is computed as follows:

$$\mathbf{Z} = \frac{\Sigma Z_i}{M} \tag{3.2}$$

The standard deviation measures the total deviation between the input evaluation values, for example, the first differences for the linear curve, and the mean for these values. If the values are equal, the Z_i values will equal the mean, Z, and the standard deviation will be zero. The larger the dispersion in the input evaluation values, the larger the standard deviation.

The computations can be simplified by using an algebraically equivalent formula for the standard deviation given in Eq. (3.3).

$$s = \left[\frac{\sum Z_i^2 - \frac{(\sum Z_i)^2}{M}}{M - 1} \right]^{1/2} \tag{3.3}$$

where

$$\sum Z_i^2 = \text{sum of squared input evaluation values}$$
$$(\sum Z_i)^2 = \text{sum of input evaluation values squared}$$
$$M = \text{number of input evaluation values}$$

This formula is easier to use because it does not require calculating the mean before computing the standard deviation.

The difference between the sum of squared input evaluation values, $\sum Z_i^2$, and the sum of input evaluation values squared, $(\sum Z_i)^2$, can be illustrated with a simple example in which the Z_i values are equal to 1, 2, and 3, respectively. $\sum Z_i^2$ is computed by squaring each value and summing the squares, that is, 1^2 (1) plus 2^2 (4) plus 3^2 (9), or 14. $(\sum Z_i)^2$ is computed by summing the values and then squaring the result, that is, 1 plus 2 plus 3 (6) squared, or 36.

The standard deviation is expressed in the same units as the input evaluation values for each curve. This is inappropriate for this application because the input evaluation values are expressed in different measurement units. The linear and parabolic curves consider the first and second differences between observations, which are often measured in thousands. The geometric curve examines the difference between logarithms, which are generally between one and ten. And the three asymptotic growth curves evaluate ratios, which are generally close to one. As a result, standard deviation scores for the various input evaluation tests vary substantially as a result of the different measurement units.

A more appropriate input evaluation statistic is the *coefficient of relative variation (CRV)*, the standard deviation expressed as a percentage of the absolute value of the mean. That is,

$$CRV = \frac{s}{|Z|} \times 100 \tag{3.4}$$

The coefficient of relative variation divides the standard deviation by the mean so that the test statistics are not affected by the measurement units employed. The mean is expressed as a positive number to ensure that the coefficient of relative variation is always positive. As a result, the test statistics for all six curves are expressed in common terms, allowing direct comparison of the extent to which each curve corresponds to the observation data.

For example, Table 3.6 illustrates the procedure for computing the coefficient of relative variation for the linear curve. The first step is computing the input evaluation values, in this case, the first differences between observations shown in column 3. The sum of the input evaluation values, ΣZ_i, and sum of squares of these values, ΣZ_i^2, must then be computed. The standard deviation for the input evaluation values is calculated by applying Eq. (3.3):

$$s = \left[\frac{\Sigma Z_i^2 - \dfrac{(\Sigma Z_i)^2}{M}}{M - 1} \right]^{1/2}$$

$$= \left[\frac{670 \times 10^6 - \dfrac{(70,000)^2}{8}}{8 - 1} \right]^{1/2}$$

$$= \left[\frac{670 \times 10^6 - 612.5 \times 10^6}{7} \right]^{1/2} \tag{3.3}$$

$$= 2,870$$

Table 3.6

Computing Coefficient of Relative Variation for Linear Curve

Year (1)	Observed Value[a] (2)	First Difference (3)	Difference Squared (4)
1940	17,000	...	...
1945	23,000	6,000	36×10^6
1950	29,000	6,000	36×10^6
1955	35,000	6,000	36×10^6
1960	43,000	8,000	64×10^6
1965	52,000	9,000	81×10^6
1970	63,000	11,000	121×10^6
1975	77,000	14,000	196×10^6
1980	87,000	10,000	100×10^6
Sum	...	70,000	670×10^6

[a] These data are from Table 3.2, column 2.

The mean is computed by applying Eq. (3.2), as follows:

$$\mathbf{Z} = \frac{\Sigma Z_i}{M}$$

$$= \frac{70,000}{8} = 8,750 \tag{3.2}$$

The number of values, M, used to compute the standard deviation and mean is equal to the number of input evaluation values, for example, the number of first differences for the linear curve, rather than the number of observations.

The coefficient of relative variation *(CRV)* for the linear curve is computed by applying Eq. (3.4).

$$CRV = \frac{s}{|\mathbf{Z}|} \times 100$$

$$= \frac{2,870}{|8,750|} \times 100 \tag{3.4}$$

$$= 32.8$$

This value can be compared with the input evaluation statistics for the other extrapolation curves shown later in the chapter in Table 3.8. The curve with the smallest *CRV* value is the preferred extrapolation curve by this criterion. A second set of evaluation criteria is considered in the next section.

OUTPUT EVALUATION PROCEDURES

The second set of procedures for selecting the most appropriate set of estimates and projections evaluate the extent to which the curve estimates match the observation data. The procedures assume that the extrapolation curve that best fits past growth trends will most accurately predict future trends. While this assumption does not always hold, it does provide a reasonable basis for evaluating alternative extrapolation curves.

Two widely used accuracy measures are the *mean error (ME)* and the *mean absolute percentage error (MAPE)*.[2] The mean error is calculated as follows:

$$ME = \frac{\Sigma(Y - Y_c)}{N} \tag{3.5}$$

where

Y = observed value for the dependent variable
Y_C = estimated value for the dependent variable
N = number of observations

Table 3.7 illustrates the procedures for computing the mean error for the linear curve. The deviations between each set of the observed and estimated values are computed and summed to determine the total deviation, recognizing sign. This value is then divided by the number of observations to yield the mean error.

As Table 3.7 illustrates, large positive and negative deviations can cancel one another, yielding a mean error score of zero. As a result, the mean error is a poor measure of the total deviation between the observed and estimated values. However, it is a useful measure of estimation error or bias, that is, the extent to which the curve estimates are consistently larger or smaller than the observation data. Thus, the mean error of zero for the linear estimates in Table 3.7 indicates that while there are significant estimation errors, the linear curve does not consistently over- or underestimate the observed values.

The mean absolute percentage error *(MAPE)* is computed as follows:

Table 3.7

Computing Output Evaluation Statistics for Linear Curve

Year (1)	Observed Value[a] (Y) (2)	Estimated Value (Y_C) (3)	Deviation $(Y - Y_C)$[1] (4)	Absolute Percentage Error (5)
1940	17,000	12,200	4,800	28.23
1945	23,000	21,000	2,000	8.70
1950	29,000	29,800	–0,800	2.76
1955	35,000	38,600	–3,600	10.29
1960	43,000	47,300	–4,300	10.00
1965	52,000	56,100	–4,100	7.88
1970	63,000	64,900	–1,900	3.02
1975	77,000	73,700	3,300	4.29
1980	87,000	82,400	4,600	5.29
Sum	...	...	0	80.46

[a] These data are from Table 3.2, column 2.

$$MAPE = \frac{\Sigma \dfrac{\left[|Y - Y_c|\right]}{Y}}{N} \times 100 \qquad (3.6)$$

where Y, Y_c, and N are defined as before. The vertical lines around the $Y - Y_c$ term indicate that the difference between the observed and estimated values is expressed as an absolute (or positive) value.

As shown in Table 3.7, the mean absolute percentage error is computed by first determining the deviation between the observed and estimated values (column 4). The deviations are then divided by the observed values and multiplied by 100 to give the percentage error (column 5). For example, the percentage error for 1940 is 4,800/17,000 × 100, or 28.23. Negative signs are dropped to yield absolute percentage errors. The absolute percentage errors are then summed and divided by the number of observations to yield the mean absolute percentage error. Thus, for this example, the mean absolute percentage error is equal to 80.46/9, or 8.94.

The mean absolute percentage error evaluates the total estimation error, regardless of sign, providing a good measure of the total variation between the observed and estimated values. It is particularly useful because it is dimensionless and is unaffected by the number of observations, making it appropriate for comparing estimates for different data sets and different numbers of observations.

APPLICATION OF THE EVALUATION PROCEDURES

The application of the input and output evaluation criteria can be illustrated by examining Table 3.8, which records the *CRV, ME,* and *MAPE* statistics for the six curve estimates computed in Appendix A. For example, the *CRV* statistics for the modified exponential and Gompertz curves are significantly smaller than the values for the other curves, suggesting that they are equally attractive extrapolation candidates. The mean errors reveal that only the linear and parabolic estimates are unbiased.

The mean absolute percentage errors indicate that the modified exponential curve provides the best fit with the logistic and parabolic curves closely tied for the second best fit. The linear curve has the largest *MAPE* value, even though the mean error is zero. This demon-

Table 3.8

Input and Output Evaluation Statistics

Curve (1)	CRV (2)	ME (3)	MAPE (4)	Upper Limit (5)
Linear	32.8	0	8.94	...
Geometric	402.3	−159	3.56	...
Parabolic	24.7	0	1.86	...
Modified Exponential	19.3	120	1.63	None
Gompertz	19.5	740	2.60	3,480,000
Logistic	20.0	20	1.82	223,000

strates once again that the linear curve parameters that minimize the sum of squared deviations do not necessarily provide the best fit for a given set of observation data.

As mentioned in Chapter 2, for appropriate values for the a and b parameters, the asymptotic growth curves define an upper growth limit for large positive values of the independent variable. The modified exponential curve does not have an upper growth limit for these data. However, the computed growth limits for the Gompertz and logistic curves are 3,480,000 and 223,000, respectively.

The input and output evaluation statistics do not unequivocally point to a single set of estimates and projections. However, they can help guide the curve evaluation process. The linear curve can be eliminated from consideration on the basis of its poor fit to the observed data revealed by an extremely high *MAPE* value and Figure A.1. The geometric curve is suspect due to its extremely high *CRV* and *ME* statistics. The parabolic curve is brought into question by its relatively high *CRV* and *MAPE* statistics. The Gompertz curve is questionable due to its extremely large mean error and extremely high upper growth limit. The modified exponential curve is recommended by the lowest *CRV* and *MAPE* scores; however it is questionable due to its relatively high systematic bias and lack of an upper growth limit. As a result, the logistic curve is perhaps the most desirable candidate because it has low scores for all three statistics and a reasonable upper growth limit.

EVALUATION

The curve-fitting/extrapolation technique is based on a simple two-stage process of curve fitting, the identification of past trends, and curve extrapolation, the extension of these trends to project the future.[3] This process is revealed most clearly in graphical extrapolations that use visual observation and manual techniques for curve fitting and extension. However, quantitative procedures for identifying and extending the "best-fitting" curve and evaluating alternative curves are only more explicit and replicable forms of these procedures.

As a result, all extrapolation forecasts are judgmental by definition. A large number of computationally correct projections can easily be prepared for a region by selecting different observation periods, assuming different growth limits, and modifying or deleting questionable observation values. Judgment is therefore required to select the extrapolation curve that best describes the past. It is also necessary to identify the relevant historical period for projecting the region's future. This choice is important because projections based on different historical periods often differ substantially.

Several procedures can be used to more fully inform the judgment process. The first and most important procedure is plotting the data. Graphs are extremely helpful for revealing anomalies or discontinuities in past trends and for determining whether an extrapolation curve adequately describes and extends observed growth patterns. Plots of the historical data for extended time periods are also useful for identifying the historical period to be used in fitting the extrapolation curves.

The long-term implications of alternative projection curves can also be determined by extending the curve beyond the projection date and by examining the computed growth curve limits. If the long-range projections or upper limits are unreasonable in the light of past trends, the short-term projections are also questioned.

Alternative curves can also be evaluated with respect to their demonstrated effectiveness in controlled test situations. For example, Isserman (1977a) used decennial census data for 1930 through 1960 to project the population of 1,777 subcounty units in Illinois and Indiana for 1960 and 1970. Projections for eight extrapolation models were compared with actual census counts in 1960 and 1970 to test the models' projection accuracy as measured by the mean absolute percentage error. While no model was superior for all subcounty units, some models were more accurate for certain types of areas. For example, the geometric model was the most accurate for areas that were rapidly growing, were moderately declining, or had fewer than 5,000 inhabitants. While these results are not strictly applicable to other regions or different time periods, they can be considered on the assumption that similar regions will exhibit comparable growth patterns in the future.[4]

The curve-fitting/extrapolation technique assumes that past trends will continue into the future. If this assumption is incorrect, the best-fitting curve will not necessarily provide the best forecasts. Unfortunately, there is no assurance in practice that past trends will continue. Close agreement with past data may result from mere coincidence or from the aggregate effect of underlying causal processes that may not continue into the future. Growth trends for rapidly growing or declining regions cannot continue forever. Many regions experience long-term cyclical patterns of growth and decline, which cannot be predicted from past trends.

Recognizing that the equation that best fits the past may not necessarily predict the future, analysts should select the equation (or equations) that produce results consistent with their views of the most likely future. A number of projections can also be prepared, reflecting a range of assumptions about the future. Alternative scenarios including a "baseline" extrapolation of past trends, a "high plausible," a "low plausible," and a "preferred" or "planning" series can be developed to inform elected officials and the public of the range of futures they may face. The planning forecast will not always be the "most likely" forecast, for example, for capital improvements planning in which the costs of high projections and initial overbuilding are substantially lower than the costs of underprojections requiring the construction of additional facilities at a later date.

Professional judgment must be exercised in forecasting, but it must also be documented. The assumptions underlying alternative forecasts should be explicitly stated, including the standard "no catastrophe" disclaimer that the forecasts are invalid in the case of war, natural disaster, and the like. The growth assumptions embodied in the extrapolation equations should be stated in nontechnical terms. The historical data used to fit the curve and the source for these data should be identified. In addition, the curve parameters and any special characteristics such as assumed or computed growth limits should be reported.

Sophisticated extrapolation and evaluation procedures cannot replace the need for an understanding of the causes for past trends and informed choices about the ways in which these trends will (or will not) continue in the future. As a result, forecast accuracy will be improved not by the development of more complex models but by paying increased attention to the "informal" elements of forecasting: learning about the forecast region and its resources and liabilities, studying national and regional trends, following the economic and demographic literature, and incorporating all of this information into the forecasting process. The more planners know about the past and present, the better they will be able to predict the future (Isserman and Fisher 1984, 44–45).

The curve-fitting/extrapolation technique is unique in using aggregate data from the past to predict the future. While extremely useful when time, resources, and information are limited, the technique's inability to deal with the causes of past trends makes it theoretically suspect. The limited empirical evidence suggests that simple extrapolation models are often as accurate as more complex projection models (see, e.g., Smith 1987a and 1987b and Beaumont and Isserman 1987). Nevertheless, it seems clear that analytic rigor and potential forecast accuracy can be improved by dealing separately with the three components of population change—deaths, births, and migration—and dividing a region's population into its sex, race, and age components. The cohort-component technique described in Part Two does exactly this.

ENDNOTES

1. The following input evaluation criteria are adopted from Croxton, Cowden, and Klein (1967, 282–83).

2. For an extended discussion of these and other measures of forecast accuracy, see Armstrong (1978, 320–33).

3. The discussion in this section draws heavily on similar discussions in Isserman (1984), Isserman and Fisher (1984), and Pittenger (1977 and 1980).

4. Also see Smith (1987b, 998–99).

Part Two

The Cohort-Component Technique

The five chapters in this part examine the cohort-component projection technique and the three components of population change that make up the cohort-component projection model. Chapter 5 examines the mortality component, Chapter 6 considers the fertility component, and Chapter 7 reviews the migration component. Each chapter illustrates computational procedures for estimating and projecting these components for the sample population data in Table 4.1. Chapter 8 demonstrates the combined application of these components in a complete projection model, reviews procedures for identifying the most appropriate projection (or projections), and evaluates the cohort-component projection technique.

Chapter 4

Cohort-Component Technique: An Introduction

Perhaps no single factor is more important for local government planning than the size and composition of a region's population and the way it will change in the future. Changes in population size, distribution, and composition place new demands on educational facilities, transportation systems, health and welfare services, and employment and recreational facilities. Even though the total population may remain constant, changes in its composition can fundamentally alter the need for public facilities and services.

The extrapolation technique described in Part One projects future populations without disaggregating the population or identifying the causes of past trends. Improved projections can be obtained by dealing separately with the three components of population change—fertility, mortality, and migration. These three factors determine overall rates of population change because a population can only change when someone is born, dies, or moves into or out of the area.

Deaths, births, and migration are largely independent processes that change by differing amounts at varying times, affecting different segments of the population in diverse ways. Death rates are very high for infants, low for children, and gradually increase with age. Death rates by age are generally higher for males than for females, higher for nonwhites than for whites, and higher for low-income groups than for the well-to-do. Fertility rates vary dramatically between the different age and racial segments of the female population. Out-migration has traditionally been highest for the better educated rural population between the ages of 18 and 35, and in-migration has been highest for economically advantaged areas, metropolitan counties, and the Sun Belt.

The age and sex differences in the components of population change are particularly important because they can interact with a region's population structure (i.e., the distribution among different age and sex categories) to affect the region's overall rates of population change. For example, retirement communities experience more deaths than numerically equivalent populations of young married couples because their population is concentrated in the older age groups that experience higher mortality rates. The area populated with young couples similarly has more births because its population is concentrated in the child-bearing ages.

The interaction between age structure and the components of population change is further complicated by substantial age- and sex-related changes over time in each component. Mortality rates for whites declined steadily until 1950; since then they have declined slowly for some age groups and increased slightly for others. Birth rates have fluctuated substantially over the past fifty years and have recently reversed long-term declines. Migration—by far the most volatile component of population change—is affected dramatically by short-term economic changes that differentially affect the various segments of a population.

These considerations suggest that population projections can be improved by dealing separately with the three components of demographic change and with the different age, sex, and racial segments of a population. Projection methods that do this are called *cohort-component* models because they disaggregate a population into uniform age, sex, and racial groups or *cohorts* and because they deal separately with the three *components* of population change.[1] Models of this type were first developed in the United States during the 1920s by Pascal K. Whelpton and Warren S. Thompson. Since then, the cohort-component model has become the most widely used technique for projecting the population of states, metropolitan areas, and counties in the United States (Smith 1986, 127).[2]

Cohort-component projection models are extremely useful because they provide disaggregated population forecasts by age, sex, and race. These forecasts are required for many areas of public administration and planning: projecting school enrollments, providing medical facilities and other services for specialized populations, and forecasting the demand for housing and population-related public infrastructure and services. They also project the number of births and deaths and migration trends. These data are often useful for health planning and other areas. Disaggregated information such as this can only be produced by projection models that divide a population into age, sex, and race cohorts and that deal separately with the three components of population change.

POPULATION COHORTS

Cohort-component projection models generally divide a population into five-year age groups, that is, the population between the ages of 0 and 4, between 5 and 9, and so forth, to an open-ended cohort made up of the population over a certain age, generally 85.[3] These models also divide a population by sex and by race when there is a significant number of persons in more than one race. These divisions are used to isolate population segments that experience significantly different demographic rates from the rest of the population.

However, the cohort-component technique can be illustrated with a simplified projection model that divides a population by sex and ten-year age intervals. The first cohort includes the population between the ages of 0 and 9; the second includes the population between 10 and 19. The ninth cohort is open-ended and includes the population aged 80 and above. The male population in a cohort, n, at any time, t, can be represented by PM_n^t; the female population in the cohort is expressed by PF_n^t, and the total population in the cohort by P_n^t.

For example, Table 4.1 reports the population of Wayne County, Ohio (site of the author's home town) in 1980. The male population in the first cohort, PM_1^t, is 8,323; the female population in the first cohort, PF_1^t, is 7,899; and the total population over the age of 80, P_9^t, is 2,216.

POPULATION PYRAMIDS

An extremely effective technique for graphically describing the age and sex composition of a population is the *population pyramid*. For example, Figure 4.1 is the population pyramid for the population data reported in Table 4.1. Population pyramids consist of horizontal bars representing the population in each age group, displayed in ascending order from youngest to oldest. The bars to the left of the vertical axis represent the male population in each age interval; the bars to the right

Table 4.1

Population by Age and Sex, 1980

Age of Cohort (1)	Cohort Number (n) (2)	Male Population (PM_n^{1980}) (3)	Female Population (PF_n^{1980}) (4)	Total Population (P_n^{1980}) (5)
0–9	1	8,323	7,899	16,222
10–19	2	9,160	8,513	17,673
20–29	3	8,866	8,817	17,683
30–39	4	6,700	6,956	13,656
40–49	5	4,915	4,956	9,871
50–59	6	4,451	4,717	9,168
60–69	7	3,211	3,691	6,902
70–79	8	1,627	2,390	4,017
80+	9	745	1,471	2,216
Total		47,998	49,410	97,408

Source: U.S. Bureau of the Census (1982, 37–358).

represent the female population. Pyramids may show either the number of persons in each age group or the percentage of the total population in each cohort.

As Figure 4.2 illustrates, population pyramids graphically describe a population's age structure. The pyramid for Costa Rica has a very broad base and narrows rapidly, indicating a relatively young population with a high proportion of children. The pyramid for Sweden has a relatively narrow base, indicating a relatively old population. The pyramids for India and the United States illustrate more normal age structures than those of Costa Rica and Sweden.

As Figure 4.3 illustrates, a population pyramid is also extremely useful for describing the changes in a population's age structure. The figure shows the observed 1980 population and the projected population in 1990 as a single population pyramid. The pyramid quickly reveals population increases in cohorts one and four through nine. In these cohorts the length of the clear horizontal bars represents the 1980 population and the combined length of the clear and crosshatched bars represents the projected 1990 population. In cohorts two and three, the length of the clear bars represents the projected population in 1990, and the length of the combined clear and crosshatched bars represents the observed 1980 population.

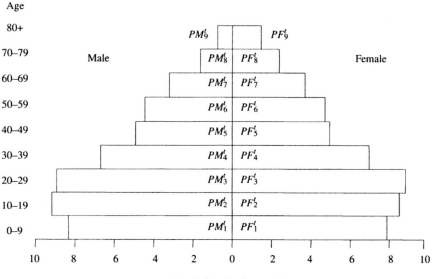

Figure 4.1   Population by Age and Sex, 1980

Source: Table 4.1.

MORTALITY COMPONENT

If the population in cohort n at time t is P_n^t, the cohort's population ten years later can be designated P_n^{t+1} to indicate the passage of one ten-year interval. The length of the projection interval equals the size of the age cohorts to facilitate the construction and interpretation of a cohort-component projection model. As a result, the illustrative cohort-component model has ten-year age cohorts and ten-year projection intervals. Five-year models have five-year age cohorts and project the population at five-year intervals.

Some of the population in each cohort at time t will die during the ten-year period between t and $t + 1$. The surviving population becomes the population of the next higher cohort at $t + 1$. For example, the population which is born at time t and survives the ten-year interval will be 10 years old at time $t + 1$. The surviving population which is 9

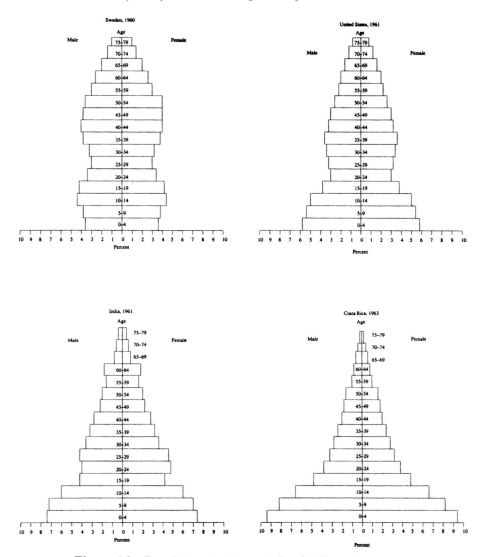

Figure 4.2   Population by Age and Sex for Four Countries

Source: U.S. Bureau of the Census (1975, 240).

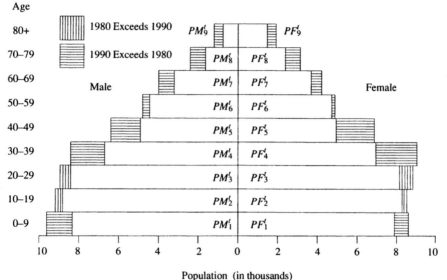

Figure 4.3   Population by Age and Sex, 1980 and 1990

Source: Table 8.1

years old at t will be 19 at $t + 1$, and the surviving population which is initially between the ages of 0 and 9 will make up the remainder of the second age cohort (ages 10 to 19) at $t + 1$.

As shown in Figure 4.4, the surviving population from the first cohort at time t becomes the population of the second cohort at $t + 1$; the surviving population from the second cohort becomes the new population of the third cohort; and so on. Therefore, if the surviving population from cohort n is represented by S_n,

$$P_{n+1}^{t+1} = S_n \quad (1 \le n \le 7) \tag{4.1}$$

for all but the first and last cohorts.

Some of the members of the open-ended cohort who are 80 or older at time t will still be alive at $t + 1$; that is, they will be aged 90 and over. As a result, the population of the last cohort in $t + 1$ includes the surviving population from the eighth cohort, S_8, plus the surviving population from the ninth cohort, S_9. That is,

$$P_9^{t+1} = S_8 + S_9 \tag{4.2}$$

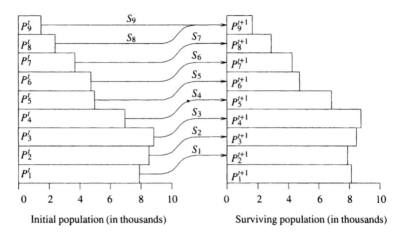

Figure 4.4   Surviving Population in a Ten–Year Period

Source: Table 8.1

The probability of surviving from cohort n to cohort $n + 1$ can be expressed as $s_{n,n+1}$. Given this probability, the surviving population from cohort n is equal to the initial population of that cohort, P_n^t, multiplied by the appropriate survival rate. That is,

$$S_n = P_n^t \times s_{n,n+1} \qquad (4.3)$$

Substituting the expression for the surviving population from Eq. (4.3) into Eq. (4.1) yields the following:

$$P_{n+1}^{t+1} = P_n^t \times s_{n,n+1} \quad (1 \le n \le 7) \qquad (4.4)$$

That is, the population of cohort $n + 1$ at $t + 1$ is equal to the population of cohort n at time t multiplied by the survival rate from cohort n to cohort $n + 1$.

Substituting Eq. (4.3) into Eq. (4.2) yields the following formula for the population of the open-ended cohort at time $t + 1$:

$$P_9^{t+1} = (P_8^t \times s_{8,9}) + (P_9^t \times s_{9,9}) \qquad (4.5)$$

That is, the population of the ninth cohort at $t + 1$ is equal to (1) the population of cohort eight at t multiplied by the survival rate from cohort eight to cohort nine; plus (2) the population of cohort nine at t multiplied by the survival rate from cohort nine to cohort nine.

Chapter 5 describes the procedures for estimating and projecting the survival rate from one cohort to another and for using these rates and the equations developed in this section to project the surviving population in each cohort.

FERTILITY COMPONENT

The surviving population from the first cohort at time t becomes the population of the second cohort at time $t + 1$, the surviving population from the second cohort becomes the population of the third cohort, and so on. As a result, and as Figure 4.5 indicates, the first cohort at time $t + 1$ must be filled with surviving children born during the ten-year period from t to $t + 1$.

The number of annual live births to women in cohort n can be represented by B_n, and the *age-specific fertility rate* (i.e., the probability that a woman in cohort n will give birth in a given year) can be expressed as $f_{n,0}$. Therefore the number of children born to women in cohort n in a year is equal to the average female population for the projection period, PA_n^{t-t+1}, multiplied by the appropriate age-specific fertility rate:

$$B_n = PA_n^{t-t+1} \times f_{n,0} \qquad (4.6)$$

The average female population for the projection period t to $t + 1$ must be used because the number of women in a cohort can change significantly in a five- or ten-year period as women die or move into or out of the region.

If children are only born to women in cohorts two (ages 10 to 19) through five (ages 40 to 49), the total number of births in a year is equal to the sum of births to women in these four cohorts. The total number of births in a ten-year period, B_T, is ten times the number of births in a one-year period. Therefore,

$$B_T = 10 \times \Sigma_2^5 B_n \qquad (4.7)$$

Substituting the expression for the number of annual births from Eq. (4.6) into Eq. (4.7) yields the following:

$$B_T = 10 \times \Sigma_2^5 (PA_n^{t-t+1} \times f_{n,0}) \qquad (4.8)$$

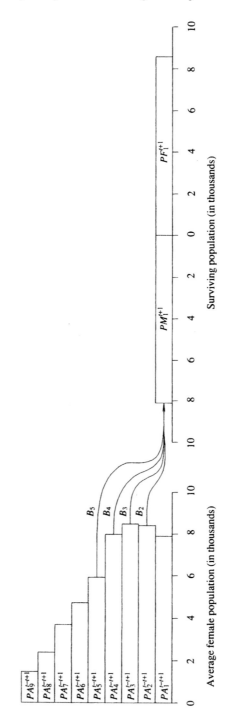

Figure 4.5   Surviving Births in a Ten–Year Period

The number of male births, B_m, and female births, B_f, in a ten-year interval can be determined by multiplying the total number of births by the proportion of male births, p_m, and female births, p_f:

$$B_f = B_T \times p_f \tag{4.9}$$

and

$$B_m = B_T \times p_m \tag{4.10}$$

Because some of the children who are born during a ten-year period will die before the end of the period, the projected population of the first cohort is equal to the number of male and female births, multiplied by the appropriate survival rates. For example, the projected female population in cohort one at $t + 1$ is equal to

$$PF_1^{t+1} = B_f \times s_{0,1}$$

where $s_{0,1}$ is the survival rate for female children born during a ten-year period and the number of female births, B_f, is computed by applying Eqs. (4.8) and (4.9). Chapter 6 describes the procedures for estimating and projecting age-specific fertility rates and applying these rates to project the number of births in a projection period.

MIGRATION COMPONENT

Migration is the most important, volatile, and difficult factor to be considered in preparing small-area population projections. Its importance is reflected in great migration flows such as the rural to urban migration of the 1900s, the northern migration of Blacks in the 1950s and 1960s, and the recent movement from the Northeast to the South and West. These migration trends have changed the face of the nation. Survey data consistently reveal that 6 to 7 percent of the U.S. population lived in a different county in the previous year. Over 15 percent of the population moves in a five-year period; migration rates for young adults are even higher. Between 1970 and 1980 migration accounted for 92 percent of Florida's population growth and 83 percent of Nevada's population growth. The impact of migration is even higher for many local areas.

Unlike death rates, which change slowly and predictably over time, and birth rates, which generally follow stable short-run trends, state and local migration rates can change tremendously in a very short time. For example, net in-migration rates for Florida averaged almost 400,000 per year between 1970 and 1974 but fell to only 160,000 per year for the next four years. Local migration rates can change even more dramatically in response to regional economic changes such as plant closings or the discovery of major resource deposits (Irwin 1977, 19; Smith 1986, 127).

The impact of migration on local population change is compounded by the fact that migration is age-, sex-, and race-related. The peak migratory ages extend from the late teens through the early thirties when people leave their parents' home to seek education and work and to establish households of their own. After this period, migration rates become progressively lower until the age of retirement, when there is a smaller spurt of migratory activity. Underlying these general trends are considerable variations in local migration rates for different segments of the population and types of communities (Pittenger 1976, 187–94).

Migration can be defined as geographical or spatial mobility involving a change of usual residence between political or administrative units.[4] Changes in usual residence are used to exclude short-term movements such as commuting trips and vacation or business excursions. Classifying migrants by political unit excludes local moves and allows migration flows to be identified at different political levels.

An *in-migrant* is a person who moves into a migration-defining area (e.g., a state or county) from outside the area but within the same country. An *out-migrant* is a person who leaves a migration-defining area for another location within the same country.[5] *Gross migration* refers to either in-migration or out-migration. *Net migration* refers to the balance between (or net effect of) in-migration and out-migration. Net in-migration (or "positive" net migration) exists when the number of in-migrants is larger than the number of out-migrants and is indicated by a plus sign. Net out-migration (or "negative" net migration) occurs when the number of out-migrants exceeds the number of in-migrants and is identified by a negative sign.

A *migration rate* is defined as the number of migrants in a time period, divided by the population at risk, that is,

$$m = \frac{M}{P} \times k$$

where

m = migration rate
M = number of migrants
P = population at risk
k = a constant, such as 100 or 1,000

Analogous rates for in-migration (m_i), out-migration (m_o), and net migration (m_n) can be defined as follows:

$$m_i = \frac{I}{P} \times k$$

$$m_o = \frac{O}{P} \times k$$

$$m_n = \frac{I - O}{P} \times k$$

where I and O are the number of in-migrants and out-migrants, respectively.

The population at risk is the population exposed to the probability of moving reflected by the appropriate migration rate. The population at risk for out-migration is the population of the area from which the migrants leave. The population at risk for in-migration is the population of the remainder of the country. Two-region models consisting of the study area and the rest of the nation are sometimes used to compute in-migration rates based on the population outside of the study area. However, in-migration rates are generally based on the population of the area of destination.

The population at risk also changes over time as people are born, die, and move into or out of the area. As a result, the population at risk can be assumed to be the initial population, the final population, or the mean of the initial and final populations. However, most cohort models use the initial population to compute migration rates.[6]

Two procedures are widely used for incorporating migration in a cohort-component projection model.[7] The first approach uses past migration data to compute net migration rates by cohort, which are applied to the current population to project the number of net migrants in the next period. In this approach, positive net migration increases the projected population and is equivalent to an increase in the region's survival and fertility rates. Negative net migration reduces the projected population and is equivalent to reduced survival and fertility rates.

Migration can also be considered by independently projecting the number of net migrants by cohort and by adding the number of net in-migrants to the surviving population. The projected number of net migrants is subtracted from the surviving population for cohorts with negative net migration. Chapter 7 illustrates these procedures and techniques for estimating and projecting net migration by cohort.

ENDNOTES

1. The term *cohort-survival* has also been used to describe models of this type. However, as Pittenger suggests (1976, 128), this term is more accurately applied to component projection models that do not explicitly consider migration.

2. For a more complete discussion of Whelpton's original model, see Pittenger (1976, 135–39).

3. The following discussion of the population pyramid is adapted from U.S. Bureau of the Census (1975, 236–42). For a more complete discussion of this and other techniques for describing the age and sex structure of a population, see Browing (1961).

4. The following definitions are taken from U.S. Bureau of the Census (1975, 616–19).

5. In-migrants and out-migrants are therefore distinguished from *immigrants,* international migrants who come from outside the country, and *emigrants,* international migrants who move to another country.

6. The migration data from the U.S. decennial censuses (e.g., U.S. Bureau of the Census 1977 and 1984b) are based on questions asked of surviving migrants. To be consistent, migration rates computed from these data should also be based on the final population. See Smith (1986) for an empirical study of the effect of the population base on cohort-component projection results.

7. A third procedure using cohort survival rates is described in Chapter 7.

Chapter 5

Mortality Component

Mortality is incorporated in a cohort-component model as the probability that a member of a cohort, n, will survive to become a member of the next higher cohort, $n + 1$, at the end of a projection period. For example, for the ten-year cohort-component model described in Chapter 4,

$$P_{n+1}^{t+1} = P_n^t \times s_{n,n+1} \qquad (1 \le n \le 7) \qquad (5.1)$$

where

$$P_n^t = \text{population of cohort } n \text{ at time } t$$
$$P_{n+1}^{t+1} = \text{population of cohort } n + 1 \text{ at time } t + 1$$
$$s_{n,n+1} = \text{survival rate (or probability of surviving)}$$
$$\text{from cohort } n \text{ to cohort } n + 1$$

For the open-ended ninth cohort consisting of the population aged 80 and above.

$$P_9^{t+1} = (P_8^t \times s_{8,9}) + (P_9^t \times s_{9,9}) \qquad (5.2)$$

The probability that an individual will survive is equal to one minus the probability that he or she will die during an interval. As a result, cohort-component projection models are based on past, present, and projected mortality rates for each age, sex, and race segment of the population. National survival rates by cohort are used by the U.S. Bureau of the Census to prepare periodic projections for the U.S. population (see, e.g., U.S. Bureau of the Census 1984a). However, national mortality rates are rarely used at the local level because they often differ substantially from local rates, generating significant projection errors.[1]

Population counts and deaths by age, sex, and race are readily available for states and counties from the decennial censuses and annual state vital statistics reports. These data could be used to compute local survival rates directly. However, the number of annual deaths in a five- or ten-year age, sex, and race cohort for a county can vary substantially from year to year, making estimates of local survival rates highly unreliable.

More reliable survival rates can be computed from the mortality data for larger areas that experience a larger number of deaths in each age, sex, and race cohort. State-level mortality data are generally used, as they best approximate local mortality rates. As a result, most small-area cohort-component models are based on survival rates computed from a state life table.

LIFE TABLES

Life tables were invented by Edmund Halley, the seventeenth-century mathematician and astronomer who also discovered the comet that bears his name.[2] Life tables are summary statistical models reporting the mortality and survivorship rates and life expectations of a population.[3] They are particularly useful for projection purposes because they provide summary mortality measures that are independent of the age distribution of a population.

Two types of life tables can be developed: (1) cohort or generation life tables and (2) current or period life tables. *Cohort* or *generation life tables* are based on the mortality rates experienced by an actual birth cohort (for example, the U.S. population born in the year 1900). These life tables record the mortality experiences of a cohort from birth until all of its members die. As a result, they require data for long time periods and cannot be completed until the entire cohort dies. *Current* or *period life tables* are based on the mortality rates experienced by the different components of a population over a short period of time, generally one to three years. This type of table is based on a cross-sectional "snapshot" of all segments of a population, in contrast to the cohort life table's longitudinal record for a small population segment. Current life tables are expressed in terms of the mortality experiences of a hypothetical population of 100,000 live births subjected throughout its life history to the mortality rates experienced by the original population in a short time period. Cohort-component projection models are based exclusively on current life tables. As a result, the term *life table* in the remainder of this discussion refers only to current life tables.

Table 5.1 contains data from a life table derived from the 1980 population census and recorded deaths for the female population of Ohio for 1979 through 1981.[4] Similar data by race and sex are prepared annually for the United States and every ten years for states and the District of Columbia (e.g., National Center for Health Statistics 1966; 1975b; 1986). The columns of a life table are interpreted as follows:

Column 1: Age Interval (x to $x + t$). The age interval shown in column 1 refers to the time interval between the exact ages (or birth anniversaries) indicated. For example, for the one-year life table shown in Table 5.1, the 0–1 age interval refers to the one-year interval between the birth date for the hypothetical population and the population's first birthday; the 5–6 interval refers to the one-year interval between the population's fifth and sixth birthdays; and so on.

Column 2: Proportion Dying ($_tq_x$). Column 2 records the proportion of the population in each age interval that is alive at the beginning of the interval but dies before reaching the end of the interval. For example, in Table 5.1, the proportion dying for the 0–1 age interval, 0.01113, indicates that approximately 11 of every 1,000 live births will die before they reach their first birthday. Column 2 is computed from the observed mortality rates for an actual population and is used to derive the remaining columns of the life table.[5]

Column 3: Number Living (l_x). Column 3 shows the number of persons who have survived to the beginning of the indicated age interval. The 100,000 persons for the first age interval represent the hypothetical population of 100,000 live births subjected to the morality rates reported in column 2. For example, Table 5.1 indicates that 98,887 of these births survive to their first birthday; 98,685 survive to their fifth birthday; and 19,100 survive to their ninetieth birthday.

Column 4: Number Dying ($_td_x$). Column 4 shows the number of persons dying during the age interval x to $x + t$. For example, for the initial population of 100,000 live births, 1,113 persons die before their first birthday and 33 die between their fifth and sixth birthdays. The number dying, $_td_x$, equals the number living at the beginning of an age interval, l_x, multiplied by the proportion dying during that interval, $_tq_x$. For example, the number dying in the first age interval, 1,113, is equal to the number living at the beginning of the interval, 100,000, multiplied by the proportion dying, 0.01113. The number living at the beginning

Table 5.1

Life Table for Ohio Females, 1979 to 1981

Age Interval (x to $x+t$)	Proportion Dying ($_tq_x$)	Of 100,000 Births		Stationary Population		Average Remaining Lifetime ($^o e_x$)
		Number Living (l_x)	Number Dying ($_td_x$)	In The Age Interval ($_tL_x$)	In This and All Subsequent Intervals (T_x)	
(1)	(2)	(3)	(4)	(5)	(6)	(7)
0–1......	0.01113	100,000	1,113	99,083	7,705,577	77.06
1–2......	0.00065	98,887	65	98,855	7,606,494	76.92
2–3......	0.00056	98,822	55	98,794	7,507,639	75.97
3–4......	0.00046	98,767	45	98,745	7,408,845	75.01
4–5......	0.00038	98,722	37	98,703	7,310,100	74.05
5–6......	0.00033	98,685	33	98,669	7,211,397	73.08
6–7......	0.00028	98,652	28	98,638	7,112,728	72.10
7–8......	0.00025	98,624	24	98,612	7,014,090	71.12
8–9......	0.00022	98,600	22	98,589	6,915,478	70.14
9–10.....	0.00020	98,578	19	98,569	6,816,889	69.15
10–11.....	0.00018	98,559	18	98,549	6,718,320	68.17
20–21.....	0.00056	98,246	55	98,219	5,733,966	58.36
30–31.....	0.00074	97,613	72	97,576	4,754,587	48.71
40–41.....	0.00164	96,596	158	96,517	3,782,873	39.16
50–51.....	0.00429	94,070	404	93,867	2,827,582	30.06
60–61.....	0.01032	88,080	909	87,625	1,912,861	21.72
70–71.....	0.02402	75,323	1,809	74,419	1,088,860	14.46
80–81.....	0.05958	51,860	3,090	50,315	442,924	8.54
90–91.....	0.14769	19,100	2,821	17,689	88,728	4.65
91–92.....	0.16141	16,279	2,628	14,965	71,039	4.36
92–93.....	0.17581	13,651	2,400	12,451	56,074	4.11
93–94.....	0.19006	11,251	2,138	10,182	43,623	3.88
94–95.....	0.20404	9,113	1,860	8,183	33,441	3.67

Source: National Center for Health Statistics (1986, 36–8 and 36–9).

of an age interval equals the number living at the beginning of the previous age interval minus the number who died during the previous interval. For example, the number living at the beginning of the second age interval, 98,887, is equal to the number of persons living at the beginning of the first age interval, 100,000, minus the number dying in the first age interval, 1,113.

Columns 5 and 6: Stationary Population. The *stationary population* is a hypothetical population in which 100,000 persons are born and die each year and the proportion dying in each age interval corresponds to the $_tq_x$ values shown in column 2 of the life table. If there is no migration and if births and deaths are evenly distributed over the year, the population is considered stationary because the total population and the number of persons in each age interval do not change. When a person dies or enters the next higher age interval, his or her place is immediately taken by someone entering from the next lower age interval. Thus the number of persons in the age interval remains the same.

Column 5: Stationary Population in the Age Interval ($_tL_x$). Column 5 shows the total number of persons in the stationary population for each age interval. Thus, in Table 5.1, the stationary population between the ages of 0 and 1 is 99,083, and the stationary population between the ages of 5 and 6 is 98,669. Because the stationary population is constant and the population remains in this age interval for exactly one year, the $_tL_x$ values are equal to the number of person-years lived by the stationary population in each age interval.

The l_x values in column 3 correspond to the number of persons who are alive on the anniversary of their birth. The $_tL_x$ values in column 5 are equivalent to the average population size between birth anniversaries, taking into account the distribution of deaths throughout the year. For example, for the 5–6 age interval, 98,685 individuals are alive at the beginning of the interval, and 98,652 are alive at the end of the interval. The $_tL_x$ value for this age interval is the average of these values, 98,669. The $_tL_x$ value for the 0–1 age interval, 99,083, is less than the average of the initial and final populations (i.e., the average of 100,000 and 98,887, or 99,444), because a large proportion of the deaths occur shortly after birth, reducing the average population in the age interval.

Column 6: Stationary Population in This and Subsequent Intervals (T_x). Column 6 records the stationary population in the indicated age interval and all subsequent intervals. For example, Table 5.1 indicates that 7,211,397 persons are aged 5 and above and 88,728 are 90 years of age and older. The T_X values equal the cumulative sum of the $_lL_X$ values for the indicated age interval and all higher age intervals. For example, the T_X value for the first age interval, 7,705,577, is equal to the T_X value for the second age interval, 7,606,494, plus the $_lL_X$ value for the first age interval, 99,083. Because the $_lL_X$ values correspond to the number of years lived by the members of each age interval, the T_X values correspond to the total number of person-years that will be lived by the stationary population in each age interval.

Column 7: Average Remaining Lifetime (^0e_x). Column 7 indicates the average remaining lifetime or life expectancy in years for a person who survives to the beginning of the indicated age interval. For example, the life table in Table 5.1 reports that female residents of Ohio who were twenty years old in 1980 will, on average, live 58.36 more years. The life expectancy is obtained by dividing the total number of years that will be lived by the persons in an age interval, T_X, by the number of persons in the interval, l_X. For example, the life expectancy for ninety-year-old women in Table 5.1, 4.65, is equal to the T_X value for this age interval, 88,728, divided by the l_X value for this age interval, 19,100.

Life tables record the life experiences of a hypothetical population exposed to the mortality rates experienced by an actual population in a particular time period. As a result, analysts can select the life table for the population whose life expectations correspond most closely to those of the study region. While state life tables are generally used for these purposes, national or other state life tables may be used when the state-level mortality rates differ significantly from local rates, for instance, for a metropolitan county located in a largely rural state.

State-level mortality rates can also be adjusted to approximate local rates by using the state rates to estimate total local deaths in a year, say, 1980. Observed local deaths for 1979 through 1981 can then be averaged to account for the variability of death rates for small areas. The state rates can then be multiplied by the ratio of the average observed local deaths to the estimated deaths derived from the state rates. For example, if the total number of local deaths is 10 percent higher than estimated by the state rates, the state mortality rates for each cohort can be increased by 10 percent to approximate the local rates.[6]

Cohort-component projection models generally use five-year cohorts and projection periods, requiring five-year survival rates. However, the procedures for deriving survival rates from a life table are most easily demonstrated for a one-year cohort-component model. The following section illustrates these procedures for the life table data given in Table 5.1. The next section uses these data to illustrate procedures for computing survival rates for periods of more than one year.

COMPUTING ONE-YEAR SURVIVAL RATES

Mortality is incorporated in a cohort-component projection model as the probability that a member of a cohort will survive to the next higher cohort at the end of a projection period:[7]

$$P_{n+1}^{t+1} = P_n^t \times s_{n,n+1} \quad (1 \le n \le 7) \tag{5.3}$$

Dividing both sides of Eq. (5.3) by P_n^t yields the following:

$$s_{n,n,+1} = \frac{P_{n+1}^{t+1}}{P_n^t} \tag{5.4}$$

That is, the survival rate from cohort n to cohort $n + 1$, $s_{n,n+1}$, can be computed by dividing the surviving population, P_{n+1}^{t+1}, by the initial population, P_n^t.

The life table population between the ages of x and $x + 1$ is reported as the stationary population $_tL_x$ value in column 5 of a life table. As a result, the life table population at the beginning of a one-year period, P_n^t, is equal to the $_tL_x$ value for that age interval, L_n. The life table population for the next one-year age interval, P_{n+1}^{t+1} is equal to the $_tL_x$ value for the next higher age interval, L_{n+1}. Substituting these values into Eq. (5.4) yields the following equation for the one-year survival rate from age n to $n + 1$:

$$s_{n,n+1} = \frac{L_{n+1}}{L_n} \tag{5.5}$$

For example, the $_tL_x$ value for the first age interval (ages 0 to 1) in Table 5.1 is 99,083, and the $_tL_x$ value for the second age interval (ages 1 to 2) is 98,855. Substitution into Eq. (5.5) yields the one-year survival rate from age 1 to age 2:

$$s_{1,2} = \frac{L_2}{L_1} = \frac{98,855}{99,083} = 0.9977$$

These survival rates are not equivalent to the proportion dying, $_tq_x$, values reported in column 2 of the life table. The $_tq_x$ values are the probabilities that an individual who is exactly x years old will die before his or her next birthday. As a result, the corresponding survival rates are the probabilities that an individual who is *exactly* x years old will survive to be *exactly* x + 1. For example, the probability that an individual who has just been born will survive to his or her first birthday is equal to one minus the $_tq_x$ value for the first age interval (ages 0 to 1), or 0.9887. The survival rate computed from the stable population $_tL_x$ values, 0.9977, is the probability that an individual who is *between* the ages of 0 and 1 will survive to be *between* the ages of 1 and 2.

Survival rates into the first and last age intervals can also be computed by applying Eq. (5.4). For a one-year cohort-component model, the survival rate into the first age interval, $s_{0,1}$, is the probability that an infant born in a one-year projection period will survive to be a member of the first age interval. As a result, the population at the end of the period, P_1^{t+1}, is equal to the $_tL_x$ value for the first age interval. The population at the beginning of the period, P_n^t, is equal to the number of births in a one-year period or 100,000. Thus for the life table reported in Table 5.1, the survival rate into the first one-year cohort is computed as follows:

$$s_{0,1} = \frac{L_1}{100,000} = \frac{99,083}{100,000} = 0.9908$$

The survival rate for the open-ended cohort consisting of persons above a certain age is equal to the probability that an individual in the open-ended cohort will live for a year and remain in the cohort. For example, the one-year survival rate for an open-ended cohort for ages 90 and older is equal to the probability that an individual who is 90 or older will survive to be 91 or older at the end of a year.

This survival rate can be computed by substituting the appropriate values into Eq. (5.4). In this case the population at the end of the period, P_{n+1}^{t+1}, is the life table population aged ninety-one and above. The population at the beginning of the period, P_n^t, is the life table population aged 90 and above. The life table population that is age x and older is reported as the T_x value in column 6 of a life table. The survival rate for an open-ended cohort n can therefore be computed by dividing the T_x value for age interval n + 1, T_{n+1}, by the T_x value for age interval n, T_n. That is, the one-year survival rate for an open-ended interval n, is computed as follows:

$$s_{n,n} = \frac{T_{n+1}}{T_n} \tag{5.6}$$

For example, for the life table data in Table 5.1, the one-year survival rate for an open-ended ninety-first cohort (ages 90 and above), $s_{91,91}$, is equal to the T_X value for the 91–92 age interval, 71,039, divided by the T_X value for the 90–91 age interval, 88,728:

$$s_{91,91} = \frac{T_{92}}{T_{91}} = \frac{71,039}{88,728} = 0.8006$$

COMPUTING MULTIPLE-YEAR SURVIVAL RATES

Cohort-component models generally disaggregate a population into five-year age cohorts and project a population at five-year intervals. Decennial state life table such as the life table in Table 5.1 (e.g., National Center for Health Statistics 1966 and 1975b) provide information on single-year age intervals. As a result, survival rates for five- or ten-year cohort models must be computed from data from one-year life tables. This section describes procedures for deriving ten-year survival rates for the simple cohort projection model introduced in Chapter 4. Equivalent procedures can be used to compute five-year survival rates.

Survival rates for multiple-year age cohorts are computed by substituting appropriate life table population values into Eq. (5.4):

$$S_{n,n+1} = \frac{P_{n+1}^{t+1}}{P_n^t} \tag{5.4}$$

where P_n^t and P_{n+1}^{t+1} are the life table stable populations in cohorts n and $n + 1$, respectively.

The life table population in a ten-year age cohort is equal to the sum of the $_tL_x$ values for a one-year life table. For example, the population in the first ten-year age cohort (ages 0 through 9) is equal to the sum of the $_tL_x$ values for age intervals 0–1 through 9–10.[8] The life table population in a ten-year interval can also be computed from the T_X values reported in the sixth column of the life table. The T_X value for the 0–1 age interval, T_0, is equal to the life table population aged 0 or older; the T_X value for the 10–11 age interval, T_{10}, is equal to the life table population aged 10 or older. The difference between these values is the life table population that is older than 0 and less than 10, (i.e., the population in the first cohort aged 0 through 9).

The life table stable population in each ten-year age interval, D_n, is therefore equal to the difference between the T_X values that define the beginning and end of the life table stable population interval. For example, in Table 5.2, the life table stable population in the first ten-year cohort, 987,257, is equal to T_x value for the 0–1 age interval, 7,705,577, minus T_x value for the 10–11 age interval, 6,718,320.

As a result, the survival rate for all but the first and last cohorts can be computed by substituting the appropriate life table stable population values into Eq. (5.7).

$$s_{n,n+1} = \frac{D_{n+1}}{D_n} \qquad (5.7)$$

where D_n and D_{n+1} are computed by taking the difference between the life table T_x values defining the beginning and end of each cohort.

For example, given the life table data from Tables 5.1 and 5.2, the survival rate from the first ten-year cohort to the second, $s_{1,2}$, can be computed as follows:

$$s_{1,2} = \frac{D_2}{D_1} = \frac{984,354}{987,257} = 0.9971$$

Table 5.2

Computing Ten-Year Survival Rates

Initial Age of Cohort	Cohort Number (n)	Life Table		Life Table Stable Population (Dn)	Survival Rate (sn,n+1)
		Age Interval (x to x+n)	Stationary Population In This and All Subsequent Intervals[a] (Tx)		
(1)	(2)	(3)	(4)	(5)	(6)
Births	0	...	...	...	0.9873
0–9	1	0– 1...	7,705,577	987,257	0.9971
10–19	2	10–11..	6,718,320	984,354	0.9949
20–29	3	20–21..	5,733,966	979,379	0.9922
30–39	4	30–31..	4,754,587	971,714	0.9831
40–49	5	40–41..	3,782,873	955,291	0.9575
50–59	6	50–51..	2,827,582	914,721	0.9008
60–69	7	60–61..	1,912,861	824,001	0.7839
70–79	8	70–71..	1,088,860	645,936	0.5483
80+	9	80–81..	442,924	354,196	0.2003
...	...	90–91..	88,728	...	...

[a] These data are from Table 5.1, column 6.

Similar computations for cohorts one through eight yield the survival rates reported in column 6 of Table 5.2

The survival rate for births into the first cohort, $s_{0,1}$, is the probability that an infant born during a ten-year projection period will survive to be a member of the first cohort at the end of the period. As before, this rate is computed by dividing the population at the end of the period (the life table stable population in the first cohort) by the population at the beginning of the period (the number of births in a period). For a ten-year cohort model, the life table stable population in the first cohort, D_1, is equal to the difference between the T_X value for the 0–1 age interval, T_0, and the T_X value for the 10–11 age interval, T_{10}. The number of births in a ten-year projection period is equal to ten times the 100,000 annual live births that provide the basis for the life table, or 1,000,000. As a result,

$$s_{0,1} = \frac{D_1}{1,000,000} \qquad (5.8)$$

For example, the survival rate into the first cohort, $s_{0,1}$, for the life table data reported in Tables 5.1 and 5.2, can be computed as follows:

$$s_{0,1} = \frac{987,257}{1,000,000} = 0.9873$$

The survival rate for the population in the open-ended ninth cohort, $s_{9,9}$ can be computed in a similar manner. For a ten-year cohort model, the population at the beginning of the period, P_n^t, is equal to the population aged 80 and above, that is, the life table stable population aged 80 or above, T_{80}. The population at the end of the period, P_{n+1}^{t+1}, is equal to the surviving population aged 90 and above, that is, the life table stable population aged 90 and above, T_{90}. Therefore, the survival rate from cohort nine to cohort nine is equal to

$$s_{9,9} = \frac{T_{90}}{T_{80}} \qquad (5.9)$$

Thus, for the life table data reported in Tables 5.1 and 5.2, the survival rate for the open-ended ninth cohort, $s_{9,9}$, is equal to

$$s_{9,9} = \frac{88,728}{442,924} = 0.2003$$

PROJECTING SURVIVING POPULATION

Table 5.3 illustrates the procedures for using the survival rates computed in Table 5.2 and the sample population data in Table 4.1 to

Table 5.3

Projecting Surviving Female Population, 1990

Initial Age of Cohort (1)	Cohort Number (n) (2)	Initial Population[a] (P_n^{1980}) (3)	Survival Rate[b] ($s_{n,n+1}$) (4)	Surviving Population (P_n^{1990}) (5)
0–9	1	7,899	0.9971	...
10–19	2	8,513	0.9949	7,876
20–29	3	8,817	0.9922	8,470
30–39	4	6,956	0.9831	8,748
40–49	5	4,956	0.9575	6,838
50–59	6	4,717	0.9008	4,746
60–69	7	3,691	0.7839	4,249
70–79	8	2,390	0.5483	2,893
80+	9	1,471	0.2003	1,605
Total	...	49,410	...	...

[a] These data are from Table 4.1, column 4.
[b] These data are from Table 5.2, column 6.

project the surviving female population in 1990. Identical procedures using survival rates for males are used to project the surviving male population in 1990. Four sets of computations using appropriate age-, sex-, and race-specific survival rates are required if the population is divided by race and sex.

The surviving female population in 1990 for all but the final cohort is equal to the female population of the next lower cohort in 1980 multiplied by the survival rate for that cohort, $s_{n,n+1}$, as shown in Eq. (5.1):

$$P_{n+1}^{t+1} = P_n^t \times s_{n,n+1} \qquad (1 \leq n \leq 7) \qquad (5.1)$$

For example, given the survival rates in Table 5.3, the projected female population in the second cohort can be computed as follows:

$$\begin{aligned} P_2^{1990} &= P_1^{1980} \times s_{1,2} \\ &= 7,899 \times 0.9971 \\ &= 7,876 \end{aligned}$$

The surviving female population in the open-ended ninth cohort can be calculated by applying Eq. (5.2), as follows: (5.2)

$$\begin{aligned} P_9^{t+1} &= (P_8^t \times s_{8,9}) + (P_9^t \times s_{9,9}) \\ P_9^{1990} &= (P_8^{1980} \times s_{9,8}) + (P_9^{1980} \times s_{9,9}) \\ &= (2,390 \times 0.5483) + (1,471 \times 0.2003) \\ &= 1,310 + 295 = 1,605 \end{aligned}$$

The pattern for computing the surviving population in Table 5.3 is the mirror image of the graphic representation in Figure 4.2. In Figure 4.2, the surviving population in each cohort moves *up* one row of the population pyramid to become the new population of the next cohort. In Table 5.3, the surviving population from each cohort (computed by multiplying the initial population by the appropriate survival rate) moves *down* one row to become the population of the next cohort. The only exception to this pattern is the open-ended cohort; in both cases the surviving population equals the surviving population from the preceding cohort plus the surviving population from the open-ended cohort.

PROJECTING MORTALITY RATES

The procedures described in the preceding sections can be used to estimate past and present survival rates from a state or national life table. Many cohort-component models assume that future mortality rates equal present rates. However, this assumption is questionable in the face of declining mortality rates resulting from general improvements in health care and life style. Given a high degree of uncertainty concerning future improvements, it seems appropriate to prepare a series of projections reflecting different mortality assumptions.

The national population projections of the U.S. Bureau of the Census (e.g., U.S. Bureau of the Census, 1984a) include three sets of survival rate projections derived from the Social Security Administration's detailed analysis of past and prospective mortality trends by age and sex for ten causes of death.[9] For example, the 1983 population projections for 1985 through 2025 include low, medium, and high mortality assumptions by race, sex, and five-year age intervals from birth to an open-ended cohort for ages 95 and older. Life expectancy at birth for the total population under the middle assumption series is projected to increase from 74.3 years in 1982 to 76.7 years in 2000 and 81.0 years in 2080. Life expectancies for the low mortality series are about two years above those for the middle series in 2000 and five to six years higher in 2080 and a similar amount lower for the high mortality series. Life expectancies for blacks are assumed to improve two to four times as rapidly as white rates but still not match the white rates by the year 2080.

The mortality projections of the U.S. Bureau of the Census can be incorporated in a cohort-component projection model by using a state life table to estimate current survival rates by age and sex. Projected national survival rates by age and sex for each mortality assumption series can then be divided by the current national rates to determine the projected rates of improvement by cohort for each series. Local survival rates can then be multiplied by the projected improvement rates to yield survival rate projections reflecting the Bureau's national mortality assumptions.

ENDNOTES

1. For example, compounding errors from a 1 percent error in local mortality rates generate errors of more than 6 percent in 30-year projections for a 5-year cohort model (Pittenger 1976, 150–51).

2. Though John Graunt conducted the first mortality analysis and produced an elementary life table in 1662, his analysis was mostly descriptive, presenting rates and numbers of deaths for various causes. Halley used life tables as a mathematical model of mortality in a work published in the Royal Society's *Transactions* in 1693 (Levine 1985, 510). Also see Newman (1956, 1416–47).

3. The following discussion is based largely on U.S. Bureau of the Census (1975, 429–33) and National Center for Health Statistics (1975b, 1–5). Pages 429 to 459 of the first reference should be consulted for a detailed discussion of the derivation, interpretation, and use of life tables. For additional information, see Cox (1976, 275–93) and Keyfitz (1977, 47–53).

4. The actual life table provides information for one-year age intervals from ages 0 to 110.

5. The data and procedures used to prepare the decennial life tables for the United States and the 50 states are described in National Center for Health Statistics (1975a). Also see U.S. Bureau of the Census (1975, 433–46) and Keyfitz (1977, 34–53).

6. This adjustment was suggested by Andrew Isserman in personal correspondence.

7. The computational procedures outlined below are described in Irwin (1977, 50–51).

8. Caution must be exercised in comparing the age intervals in a life table to those in a cohort-component projection model because they use different nomenclature. In a life table, the x to $x + t$ age interval refers to the period between a person's xth birthday and the day before his or her x plus first birthday. Thus, the life table population in the 0–1 through 9–10 age intervals includes the population between the ages of 0 and 10, that is, those aged 0 through 9.

The age interval in a cohort-component projection model refers to the population included in the ages indicated. Thus the 0–9 age interval includes the population aged 0 through 9, that is, the population included in life table age intervals 0–1 through 9–10.

9. For a more complete discussion of this and other mortality projection methods, see U.S. Bureau of the Census (1975, 778–81).

Chapter 6

Fertility Component

Fertility is incorporated in a cohort-component projection model as infants born to women in the fertile age cohorts who survive to become the projected population in the first cohort. Most cohort-component models separate the birth and survival computations by first projecting the number of live births and then projecting the surviving population in the first cohort. Procedures for computing the survival rate for infants are described in Chapter 5. This chapter discusses the procedures for estimating fertility rates, projecting the number of male and female births, and predicting future fertility rates.

The number of births in a projection period is computed by multiplying the female population in the childbearing cohorts by the appropriate age-specific birth rates. Data on the number of resident births by age and race of mother are generally available at the county and city level from state vital statistics offices (see, for example, Ohio Department of Health 1972 and 1982). "Resident" births, recorded by the mothers' usual residence, are used to measure and project an area's fertility. "Occurrence" births, reported by the location in which births occur, are useful for applications such as determining regional demand for maternity services.[1]

Resident birth data can be combined with census population data to estimate fertility rates by age and race of the mother. That is, the fertility rate for women in cohort n, $f_{n,0}$, is equal to the number of resident live births to women in the cohort, B_n, divided by the female population in the cohort, PF_n^t:

$$f_{n,0} = \frac{B_n}{PF_n^t} \tag{6.1}$$

81

Caution must be exercised, however, in computing age-specific fertility rates from small-area birth data. The number of local births to women in a given age and race cohort is generally quite small and highly variable, making fertility estimates for a single year very unreliable. This variability can be reduced by computing fertility rates from the average number of births for a three-year period centered around the census year, for instance, 1979, 1980, and 1981.

Table 6.1 illustrates the procedure for computing age-specific fertility rates for the sample population considered in Chapters 4 and 5. For example, the estimated fertility rate for the second cohort (ages 10 to 19), 0.0202, is equal to the average number of resident births to women in this cohort, 172, divided by the cohort's population, 8,513.

Small-area fertility estimates can also be affected by the unknown "contamination" effects of migration. The classic example is a rapidly suburbanizing county initially having a rural population and a high birth rate. Twenty years later the population is largely white collar and suburban with a low birth rate, invalidating population forecasts based on the earlier fertility rates (Pittenger 1976, 156). Because white/ nonwhite and urban/rural birth rates differ substantially, extreme care must be used in applying fertility rates. If the area's demographic composition differs substantially from the county's (e.g., a small town in a metropolitan county), fertility rates for the state or other comparable areas can be used.

County- or state-level fertility rates can also be adjusted to more closely approximate local rates by using the published county or state fertility rates to estimate total local births in a year, say 1980. The

Table 6.1

Estimating Age-Specific Fertility Rates, 1980

Initial Age of Cohort	Cohort Number (n)	Female Population[a] (PF_n^{1980})	Average Births 1979–1981[b] (B_n)	Fertility Rate $(f_{n,0})$
(1)	(2)	(3)	(4)	(5)
10–19	2	8,513	172	0.0202
20–29	3	8,817	1,170	0.1327
30–39	4	6,956	326	0.0469
40–49	5	4,956	17	0.0034
Total	...	...	1,685	...

[a] These data are from Table 4.1, column 4.
[b] These data are from Ohio Department of Health. *Report of Vital Statistics for Ohio* (1979 to 1981).

average number of local births for a three-year period can then be divided by this estimate to compute an adjustment factor that is applied to the county-level age-specific fertility rates. For example, if the average number of local births is 5 percent lower than the estimate obtained by applying the county-level age-specific fertility rates, these rates should be reduced by 5 percent.[2]

PROJECTING MALE AND FEMALE BIRTHS

As pointed out in Chapter 4, the projected number of births in a year to the women in a cohort, B_n, is computed by multiplying the projected average female population, PA_n^{t-t+1}, by the appropriate age-specific birth rates, $f_{n,0}$. The average female population is used because the number of women in a cohort can change significantly during a projection period as women die or move into or out of the region.

The average female population in a cohort is the average of the initial population, P_n^t, and the final population, P_n^{t+1}. The initial population is the observed population in a census year or the projected population from a previous census year. The final population equals the surviving population from the preceding cohort plus the number of net migrants (in-migrants minus out-migrants) for the projection period, as follows:

$$P_n^{t+1} = (P_{n-1}^t \times s_{n-1,n}) + NM_n^{t-t+1}$$

and

$$PA_n^{t-t+1} = [P_n^t + (P_{n-1}^t \times s_{n-1,n}) + NM_n^{t-t+1}] \tag{6.2}$$

where

P_n^t = initial population in cohort n
P_{n-1}^t = initial population in cohort $n - 1$
$s_{n-1,n}$ = survival rate from cohort $n - 1$ to cohort n
NM_n^{t-t+1} = projected net migration into cohort n

For example, Table 6.2 illustrates the procedure for projecting the average female population for the sample population considered previously. Column 3 lists the observed female population by cohort in 1980; column 4 lists the survival rates computed in Chapter 5; and column 6 lists the projected number of net migrants in each cohort

Table 6.2

Projecting Average Female Population, 1980 to 1990

Age of Cohort (1)	Cohort Number (n) (2)	Initial Population[a] (PF_n^{1980}) (3)	Survival Rate[b] $(s_{n,n+1})$ (4)	Surviving Population PF_n^{1990} (5)	Projected Net Migration[c] $(NM_n^{1980-1990})$ (6)	Average Population $(PA_n^{1980-1990})$ (7)
0–9	1	7,899	0.9971	...	...	...
10–19	2	8,513	0.9949	7,876	405	8,397
20–29	3	8,817	0.9922	8,470	−323	8,482
30–39	4	6,956	0.9831	8,748	285	7,994
40–49	5	4,956	0.9575	6,838	37	5,916

[a]These data are from Table 4.1, column 4.
[b]These data are from Table 5.2, column 6.
[c]These data are from Table 5.3, column 5.

derived in Chapter 7. The average female population in each cohort is computed by applying Eq. (6.2). For example, for cohort two,

$$
\begin{aligned}
PA_2^{1980-1990} &= \frac{P_2^{1980} + (P_1^{1980} \times s_{1,2}) + NM_2^{1980-1990}}{2} \\
&= \frac{8,513 + (7,899 \times 0.9971) + 405}{2} \\
&= \frac{8,513 + 7,876 + 405}{2} = 8,397
\end{aligned}
$$

The total number of births in a ten-year projection period, B_T, is ten times the total number of annual births in all of the fertile cohorts:

$$B_T = 10 \times \Sigma_2^5 (PA_n^{t-t+1} \times f_{n,0}) \tag{4.8}$$

Table 6.3 illustrates the use of this equation to project the total births between 1980 and 1990. For example, the number of annual births to women in the second cohort, 170, is equal to the projected average number of women in the cohort, 8,397, multiplied by the estimated fertility rate, 0.0202. The total number of births in a ten-year period is ten times the projected number of annual births, or 16,900.

Total births in a projection period, B_T, can be divided into male births, B_m, and female births, B_f, by applying the estimated proportion of male births, p_m, and female births, p_f, respectively. These proportions are generally computed from national data on the *sex ratio (SR) at birth,* that is, the number of male births, B_m, per 100 female births, B_f. In other words,

$$SR = \frac{B_m}{B_f} \times 100$$

Table 6.3

Projecting Annual Births, 1980 to 1990

Age of Cohort (1)	Cohort Number (n) (2)	Average Female Population[a] ($PA_n^{1980-1990}$) (3)	Fertility Rate[b] ($f_{n,0}$) (4)	Projected Annual Births (B_n) (5)
10–19	2	8,397	0.0202	170
20–29	3	8,482	0.1327	1,126
30–39	4	7,994	0.0469	374
40–49	5	5,916	0.0034	20
Total	...	...	...	1,690

[a] These data are from Table 6.2, column 7.
[b] These data are from Table 6.1, column 5.

A sex ratio of 100 indicates an equal number of male and female births; a sex ratio larger than 100 indicates an excess of male births; and a sex ratio smaller than 100 indicates an excess of female births.

The average sex ratio at birth for the total population of the United States for 1915 through 1964 was 105.4 with a standard deviation of 0.3, indicating that the ratio is quite stable. Average sex ratios at birth were 105.7 for whites and 102.3 for nonwhites. The ratios show relatively little geographic variation for the United States and are inversely related to the age of the mother and the birth order of the child (U.S. Bureau of the Census 1975, 195–96).

Given a value for the sex ratio at birth, the proportion of male births, p_m, and female births, p_f, can be computed by applying the following equations:

$$p_f = \frac{100}{100 + SR} \qquad (6.3)$$

$$p_m = \frac{SR}{100 + SR} \qquad (6.4)$$

For example, the proportion of female births for the total population can be estimated as follows:

$$p_f = \frac{100}{100 + SR}$$
$$= \frac{100}{100 + 105.4}$$
$$= 0.487$$

The proportion of male births for the total population and the male and female proportions by race can similarly be computed by substituting appropriate sex ratios into Eqs. (6.3) and (6.4).

The projected number of male and female births in a projection period can be determined by substituting the projected number of total births, B_T, and the proportion of male or female births into the following equations:

$$B_f = B_T \times p_f \qquad (6.5)$$
$$B_m = B_T \times p_m \qquad (6.6)$$

For example, given the projected number of total births and the proportion of female births computed above, the projected number of female births between 1980 and 1990 can be calculated as follows:

$$
\begin{aligned}
B_f &= B_T \times p_f \\
&= 16{,}900 \times 0.487 \\
&= 8{,}230
\end{aligned}
$$

The projected number of male births can be determined by substituting the projected number of total births and the projected proportion of male births into Eq. (6.6). Similar procedures using projected total births and male and female proportions by race can be used to project the number of births by race and sex. Chapter 8 reviews the procedures for calculating the surviving population in the first cohort from the projected number of births.

PROJECTING FERTILITY RATES

The procedures described in the previous section can be used to estimate present and past fertility rates from readily available published data for states, counties, and cities. Although many cohort-component models assume that the most recent fertility rates will continue without change, models that incorporate a range of fertility assumptions are clearly preferable in the face of dramatic long-term changes in fertility rates.

The national population projections of the U.S. Bureau of the Census incorporate three fertility assumption series comparable to the mortality assumption discussed in Chapter 5. The series are based on assumptions concerning average family size and mean age of childbearing derived from current information on the birth expectations of women and other variables affecting future fertility rates.[3]

For example, the projections of the U.S. Bureau of the Census for 1983 through 2080 include a low, medium, and high fertility assumption series. The middle assumption series is based on an ultimate fertility level or completed family size of 1,900 births per 1,000 women. This was reduced from a middle assumption of 2,100 births per 1,000 women in previous projections to reflect the declining birth expectations of women aged 18 to 24, the increasing proportion of working women, the rise in female age at marriage, and the increased incidence of divorce. The low series assumes a completed family size of 1,600 births per 1,000 women. The high series assumes a completed family size of 2,300 births per 1,000 women, which is lower than fertility has been in the United States except during the Great Depression and in the period since 1972. The ultimate mean age at childbearing for all three series is 26.5 years, up from 26.0 for the last several national projections (U.S. Bureau of the Census 1984b, 15–17).

Three sets of age- and race-specific fertility rate projections are provided for total females, white females, and black females and for eight five-year age cohorts (ages 10 to 14 through 45 to 49). Projections are provided at one-year intervals from 1983 to 1990, at five-year intervals from 1990 to 2030, and at ten-year intervals for 2040 and 2050 and beyond. The fertility rate projections are prepared by linear age-specific interpolation between observed fertility rates for women born in 1959 and projected rates for women born in 1985 (U.S. Bureau of the Census 1984b, 22–24).

The U.S. Bureau of the Census also projects age- and race-specific birth rates for states (see, e.g., U.S. Bureau of the Census 1979). The rates are prepared by (1) computing the ratio of observed birth rates by age and race to the corresponding national birth rates; (2) linearly projecting the ratios so that the state and national fertility rates converge in the year 2000; and (3) multiplying the projected ratios by the middle fertility assumption series to obtain the projected state fertility rates.[4]

The national fertility projections of the U.S. Bureau of the Census can be used to produce alternative local fertility projections by dividing the three sets of age-specific fertility projections by the corresponding current national rates to identify the projected changes in national fertility rates. The projected rates of change for the nation can then be applied to current local fertility rates to produce local fertility and population projections consistent with the Bureau's national fertility assumptions.

ENDNOTES

1. For a more complete discussion of these and other fertility measures including an analysis of data reliability, see U.S. Bureau of the Census (1975, 462–522).

2. This adjustment was suggested by Andrew Isserman.

3. For a more complete discussion of this and other fertility projection methods, see U.S. Bureau of the Census (1975, 781–91) and Pittenger (1976, 155–75).

4. See Isserman (1985, 26–32) for a comprehensive review and assessment of current theoretical perspectives on fertility and current and prospective economic-demographic strategies for forecasting national and state fertility rates.

Chapter 7

Migration Component

Two approaches can be used to incorporate migration into a cohort-component projection model. The *cohort-survival* method combines migration and mortality into a single rate of overall population change. A cohort survival rate is computed by dividing the observed population in each cohort at the beginning of a period into the observed population in the next higher cohort at the end of the period. For example, a ten-year cohort survival rate for the third cohort is obtained by dividing the observed population of the fourth cohort in 1980 by the observed population of the third cohort in 1970. This rate could then be applied to the 1980 population in the third cohort to project the population of the fourth cohort in 1990, considering the joint effect of migration and mortality.

This approach is theoretically unsatisfactory because it fails to separate the mortality and migration components of population change. The method unrealistically assumes that mortality and net migration rates will remain constant or will change in the same way and at the same time. As neither assumption is reasonable, it is preferable to isolate migration from the other components of demographic change.

As a result, cohort-component projection models generally estimate migration from past population data and modify these estimates as appropriate to project future migration. Most models divide a population into five-year age groups and require migration estimates and projections for five-year periods. However, net migration estimation techniques are best introduced with the ten-year cohort-component model discussed in previous chapters. After reviewing ten-year net migration estimation procedures, this chapter considers five-year migration estimation procedures. It concludes by examining techniques for adjusting the net migration estimates to project future migration.

ESTIMATING TEN-YEAR NET MIGRATION

In- and out-migration by age, race, and sex can be determined directly from census questions and survey information on place of birth, place of residence at a fixed date in the past, number of moves, and so forth. For example, the 15 percent sample questions of the U.S. decennial population censuses include questions on place of residence five years previously. The information on place of residence in, say, 1975 and 1980 is used to estimate gross migration for counties for the five-year period. In-migrants for a county include all persons aged five years or older who lived in the county on April 1, 1980, and who reported a different county (or country) of residence in 1975. Out-migrants include all persons aged five years or older who resided in the county in 1975 and in another county in 1980. Net migration is computed by subtracting the number of out-migrants from the number of in-migrants (U.S. Bureau of the Census 1977 and 1984b).[1]

These data understate the actual migration in two ways. Persons who migrated after April 1, 1975, and who died before April 1, 1980, and persons who left a county after April 1, 1975, and who returned to it prior to April 1, 1980, are not counted as migrants. Also persons who made multiple moves during the five-year period are assumed to have made only one move—from their residence on April 1, 1975, to their residence on April 1, 1980 (U.S. Bureau of the Census 1977, 1).

County-to-county migration counts are also compiled each year by the U.S. Bureau of the Census for preparation of its annual county population and per capita income estimates. One-year migration estimates are prepared by comparing the addresses on individual tax returns for two consecutive years. If the addresses match, no migration is assumed. If they differ, the addresses are assigned to counties and the total number of personal exemptions indicated on the return is allocated to the county-to-county flow. The estimates report significant migration flows into and out of every county in the United States based on all of the individual tax returns that are filed in the two years and that can be assigned to counties.[2]

Net migration can also be measured indirectly from observed population counts for two census years and observed or estimated natural increase (births minus deaths) for the intercensal period.[3] *Residual net migration estimation* methods recognize that an area's population can only change if a person is born, dies, or moves into or out of the area. As a result, the area's population at time t, P^t, is equal to (1) the population at an earlier time period, P^{t-1}; plus (2) the number of births (B) between $t - 1$ and t; minus (3) the number of deaths during the period, D; plus (4) the number of net migrants (NM) (in-migrants minus out-migrants) between $t - 1$ and t:

$$P^t = P^{t-1} + B - D + NM$$

Rearranging terms yields the following:

$$NM = (P^t - P^{t-1}) - (B - D) \qquad (7.1)$$

where $(P^t - P^{t-1})$ is the total population change between $t - 1$ and t, and $(B - D)$ is the population change due to natural increase.[4]

Net migration is thus assumed to equal the residual population change for an observation period that cannot be accounted for by natural increase. Population growth can only exceed natural increase if positive net migration (more in-migrants than out-migrants) has added to the area's population. Conversely, population growth will only be less than natural increase if negative net migration (more out-migrants than in-migrants) has reduced the area's population.

The observed population by age, sex, and race at ten-year intervals can be obtained directly from the decennial population censuses. The *vital statistics* estimation method uses recorded births and deaths by age, sex, and race for the intercensal period to estimate population change due to natural increase. As a result, this method requires complete and reliable information on births and deaths by age, sex, race, date of occurrence, and place of residence. Because these data are generally not available for small areas, this method is used primarily to estimate net migration for states and multistate regions.

The *survival-rate* estimation method applies estimated survival rates and observed or estimated births for the intercensal period to project the expected population by age, sex and race at the end of the observation period. Survival rates can be derived from the appropriate life table using the procedures described in Chapter 3. Information on the annual number of resident births is generally available for states, counties, and cities from the state vital statistics reports (e.g., Ohio Department of Health 1972). Annual births for each of the years within the migration estimation period can be summed to determine the number of births for the migration estimation period.[5]

The number of births in a migration estimation period can also be estimated by applying age- and race-specific fertility rates for a larger area (e.g., a state or county) to the average female population in the study area. The procedure is identical to the fertility projection procedure described in Chapter 6 except that the average female population in each cohort is computed from the observed population at the beginning and end of the estimation period. For example, the average female population in a cohort for the 1970 to 1980 period is computed by averaging the cohort's population in 1970 and 1980.

Table 7.1 illustrates the use of the survival rate method to estimate net migration by age for the 1970 to 1980 period for the sample population considered in Chapters 5 and 6. Columns 3 and 6 list the observed female population in 1970 and 1980. The number of female births in the ten-year period is obtained from the state vital statistics reports for 1970 through 1979. The survival rates in column 4 are computed from the 1970 state life table using the procedures described in Chapter 5.

The expected population values for 1980 in column 5 are obtained by applying the survival rates to the observed population in 1970. For

Table 7.1

Estimating Female Net Migration by Age, 1970 to 1980

Age of Cohort (1)	Cohort Number (n) (2)	Initial Population[a] (P_n^{1970}) (3)	Survival Rate[b] $(s_{n,n+1})$ (4)	Expected Population (PE_n^{1980}) (5)	Observed Population[c] (P_n^{1980}) (6)	Estimated Net Migration $(NM_n^{1970-1980})$ (7)
Births	0	7,598[d]	0.9816	...	...	...
0– 9	1	8,165	0.9961	7,458	7,899	441
10–19	2	9,218	0.9939	8,133	8,513	380
20–29	3	6,753	0.9904	9,162	8,817	−345
30–39	4	5,031	0.9781	6,688	6,956	268
40–49	5	4,840	0.9487	4,921	4,956	35
50–59	6	4,206	0.8886	4,592	4,717	125
60–69	7	2,869	0.7504	3,737	3,691	−46
70–79	8	2,084	0.4763	2,153	2,390	237
80+	9	1,095	0.1584	1,166	1,471	305
Total	...	44,261[e]	...	48,010	49,410	1,400

[a] These data are from U.S. Bureau of the Census (1973, 37–273).
[b] These data are derived from National Center for Health Statistics (1975, 36–10 – 36–11).
[c] These data are from Table 4.1, column 4.
[d] This figure is from Ohio Department of Health, Division of Vital Statistics, *Report of Vital Statistics for Ohio*, (1970 to 1979). Columbus, Ohio: Ohio Department of Health.
[e] This total excludes births.

example, the expected 1980 population for the first cohort, 7,458, is equal to the observed number of female births in the ten-year period, 7,598, multiplied by the survival rate for births, 0.9816. The net migration estimates in column 7 are computed by subtracting the expected 1980 population in each cohort from the observed population in 1980. For example, the estimated net migration for the first cohort, 441, is equal to the observed 1980 population, 7,899, minus the expected 1980 population, 7,458.

Positive net migration values (indicating that in-migration exceeds out-migration) are obtained when the observed population in 1980 exceeds the expected population. Negative net migration values (indicating that out-migration exceeds in-migration) are obtained when the observed population in a cohort is smaller than the expected population.

ESTIMATING FIVE-YEAR NET MIGRATION

Theoretical and practical problems are encountered in adapting the estimation procedures described in the previous section to a five-year cohort-component model. The problems result from the fact that a five-year age cohort experiences two migration rates in a ten-year period. For example, the population between the ages of 20 and 29 experiences the migration probabilities for the 20–24 age cohort in the first half of a decade and the migration probabilities for the 25–29 age cohort in the second half. The question is determining which migration rate should be applied to the population in each period.

The *adjacent cohort technique* averages the net migration rates for adjacent cohorts and applies the average migration rates in both time periods. However, this approach is only appropriate if migration rates are roughly consistent from one age group to another, a situation that rarely occurs at the local level. For example, growing suburban areas typically experience large net in-migration flows for children under the age of fifteen and substantial out-migration flows for persons between the ages of fifteen and twenty-four, who leave their parents' homes to attend college, take jobs, or marry. These young adults often migrate to central cities, generating age-specific migration flows that are the reverse of those in suburban counties. As a result, migration rates for adjacent cohorts are often substantially different in both areas, generating significant estimation errors from the application of average migration values (Irwin 1977, 21–22).

Five-year net migration estimates are best obtained by applying the survival rate method to the observed and estimated population by age and sex at five-year intervals. Population counts by age, sex, and race can be obtained from the decennial population censuses and estimated for the decennial midpoints—1965, 1975, and so on—from the annual population estimates for counties (see, e.g., U.S. Bureau of the Census 1978).

Table 7.2 illustrates the procedure for estimating the 1975 female population by five-year age cohort for the sample population data previously considered. Columns 3 and 4 record the observed female population by five-year cohort in 1970 and 1980 and the total population in these years. The published estimate for the total county population in 1975 is 94,500 (U.S. Bureau of the Census 1978, 76). However, the population estimate is for July 1, 1975, and the census counts are for April 1, 1970, and April 1, 1980. As a result, the population estimate

Table 7.2

Estimating Female Population by Five-Year Age Cohort, 1975

Age of Cohort	Cohort Number	Observed 1970	Observed 1980	Total	Estimated 1975
	(n)	Population[a] (PF_n^{1970})	Population[b] (PF_n^{1980})	Population	Population (PF_n^{1975})
(1)	(2)	(3)	(4)	(5)	(6)
0– 4	1	3,729	3,920	7,649	3,903
5– 9	2	4,436	3,979	8,415	4,293
10–14	3	4,766	3,890	8,656	4,416
15–19	4	4,452	4,623	9,075	4,630
20–24	5	3,795	4,712	8,507	4,340
25–29	6	2,958	4,105	7,063	3,604
30–34	7	2,625	3,963	6,588	3,361
35–39	8	2,406	2,993	5,399	2,755
40–44	9	2,384	2,599	4,983	2,542
45–49	10	2,456	2,357	4,813	2,456
50–54	11	2,304	2,380	4,684	2,390
55–59	12	1,902	2,337	4,239	2,163
60–64	13	1,568	2,053	3,621	1,847
65–69	14	1,301	1,638	2,939	1,499
70–74	15	1,141	1,318	2,459	1,255
75–79	16	943	1,072	2,015	1,028
80–84	17	644	738	1,382	705
85+	18	451	733	1,184	604
Total population[c]		87,123	97,408	184,531	94,149

[a] These data are from U.S. Bureau of the Census (1973, 37–273).
[b] These data are from U.S. Bureau of the Census (1982, 37–358).
[c] These data include the male and female population.

for 1975 must be reduced by 4.76 percent of the change for 1970 through 1975 (i.e., by the estimated change in one of 21 quarter years between April 1, 1970, and July 1, 1975) to yield an equivalent population estimate for April 1, 1975.

For example, if the estimated population for July 1, 1975, is 94,500 and the observed population for April 1, 1970, is 87,123, the estimated population for April 1, 1975, P^{1975}, is computed as follows:

$$P^{1975} = 94,500 - 0.0476 (94,500 - 87,123) = 94,149$$

Given the total population estimate for April 1, 1975, the population by age can be estimated by summing the female populations in each cohort for 1970 and 1980 to yield the female population totals reported in column 5. These values reflect the average population distribution by cohort in 1970 and 1980, which must be adjusted to match the estimated 1975 total population, 94,149. This can be done by computing an adjustment factor equal to the desired total population value, 94,149, divided by the total female population for 1970 and 1980, 184,531. This ratio, 0.5102, can then be applied to the total female population values in column 5 to yield the population estimates for 1975 reported in column 6. For example, the estimated female population in the first cohort for April 1, 1975, 3,903, is equal to the total female population in the first cohort, 7,649, multiplied by the adjustment factor, 0.5102.

Five-year net migration estimates for 1970 to 1975 can then be developed by applying the survival rate method described in the previous section. Thus, the five-year survival rates can be applied to the observed population in 1970 and observed or estimated births between 1970 and 1975 to project the expected population in 1975. The expected population can be subtracted from the estimated population for 1975 to estimate net migration for the 1970 to 1975 interval. Net migration estimates for 1975 through 1980 can be developed by using the estimated population in 1975 to project the expected population in 1980 and subtracting these values from the observed population in 1980.

PROJECTING FUTURE NET MIGRATION

Migration can be incorporated into a cohort-component model by projecting future net migration rates that are applied to the observed or projected population in an area to predict the net migration in the next period.[6] Positive net migration is comparable to an increase in the survival and fertility rates because it increases the projected population. Similarly, negative net migration is equivalent to a reduction in survival and fertility rates. This procedure assumes, however, that migration is a function of population size (e.g., if an area's population doubles, net migration will also double). In fact, migration is largely determined by regional employment opportunities, the availability of developable land, the presence of social amenities, and so on, which may be unrelated to an area's population.

Net migration by cohort can also be projected independently and added to surviving population to predict the future population. Sophisticated projection models have also been developed that attempt to relate future migration to the migration for a larger region or to regional economic variables such as relative wages and employment (see, e.g., Isard et al. 1960, 64–69; Pittenger 1976, 183–97; and Isserman 1985, 36–40). However, most cohort-component models do not attempt to model future migration behavior and merely assume that it will be identical to or an extension of past migration trends.

A range of migration alternatives can easily be generated from net migration estimates for two or more periods. For example, future net migration by sex and race can be assumed to equal one of the following: (1) the most recent net migration; (2) the high net migration observed in the past; (3) the low observed net migration; or (4) the average of the observed net migration values. Linear and geometric projections can also be obtained by applying the curve-fitting/extrapolation procedures described in Part One. Analysts can also draw on their knowledge of the study area and comparable regions to independently forecast future net migration rates (e.g., they can forecast that net migration rates will decline from 10 percent in the previous decade to 8 percent for the next ten years and to 5 percent in twenty years). Factors that should be considered in choosing between alternate migration projections are discussed in Chapter 8.

Net migration projections and forecasts require that net migration estimates by age, sex, and race be adjusted to correspond to the projected number of total net migrants. This adjustment could be accomplished by applying an adjustment factor equal to the ratio of the projected total net migration and the estimated total net migration. For example, if total net migration is projected to increase by 10 percent, the number of net migrants in each cohort could be increased by 10 percent.

Application of a uniform adjustment factor is theoretically unappealing, however, because positive and negative net migration values are treated the same. For example, a uniform adjustment of 10 percent would simultaneously increase positive net migration values (indicating more in-migration than out-migration) and negative net migration values (indicating more out-migration than in-migration) by 10 percent.

It is more reasonable to assume that total net migration will increase by enlarging the positive net migration values for cohorts with net migration gains and reducing the negative net migration values for cohorts with net migration losses. Similarly, total net migration should be diminished by reducing the positive net migration values for cohorts with net migration gains and increasing the negative net migration values for cohorts with net migration losses.

These modifications can be obtained by applying the "plus-minus" adjustment factors shown in Eqs. (7.2) and (7.3) (U.S. Bureau of the Census 1975, 705–706):

$$f_1 = \frac{\Sigma|n_i| + (N - n)}{\Sigma|n_i|} \qquad (n_i > 0) \qquad (7.2)$$

$$f_2 = \frac{\Sigma|n_i| - (N - n)}{\Sigma|n_i|} \qquad (n_i < 0) \qquad (7.3)$$

where

f_1 = adjustment for positive net migration values
f_2 = adjustment for negative net migration values
n_i = observed net migration by age and sex
n = observed total net migration recognizing signs
$\Sigma|n_i|$ = sum of absolute net migration values
N = desired total net migration recognizing signs

The use of the plus-minus correction factors is illustrated in Table 7.3, which assumes that the total net migration for 1980 through 1990 will be 10 percent larger than the total net migration estimate derived in Table 7.1. The observed total net migration for the 1970 to 1980 period, n, is 1,400. The sum of the absolute values, 2,182, is computed by summing the absolute net migration values (i.e., by treating all of the net migration values as positive numbers). The desired total net migration for the 1980 to 1990 period, N, is 1,540. Substituting these values into Eqs. (7.2) and (7.3) yields the following:

$$f_1 = \frac{2,182 + (1,540 - 1,400)}{2,182} = 1.0642$$

$$f_2 = \frac{2,182 - (1,540 - 1,400)}{2,182} = 0.9358$$

Table 7.3

Projecting Female Net Migration by Age, 1980 to 1990

Age of Cohort	Cohort Number (n)	Estimated Net Migration[a] $(NM_n^{1970-1980})$	Absolute Net Migration	Projected Net Migration $(NM_n^{1980-1990})$
(1)	(2)	(3)	(4)	(5)
0– 9	1	441	441	469
10–19	2	380	380	405
20–29	3	−345	345	−323
30–39	4	268	268	285
40–49	5	35	35	37
50–59	6	125	125	133
60–69	7	−46	46	−43
70–79	8	237	237	252
80+	9	305	305	325
Total	...	1,400	2,182	1,540

[a] These data are from Table 7.1, column 7.

The projected net migration in each cohort is computed by multiplying the positive net migration values in column 3 by the f_1 adjustment factor and the negative net migration values by the f_2 adjustment factor. For example, the projected net migration value for the first cohort, 469, is equal to the estimated net migration for this cohort, 441, multiplied by the f_1 adjustment factor, 1.0642. The projected net migration value for the third cohort, −323, is equal to the estimated net migration for this cohort, −345, multiplied by the f_2 adjustment factor, 0.9358.[7]

These adjustments expand the total number of net migrants by 10 percent by increasing the positive net migration values and reducing the negative net migration values, as desired. Procedures for combining these net migration forecasts with the mortality and fertility components of population change are discussed in Chapter 8.

ENDNOTES

1. The published data from the 1980 population census (U.S. Bureau of the Census 1984b) provide gross and net migration counts for states and counties by race, sex, and Spanish origin and for the total population by five-year intervals for ages 0 to 4 through 30 to 35 and ten-year intervals for ages 35 to 45 up to an open-ended cohort for ages 65 and above. The published data from

the 1970 population census (U.S. Bureau of the Census 1977) provide gross and net migration counts for states and counties by race and sex and for the total population for the following age groups: 0 to 14, 15 to 19, 20 to 24, 25 to 29, 30 to 44, 45 to 64, and over 65.

2. Area-to-area migration flow estimates are available on computer tape and in print by writing: Director, Statistics of Income Division, TR:S, U.S. Internal Revenue Service, 1111 Constitution Avenue, Washington, D.C. 20224.

3. The following discussion draws heavily on U.S. Bureau of the Census (1975, 627–37).

4. Equation (7.1) does not always hold. For example, a person who moves into an area and dies before the end of the observation period would be counted as a death but would not be included in the initial or final population. As a result, the number of net migrants into the area would be underestimated by one. This problem is particularly severe in retirement areas such as Florida.

5. For example, the survival rate method was used with observed local births and national survival rates to estimate net migration by age, sex, and race for regions, states, and counties in the United States for the 1950 through 1960 and 1960 through 1970 decades (Bowles and Tarver 1965; Bowles, Beale, and Lee 1975).

6. Peter Morrison expressed the difficulty of forecasting migration best in stating that "Demographers who know enough to forecast migration also know better" (quoted in McEvoy and Dietz 1977, 65). Unfortunately analysts can rarely escape the responsibility of preparing long-range population (and migration) forecasts by merely stating that they "know better."

7. The sum of the f_1 and f_2 adjustment factors is always two (except for any rounding errors), providing a quick check for computational errors.

Chapter 8

Cohort-Component Projection Model

The cohort-component technique projects an area's population by dividing it into uniform age, sex, and race groups, or cohorts, and applying the three components of population change—mortality, fertility, and migration—to each cohort. Chapters 5 through 7 have reviewed the procedures for estimating present and past rates of change for each component and projecting these components into the future. This chapter demonstrates how these components can be combined into a complete projection model, examines criteria that can be used to evaluate alternate projections, and evaluates the cohort-component projection technique.

By considering the three components of demographic change, a cohort-component model can be used to project an area's population by age, sex, and race at intervals equal to the length of its age cohorts. That is, ten-year cohort models project a population at ten-year intervals, and five-year models project a population at five-year intervals. The projection periods and age intervals are generally equal to allow the population in each cohort to move completely into the next cohort.

For example, Table 8.1 illustrates the combined application of the mortality, fertility, and migration components to project the study area's female population in 1990. As pointed out in Chapter 5, the surviving population in all but the first and last cohorts is calculated by multiplying the initial population in the previous cohort by the appropriate survival rate. For example, the surviving population in the second cohort, 7,876, is equal to the initial population in the first cohort, 7,899, multiplied by the survival rate from the first to the second cohort, 0.9971. The surviving population in the last cohort,

Table 8.1

Projecting Female Population by Age, 1990

Age of Cohort (1)	Cohort Number (n) (2)	Initial Population[a] (P_n^{1980}) (3)	Survival Rate[b] $(s_{n,n+1})$ (4)	Surviving Population (5)	Net Migration[c] $(NM_n^{1980-1990})$ (6)	Projected Population (P_n^{1990}) (7)
Births	0	8,230[d]	0.9873	...	...	...
0– 9	1	7,899	0.9971	8,125	469	8,594
10–19	2	8,513	0.9949	7,876	405	8,281
20–29	3	8,817	0.9922	8,470	–323	8,147
30–39	4	6,956	0.9831	8,748	285	9,033
40–49	5	4,956	0.9575	6,838	37	6,875
50–59	6	4,717	0.9008	4,746	133	4,879
60–69	7	3,691	0.7839	4,249	–43	4,206
70–79	8	2,390	0.5483	2,893	252	3,145
80+	9	1,471	0.2003	1,605	325	1,930
Total	...	49,410[e]	...	...	1,540	55,090

[a] These data are from Table 4.1, column 4.
[b] These data are from Table 5.2, column 6.
[c] These data are from Table 7.3, column 5.
[d] Births are computed using the data in column 5 of Table 6.3 and the procedures outlined in Chapter 6.
[e] This total excludes births.

1,605, includes the surviving population from the eighth cohort, 2,390 times 0.5483, plus the surviving population from the ninth cohort, 1,471 times 0.2003.

As pointed out in Chapter 6, the surviving population in the first cohort, 8,125, is calculated by multiplying the projected number of female births in the projection period, 8,230, by the survival rate for female infants, 0.9873. The projected number of female births is computed by summing the projected number of births in each cohort and estimating the proportion of female births. The projected number of births in each cohort is computed by multiplying the projected average female population in the fertile age groups by the corresponding age-specific fertility rates.

As pointed out in Chapter 7, the projected population in each cohort is computed by adding the surviving population and projected net migration in each cohort. For example, the projected 1990 population in the second cohort, 8,594, is equal to the surviving population in the cohort, 8,125, plus the projected net migration, 469. Negative net migration projections are subtracted from the surviving population. For example, the projected population in the third cohort, 8,147, is equal to the surviving population, 8,470, minus the projected net migration, 323.

This procedure can be repeated to project the population in 2000 and at ten-year intervals thereafter. For example, Table 8.2 illustrates the procedures for projecting the female population in the year 2000. The surviving population in 2000 can be computed by applying the appropriate survival rates to the projected population in 1990. The projected population in the first cohort is calculated by projecting the average female population for the projection period and applying age-specific fertility rates, the proportion of female births, and survival rates for infants. The projected population in the year 2000 for each cohort is then computed adding the projected number of net migrants to the projected surviving population. Similar procedures can be used to project the population at other ten-year intervals or to project the male and female population by age and race.

Table 8.2 assumes that the survival and fertility rates and number of net migrants for the 1990–2000 period are identical to those for 1980 to 1990. However, each component can also be projected independently

Table 8.2

Projecting Female Population by Age, 2000

Age of Cohort (1)	Cohort Number (n) (2)	Initial Population[a] (P_n^{1980}) (3)	Survival Rate[b] ($s_{n,n+1}$) (4)	Surviving Population (5)	Net Migration[c] ($NM_n^{1990-2000}$) (6)	Projected Population (P_n^{2000}) (7)
Births	0	8,154[d]	0.9873	...	...	...
0– 9	1	8,594	0.9971	8,049	469	8,518
10–19	2	8,281	0.9949	8,569	405	8,973
20–29	3	8,147	0.9922	8,238	−323	7,915
30–39	4	9,033	0.9831	8,083	285	8,368
40–49	5	6,875	0.9575	8,881	37	8,918
50–59	6	4,879	0.9008	6,583	133	6,716
60–69	7	4,206	0.7839	4,395	−43	4,352
70–79	8	3,145	0.5483	3,297	252	3,549
80+	9	1,930	0.2003	2,111	325	2,436
Total	...	55,090[e]	...	...	1,540	59,745

[a] These data are from Table 8.1, column 7.
[b] These data are from Table 5.2, column 6.
[c] These data are from Table 7.3, column 5.
[d] These data are computed by applying the fertility rates from Table 6.1 to the projected average female population for 1990 to 2000.
[e] This total excludes births.

using the procedures described in the preceding chapters and then used to project the population in each cohort. This allows analysts to evaluate the implication of different assumptions concerning future changes in each component.

Cohort-component projection models can also provide for "special" populations such as college students, military personnel and their dependents, and the residents of prisons, reformatories, and hospitals. These populations are important because their locations generally result from an administrative decision or legislative fiat rather than from normal demographic processes. In addition, they are often concentrated in a few age categories and have demographic characteristics that differ significantly from the remainder of the population, thus distorting normal projection procedures.

Special populations can be ignored if they are small relative to the population being projected.[1] Significant special populations should be removed from the base population, given special migration, fertility, and perhaps mortality treatment, and then added to the projected population. Future values for the special population can also be obtained from the responsible organization or agency. For example, college and university officials generally have a good idea of the future size and composition of their student bodies. This information can be incorporated directly into the population projections for their communities (Pittenger 1976, 205–206).

SELECTING APPROPRIATE PROJECTIONS

By incorporating detailed information on the age, sex, and racial segments of a population and the three components of population change, the cohort-component projection technique is theoretically superior to the curve-fitting/extrapolation technique described in Part One. However, the technique is still only an accounting framework that determines the effects of birth, death, and migration rates that have been specified externally to the model. The cohort-component model itself does not forecast these rates but merely accepts them as inputs that are applied within the model's accounting framework to determine future population values.

The previous chapters have described a number of options that can be incorporated into a cohort-component projection model. For example, future mortality rates can be assumed to equal current rates or to correspond to the low, medium, or high national mortality projections of the U.S. Bureau of the Census. Future fertility rates can similarly be assumed to equal current rates or to correspond to the Bureau's low, medium, or high fertility projections. Future net migration by sex and race can be assumed to equal the high, low, or average net migration value observed in the past, a linear or geometric extrapolation of observed net migration trends, or net migration rates specified by the analyst.

No reliable procedure exists for determining future mortality, fertility, and migration rates that reflect future life styles and health and economic conditions that cannot be known in advance. As a result, the cohort-component projection technique requires independent judgment and discretion in selecting the most appropriate projection (or projections) for a region. Thus, as was true for the curve-fitting/ extrapolation technique described in Part One, the cohort-component projection technique is only a computational procedure for determining the implications of a set of assumptions concerning the future.

While perfect population forecasts are impossible, steps can be taken to identify the most appropriate projection (or projections), given the limits of available information.[2] Assumptions about the future must be based largely on an analysis of the relevant past. As a result, the projection process must begin by examining historical trends for the study population and the three components of population change in an attempt to identify the causes of these trends. Particular attention should be given to past migration trends that reflect the region's economic and social history and to any systematic differences between local and national mortality and fertility rates that may undermine the use of the national projection series.

The forecast results should also be evaluated carefully to ensure that they are realistic, given the region's demographic history and the modeling assumptions for the future. Summary statistics that can be used to compare the projected values with the region's historical trends include (1) the total population; (2) the total population by sex and race; (3) the number of live births and deaths by category; (4) birth, death, and net migration rates by category; and (5) net migration rates for broad age categories.

These summary statistics are particularly useful if they are graphed as a function of time; for example, if the observed and projected birth, death, and migration rates by race are plotted as a function of time. These graphs quickly reveal sharp discontinuities in past trends or anomalous projection results for the underlying demographic processes. Summary statistics for the region and its constituent parts can also be compared if projections are being prepared at the regional and subregional levels.

Population pyramids for the total population and the population by race for the past, present, and future also provide valuable reliability checks. Population pyramids succinctly portray changes in a region's age structure, graphically revealing bulges or depressions resulting from the use of unrealistic migration, fertility, or mortality assumptions. Unusual changes in the community's age structure over time may also reveal undetected special populations such as large college or military populations requiring special demographic treatment.

Given the fundamental uncertainty concerning future demographic changes, it is generally desirable to prepare a range of alternative forecasts. A *high plausible projection* series can be prepared to incorporate the highest fertility rates, lowest mortality rates, and highest net in-migration rates that can reasonably be expected in the future. A corresponding *low plausible projection* can also be developed based on the lowest fertility rates, highest mortality rates, and lowest net in-migration rates that can be anticipated in the forecast period. A third projection called the *baseline* or *no-change projection,* reflecting the continuation of current fertility, mortality, and net migration rates can also be prepared. Together these three sets of projections represent judgmental confidence limits that can be used to evaluate the final *preferred forecast.*

The preferred forecast forms the basis for future planning efforts and is normally the most likely prediction for the future. However, for some purposes the preferred or *policy forecast* may not necessarily be the "most likely" forecast. For example, the lifetime of capital facilities is measured in decades and such facilities are often extremely difficult to expand at a later date. As a result, if the cost of initially overbuilding a facility is substantially lower than the cost of expanding it later, the preferred forecast may embody assumptions judged to be on the high side. Exactly how far the planning forecast assumptions should vary from the "most likely" assumptions is, of course, itself a matter of judgment (Pittenger 1977, 367–68; 1980, 137).

Three sets of assumptions underlying a cohort-component projection must be documented in detail, particularly when a range of forecasts is being prepared. The first set includes the standard *ceteris paribus* assumptions that there will be no wars, economic depressions, or natural catastrophes. These assumptions underlie virtually all forecasts.

The *scenario assumptions* specifying the general demographic trends that underlie the projection results should be stated so that they can be easily interpreted by nonspecialists. For example, a "high plausible" projection might compare past birth, death, and migration rates with those for the state and other regions. It could then state that the projected mortality rates parallel the U.S. Bureau of the Census's low mortality assumption series, fertility rates parallel the Bureau's high assumption series, and net in-migration rates equal the highest rates observed in the last twenty years. The discussion could conclude by describing the conditions under which these assumptions could be expected to hold (Pittenger 1976, 224–26; 1980, 138).

Cohort-component projections should also identify the detailed demographic assumptions concerning future mortality, fertility, and migration rates for different segments of the population and projected changes in these rates over time. In a real sense, these assumptions *are* the projections because they largely determine the population values generated by a cohort-component model. Specialists and nonspecialists will generally find the statement of the scenario assumptions most useful for evaluating the forecast and its assumptions. However, the detailed demographic rates that underlie the projections should also be identified to allow other specialists to fully interpret the projection procedures and results.

EVALUATION

The cohort-component technique is widely used because it provides detailed information on an area's future population, births, deaths, and migrants by age, sex, and race. This information is useful for many areas of planning and public administration.[3] However, cohort-component models also require more detailed information and more extensive computations than less complex models such as the extrapolation models considered in Part One. Computers can reduce the computational difficulties but cannot eliminate the need for reliable data at the proper level of geographic and demographic detail. Logically, the cohort-component technique is equally appropriate for any region with fixed geographic boundaries for which the required data can be obtained. However, in practice, as the analysis area becomes smaller, both in area and in population size, the difficulty of using the cohort-component technique increases.

The technique works best for regions such as metropolitan statistical areas (MSAs) and for counties for which the required data are readily available from published sources and for which mortality and fertility rates generally approximate state rates. Subcounty areas often contain diverse populations with dramatically different mortality and fertility rates and much higher rates of in- and out-migration. At this level the construction of a single large apartment building or subdivision may generate extremely high short-term in-migration rates. As a result, extreme caution must be used in applying the cohort-component technique to small areas. Other projection methods based on housing change models or population densities often yield more accurate results.

The cohort-component technique is particularly useful because it independently examines and projects each component of demographic change and enables local projections to incorporate sophisticated national-level mortality and fertility projections. This disaggregated analysis allows cohort-component projection models to deal explicitly with the demographic assumptions that remain hidden in more aggregate projection models.

The cohort-component technique is also helpful for illuminating alternative futures and their public policy implications. As a result, cohort-component projections are best conducted in close consultation with local elected officials and the general public. Local residents have an intimate knowledge of short-run events such as potential residential developments or plant closings that can dramatically affect the region's demographic future. It must be remembered, however, that local residents are naturally optimistic—generally, overly optimistic—concerning their region's long-term prospects. This inevitable "Chamber of Commerce" attitude must be countered by a disinterested and realistic evaluation of the region's long-term economic and demographic prospects.

More important, public involvement is required because a cohort-component projection, like all projections, is ultimately a political document. Projections of a region's demographic future help shape public perceptions of problems (and nonproblems), their definitions of potential solutions, and the nature of public actions or inaction. A change in a model's assumptions from optimistic projections for high net in-migration and fertility rates to pessimistic projections for net out-migration and low fertility rates can change public perceptions of a rosy future to despairing visions of decline and stagnation. With this pessimism comes a shift in public priorities from growth management and the provision of additional public and private facilities to strategies for local economic development and budget cutbacks.

Because it is impossible to know the future, it is equally impossible to objectively evaluate a given projection or set of conflicting projections. As a result, advocates for different public policies can use different sets of underlying assumptions to develop conflicting and "computationally correct" scenarios for the future that support their position in the policy debate. It is thus essential that the assumptions that underlie the projection (or projections) be stated explicitly so that other analysts and interested parties can understand, examine, and question the foundations on which the projection results rest. The sheen of technical sophistication can hide but not eliminate fundamental political choices in which the public has a right to be involved (Klosterman 1988).[4]

ENDNOTES

1. Information on the number of persons in group quarters by age, sex, and race are available for metropolitan statistical areas (MSAs) from the decennial population censuses. See, for example, U.S. Bureau of the Census (1983, Table 207.)

2. The discussion in this section draws heavily on similar discussions in Pittenger (1976, 214–15 and 221–27; 1977; and 1980).

3. The following discussion draws heavily on similar discussions in Irwin (1977, 23–24) and U.S. Bureau of the Census (1975, 796).

4. See Light (1985) for a particularly interesting example of the role of demographic and economic assumptions in public policymaking.

Part Three

Economic Analysis Techniques

Chapters 9 through 13 examine the economic base and related economic analysis techniques and use data from an actual community to illustrate the procedures for conducting an economic base study. Chapter 9 introduces the economic base technique and discusses preliminary issues that must be considered in undertaking an economic base study. Chapters 10 and 11 examine and evaluate three procedures for estimating the basic and nonbasic employment in a regional economy—the assumption, location quotient, and minimum requirements approaches. Chapter 12 describes and evaluates two procedures for projecting the total employment and the employment in the basic industries—the constant-share and shift-share approaches. Chapter 13 completes the discussion by examining procedures for converting the basic industry projections into projections for the entire local economy and assessing the economic analysis techniques.

Chapter 9

Economic Analysis Techniques: An Introduction

The curve-fitting/extrapolation and cohort-component projection techniques are generally used to project the population of cities and small regions. Information about an area's future population is incomplete without a parallel understanding of the local economy that largely shapes its future. If the local economy prospers, expanding employment and investment opportunities will attract new residents and stimulate additional development, ensuring future growth. If the economy falters, the lack of employment and business opportunities may force people to leave in search of better prospects, reducing the community's population and long-term development prospects.

The economic base technique is the oldest, simplest, and most widely used technique for regional economic analysis and projection.[1] The technique was first proposed by planners and geographers in the 1920s and was developed in essentially its current form by Homer Hoyt in the 1930s. It was also developed independently in the 1950s by economists applying the income and employment multipliers of Keynesian macroeconomic growth theory to urban areas.[2] Only later were these independent strands joined in a coherent theory combining the intuitive insights of practitioners with the formal theory of modern economics.[3]

BASIC AND NONBASIC SECTORS

The economic base technique assumes that the local economy can be divided into two sectors: (1) a *basic* or *nonlocal sector* and (2) a *nonbasic* or *local sector*.[4]

The *basic sector* consists of firms and parts of firms whose economic activity is dependent on factors external to the local economy. The most obvious examples are manufacturing firms, mines, and farms that produce goods for export outside of the local economy. Exporting firms are included in the basic sector because the level of economic activity in these firms—income, employment, sales, and so on—is largely dependent on the external demand for the products they produce.

The basic sector also includes federal and state government employment and purchases that are paid for by taxes collected at the national or state level and that are determined primarily by nonlocal economic conditions. As a result, federal and state government employment and purchases are assumed to be basic, even in state and national capitals that provide the government's physical location but not its economic base.

Firms and organizations that sell to tourists and temporary community residents such as convention attendees and college or university students are also included in the basic sector. Local economic activity generated by tourists and temporary residents is dependent largely on national- or state-level economic conditions over which the community has little control in the short run. As a result, these economic activities are basic, by definition.

The *nonbasic sector* consists of firms and parts of firms whose economic activity is dependent largely on local economic conditions. The most obvious examples are local firms and organizations providing goods and services to community residents. Local government is also assumed to be nonbasic because local government employment and purchases are largely determined by the state of the local economy. Thus local government expenditures are generally higher for prosperous areas than for areas experiencing economic hard times. The only exceptions are activities mandated by state and federal governments that stipulate minimal health, safety, and education levels, independent of local economic conditions.

The economic base technique assumes that all local economic activities can be assigned to either the basic or the nonbasic sector. Firms that sell to both the local and the export market are divided between the basic and nonbasic sectors. Techniques for making these allocations are described in Chapters 10 and 11.

For example, if economic activity is measured by the number of employees in each industry, the economic base technique assumes that the total local employment in an industry i in year t, e_i^t, can be divided into the basic sector employees, b_i^t, and the nonbasic sector employees, n_i^t:

$$e_i^t = b_i^t + n_i^t \tag{9.1}$$

Total local employment, e_T^t, is similarly divided into total basic employment, b_T^t, and total nonbasic employment, n_T^t:

$$e_T^t = b_T^t + n_T^t \tag{9.2}$$

And the total local employment, e_T^t, total basic employment, b_T^t, and total nonbasic employment, n_T^t, are computed by summing the total employment, basic employment, and nonbasic employment in all industries, as follows:

$$e_T^t = \Sigma e_i^t \tag{9.3}$$
$$b_T^t = \Sigma b_i^t \tag{9.4}$$

and

$$n_T^t = \Sigma n_i^t \tag{9.5}$$

ECONOMIC BASE PROJECTION MODEL

The curve-fitting/extrapolation technique can be used to project any variable for which reliable observations are available at regular intervals, including an area's employment, income, and other economic characteristics. However, the curve-fitting/extrapolation technique is limited by its inability to deal directly with the underlying causes for past changes and identify economic subcomponents that change by different rates at different times.

The economic base technique improves on the curve-fitting/extrapolation technique by incorporating an explicit model for regional economic growth and isolating the industrial sectors making up a local economy. The economic base technique is based on a simple causal model that assumes that the basic sector is the prime cause of local economic growth, that it is the economic base of the local economy.[5] This model is expressed in terms of a *base multiplier (BM)*, which can be expressed as the ratio of the total local employment in year t, e_T^t, to the total basic employment in that year, b_T^t, as follows:

$$BM = \frac{e_T^t}{b_T^t} \tag{9.6}$$

The base multiplier can also be expressed in income units by replacing the employment terms in Eq. (9.6) by the corresponding income terms, as follows:

$$BM = \frac{y_T^t}{y_B^t} \tag{9.7}$$

where y_T^t is the total region income in year t and y_B^t is the total basic sector income in year t.

Equations (9.6) and (9.7) assume that the ratio of total local economic activity to total basic economic activity, the base multiplier, is invariant over time. This implies that changes in the basic sector are accompanied by corresponding changes in the total economy. For example, if basic sector employment increases (or decreases) by 10 percent, total local employment will also grow (or decline) by 10 percent. Given this assumption, the base multiplier can be computed from historical data and used to project future changes in the total economy, a procedure that is the key to the economic base technique (Isserman 1977c, 34).

The reasoning underlying the economic base model proceeds as follows. Basic sector activities such as the sale of exports bring additional money into the local economy. Some of this money remains in the local economy, increasing the demand for local goods and services supplied by the nonbasic sector. As a result, if the basic sector prospers, that is, if regional exports increase, the increased demand for local goods and services causes the local sector and the entire regional economy to prosper. Conversely, hard times for the basic sector reduce the demand for local goods and services, causing the nonbasic sector and the entire local economy to suffer. In either case, the level of the induced activity in the local sector reflects the basic sector activity, making the basic sector the prime cause of local economic change.

This causal model is revealed most clearly in small "one industry" towns such as an isolated community in which a large steel mill employs the majority of the town's work force. In this case, the basic sector consists of the mill's employees who manufacture products for export. The nonbasic sector includes the firms and individuals who provide goods and services (food, clothing, entertainment, etc.) to the mill's employees and to other community residents.

The basic sector is clearly the prime stimulant for economic change in this situation. The mill's income and employment are dependent almost exclusively on nonlocal factors such as the national and international demand for the steel products the mill produces. If the external demand for these products increases, the resulting increase in regional income and employment expands the demand for local goods and services, stimulating a chain of income, sales, and employment increases that will ripple through the local economy. If the external demand for the mill's products decreases, the resulting decline in regional income and employment reduces the demand for local goods and services, negatively affecting the entire local economy. If the mill is closed, the economic viability of the entire community may be threatened.

Given this model of local economic growth, the economic base technique directs analysts' attention to the portion of the local economy that makes up the basic sector. The technique can be used to better understand the present state of the local economy by identifying industries and firms that serve nonlocal demand and that are, by hypothesis, the prime causes of local economic growth or decline. Using this information, local officials can identify weaknesses in the local economy such as an overdependence on a single exporting firm or industrial sector and they can assess the region's ability to attract or retain basic industries that stimulate future economic growth (Tiebout 1962, 15–16).

However, the economic base technique is generally used to determine the impact of local economic changes and to project future states of the local economy. For these applications the technique serves as a simplifying device, allowing analysts to focus their attention on the industries and firms making up the basic sector and to use the base multiplier to determine the induced effect on the entire local economy.

Preliminary issues of identifying the study area and selecting the units for measuring and classifying economic activity are discussed in the next section. Techniques for estimating basic and nonbasic employment, computing the base multiplier, and projecting economic change are discussed in Chapters 10 through 13.

PRELIMINARY CONSIDERATIONS

Identifying Study Area

The economic base technique assumes a fundamental distinction between basic sector activities dependent on factors external to the local economy and nonbasic activities dependent largely on local economic conditions.[6] As a result, economic base studies must first identify the geographic boundary separating the local community (and associated nonbasic demand) from the external world (and corresponding basic demand).

Economic base studies can be conducted for areas of any size for which the required data can be obtained—from a small town or suburban community to a state or nation. Although no geographic unit is most appropriate, the geographic unit selected is important because it affects the relative proportion of basic and nonbasic activity.

For example, the economic activity of an individual household is almost entirely basic because virtually all of its income is derived from wages, transfer payments, returns on investments, and so on, which are generated outside of the household. The only nonbasic economic activities are income transfers between household members, such as gifts and children's allowances. At the other extreme, economic activity for the earth as a whole is entirely nonbasic because the only exports are satellites and space probes, which generate no external demand.

As these extremes illustrate, the proportion of the local economic activity which is basic decreases as the size of the analysis region increases. Suburban communities and small towns generally have small, specialized economies and relatively large export or basic sectors. Large and diversified metropolitan regions, which provide a wide range of goods and services to local residents, generally have a relatively small export or basic sector.

Economic base theory suggests that the base area should be a viable economic entity with integrated, interdependent, and largely self-sufficient productive and distributive activities. Criteria for defining meaningful economic communities include the limits of local commuting and shopping patterns, the area served by local communications and advertising media, and the boundaries of regional shipping and wholesaling functions.[7]

Counties and multicounty regions are the most widely used analysis units, largely because a wealth of reliable economic data is provided annually at the county level. However, county boundaries are also theoretically appealing for relatively isolated communities for which the county boundaries roughly approximate the community's economic boundaries. Municipal boundaries should only be used in the rare situations in which they correspond to the community's economic and social boundaries.[8]

Economic base studies for urban areas generally adopt the boundaries for the metropolitan statistical area (MSA) in which the city is located.[9] MSA boundaries provide a readily accessible and reasonable representation of the concept of an economic region and are widely used by many government and nongovernment agencies, giving them a degree of independent validity. And, most important from a practical standpoint, the wealth of county-level data greatly facilitates data collection and analysis.

Selecting Measurement Units

The second preliminary consideration is selecting the units for measuring economic activity.[10] Several alternatives are available, none of which is totally acceptable. The unit that is selected depends on the purpose of the study, the available resources, and, most important, the availability of appropriate data.

Employment. Employment or number of jobs is by far the most widely used measurement unit, largely because annual employment data are readily available for counties from published sources such as the *County Business Patterns* reports prepared by the U.S. Bureau of the Census. Employment is also an attractive unit because a job is a readily understood concept and employment levels are a major concern of planners, public officials, and the public.

Despite its popularity, employment is only an imperfect measure of economic activity. For example, a part-time employee has one job, as does an employee who is working overtime; individuals who "moonlight" have two jobs; and seasonal employees only have jobs for a portion of the year. As a result, the number of employees does not accurately reflect increases in a firm's activity that may require part-time workers to work full-time, some employees to work overtime, and others to give up part-time second jobs.

Employment also cannot account for economic changes resulting from productivity increases such as the tremendous advances in agricultural productivity that have allowed American farm output and income to increase dramatically in the face of steady employment declines. It also cannot account for economic activity from non–job-related sources such as government transfer payments and returns on investments or savings, which are particularly important in areas with large retired or low-income populations.

Economic base theory assumes that changes in the basic sector will stimulate changes in local demand that will ultimately impact the entire local economy. These impacts result not only from employment changes but also from higher wage rates, more overtime work, increased productivity, and improved returns on investment, which are not reflected in changes in the number of jobs in the community. The limitations of employment data are compounded by severe practical problems of obtaining reliable information for subcounty areas and for firms protected by the government's disclosure prohibitions.

Payroll. Annual payroll is an attractive measurement unit because it accounts for overtime, part-time, and seasonal employment and recognizes that different types of jobs have different impacts on a community. For example, one job paying $50,000 a year has approximately the same impact on the local service expenditures and tax revenues as two jobs paying $25,000 a year. However, ten jobs paying $25,000 per year are not equivalent to one job paying $250,000 per year because high-income individuals generally save more and spend differently than low- or moderate-income individuals. Employment measures economic opportunity, that is, the potential number of persons to be supported at a given level of economic activity. Payroll reflects the standard of living to be expected after a job has been obtained. Both are important and neither is sufficient by itself.

Annual and first-quarter payroll data are readily available for counties from published sources such as the *County Business Patterns* reports, published by the U.S. Bureau of the Census. However, these data can be distorted in periods of rapid inflation or deflation and by strikes, extended layoffs, or periods of heavy overtime employment.

Sales and Value Added. Sales is a useful unit because most firms define their markets in terms of dollar sales and are particularly interested in sales forecasts. In addition, local governments whose tax revenues are based on sales are interested in sales forecasts for projecting potential revenues.

Regional sales data, such as the gross national product (GNP) statistics, record the total level of transactions in an economy. As a result, regional sales data can be inflated by "double counting" of intermediate sales to other regional firms. Consider, for example, a manufacturing firm with $5 million in direct sales to the export market and $5 million in sales to other local firms who incorporate these products into export goods sold for $10 million. Total regional sales are $20 million even though only $15 million has been added to the regional income.

Value added eliminates double counting by subtracting the costs of a firm's purchases from its final sales to individuals and other firms. In this example, the total value added is $15 million: $10 million by the first firm ($5 million in export sales plus $5 million in sales to other local firms) and $5 million by the other local firms ($10 million in sales less the $5 million purchased from the first firm.)

Regional sales data can also be distorted by changes in the regional sales and distribution patterns. Consider what will happen in the preceding example if the first firm's local sales are to a distributor who sells its goods to the other local firms for $7 million. Total regional sales are $27 million, even though the total physical output and regional exports are unchanged. The wholesaler's sales have simply been added to the previous sales. However, the total *value added* remains $15 million: $10 million by the first firm; $2 million by the wholesaler ($7 million in sales minus $5 million in purchases); and $3 million by the final exporters ($10 million in sales minus $7 million in purchases).

Value added is rarely used in local economic analyses, however, because reliable data on the value added by individual firms are extremely difficult to obtain at the local level.[11] Value added data also encounter severe practical difficulties in dealing with intangible inputs and outputs such as services and with corporate income from branch plants.

Other Measurement Units. Several other measurement units have been proposed in the literature but rarely used in practice, largely because of the difficulty of obtaining the required data at the local level. For example, the *direct measurement* of a community's monetary trans-actions—income, expenditures, and internal circulation—provides the most complete and satisfactory picture of the local economy. However, this type of analysis is out of the question for cities of any size due to the vast quantity of required information.[12]

Personal income including wages and salaries, dividends, interest, and proprietors' income is particularly useful for measuring non–job-related income, but these data are only available for counties and states.[13] Measuring the *quantity of goods produced* is appropriate for activities such as manufacturing or agriculture, but inappropriate for nonphysical outputs such as services or for regional income that is not related to the production of goods.

Most economic base studies rely exclusively on employment data, largely because these data are readily available at the county level. However, it must be remembered that the number of jobs in a commu-nity does not accurately reflect all economic changes in a community; nor does it account for non–job-related income. As a result, a more accurate picture of the local economy can be obtained using other measurement units appropriate for different sectors of the economy and different communities. For example, employment and payroll data might be used to obtain two pictures of a traditional economy, and personal income data might be used for retirement and low-income areas.

STANDARD INDUSTRIAL CLASSIFICATION SYSTEM

A classification system must also be used to assign economic activities to a consistent set of categories. Most government and nongovernment agencies rely on the Standard Industrial Classification (SIC) system developed by the U.S. Office of Management and Budget (OMB) to standardize data collection efforts within the federal government. The SIC system assigns economic activities to categories derived from product groupings with similar production processes, materials, customers, and so forth.

The SIC classification system assigns economic activities to increasingly refined categories identified by numeric labels containing increasingly more digits. All economic activities are first assigned to ten major categories or *Divisions,* which are identified by a letter. For example, SIC Division A includes agriculture, forestry, and fishing; SIC Division B includes mining. The ten SIC divisions are divided into *Major Groups,* which are identified by two-digit numbers. For example, Division B, Mining, is divided into five two-digit Major Groups: 10, Metal Mining; 11, Anthracite Mining; and so on. The Major Groups are divided into *Industry Groups,* which are identified by three-digit numbers. For example, Major Group 10, Metal Mining, is divided into eight three-digit Industry Groups: 101, Iron Ores; 102, Copper Ores; and so on. Finally, the Industry Groups are subdivided into *Industries,* which are identified by four-digit numbers. For example, Industry Group 104, Gold and Silver Ores, is divided into two four-digit Industries: 1041, Gold Ores, and 1042, Silver Ores.

The SIC system provides a convenient and widely used system for classifying all economic activities, including a residual category of "nonclassifiable establishments." Different aggregation levels are easily identified by examining the SIC code number. For example, information provided at the two-digit SIC code level is more aggregated than information at the three-digit SIC code level. And information provided at the four-digit SIC level is more refined than information provided at the three-digit SIC level.

The first SIC classification manual was issued in 1939. The system has been revised periodically to reflect the economy's changing industrial organization. The most recent major revisions were made in 1987 to improve industry detail and to take into account technological changes, institutional changes (such as the deregulation of the banking and transportation industries), and the tremendous expansion of the service sector. The complete list of SIC categories and the definitions used to assign activities to each category are included in U.S. Office of Management and Budget, *Standard Industrial Classification Manual* (1987).

ENDNOTES

1. For reviews of more sophisticated economic projection techniques see Richardson (1978b and 1985) and Pleeter (1980).

2. The early development of the economic base technique by Hoyt and others is described by Andrews (1953) and Lane (1966). The pioneering attempt to apply the multiplier analysis to the urban economy is described in Hildebrand and Mace (1950). For other early articles on economic base theory, see Pfouts (1960) and Isard et al. (1960, 189–205); for a review of more recent articles, see Richardson (1978b, 11–14).

3. Tiebout (1956b) was one of the first to recognize the connection between planners' and geographers' economic base theory and economists' multiplier theory. See Krueckeberg and Silvers (1973, 400–406) and Oppenheim (1980, 72–107) for formal demonstrations of the connection between these two bodies of theory.

4. Many synonyms and near-synonyms exist for the terms *basic* and *nonbasic*. Ullman, Dacey, and Brodsky (1969, 3) identify 11 related terms for *basic*, including export, exogenous, and nonlocal. They propose 15 terms for *nonbasic*, including service, local, and residentiary. Whether they are synonyms or near-synonyms depends on whether the basic sector is defined narrowly to include only exports or broadly to include other forms of exogenous demand such as state and federal expenditures, certain transfer payments, and tourist expenditures. The broader definition is used here, following Gerking and Isserman (1981, 451).

5. The following discussion draws heavily on Lane (1966, 344–45) and Tiebout (1962, 13–19). For an early and persuasive statement of this underlying model, see North (1955).

6. The following discussion draws heavily on Tiebout (1962, 21–23) and Andrews (1954b).

7. Early attempts to identify metropolitan boundaries include the work of William Reilly (1931) and the criteria proposed by N. S. B. Gras in 1929, listed in Pfouts (1955, 122).

8. However, Oakland et al. (1971) use a variation of the economic base model to examine the effect of government antipoverty programs on low-income neighborhoods.

9. As defined by the U.S. Office of Management and Budget, an MSA consists of one or more counties containing a central city or contiguous, densely settled area of 50,000 or more inhabitants. Adjacent counties are included in the MSA if they are socially and economically integrated with the central city. A sliding scale that jointly considers population density and daily commuting patterns is used to identify outlying counties that are included in an MSA. For example, a county adjacent to a county or counties containing a city of 50,000 inhabitants is included in the MSA if at least 50 percent of the employed workers in the county commute to the central county (or counties) and if its population density is at least 25 persons per square mile. Prior to June 30, 1983, metropolitan statistical areas (MSAs) were called standard metropolitan statistical areas (SMSAs). The designations and nomenclatures for SMSAs were used for the 1980 Census of Population and Housing and the 1982 Economic Censuses. The new boundaries have been used to prepare U.S. Bureau of the Census reports since 1983.

10. The following discussion is based largely on similar discussions in Andrews (1954c) and Tiebout (1962, 45–46).

11. One notable exception is Charles Leven's study of Sioux City, Iowa (Leven 1961).

12. However, this unit was used in an early study of Oskaloosa, Iowa, underwritten by *Fortune* magazine ("Oskaloosa Versus the United States," *Fortune,* April 1938).

13. Gibson and Worden (1981) and Mulligan and Gibson (1984) used average wage rates by sector and government transfer payments to estimate personal income for 20 Arizona communities. Bolton (1966) used published data on inflation-adjusted personal income to investigate the effect of defense expenditures on multistate regions in the United States.

Chapter 10

Assumption and Location Quotient Approaches

The economic base technique assumes that a local economy can be divided into a basic or nonlocal sector dependent on factors external to the local economy and a nonbasic or local sector dependent largely on local market conditions. Although a clear conceptual distinction can be drawn between these sectors, it is extremely difficult in practice to determine whether a good or service is exported or sold locally. The market served is dependent on a number of factors: the characteristics of the item, the marketing practices of the producing firm(s), the existence and characteristics of other local firms, the community's capacity to produce the item, and the nature of local and external demand.

For example, manufactured and nonperishable processed goods are generally exported but are also sold locally. Services and perishables such as fruits and vegetables tend to be sold locally because proximity between consumers and producers is preferred. However, national service centers such as New York City and Hartford serve primarily nonlocal markets, and perishable goods can be shipped long distances if nonlocal demand is sufficient. As a result, most of the goods and services produced in an area are sold in both the local and nonlocal markets, and the relative proportions can change substantially over time (Hirsch 1973, 187–88).

Field surveys and interviews directly measuring regional sales, distribution, and income flows provide the most accurate measure of a region's basic and nonbasic sectors. For example, the managers of

125

local firms can be interviewed to identify their local and external sales. Surveys can be also used to estimate the income of community residents, the geographic source of this income, and the shopping patterns of local consumers.[1]

Personal interviews and surveys are rarely used, however, because they are extremely expensive and time consuming. They also may not identify indirect exports such as cans sold by a local can company to other local firms that use these cans to export processed food products. As a result, most economic base studies use secondary data sources and indirect measurement techniques to estimate the basic and nonbasic sectors of an economy. This chapter examines two widely used indirect measurement techniques: the assumption approach and the location quotient approach. Chapter 11 examines a third technique—the minimum requirements approach—and evaluates the three estimation approaches.[2]

ASSUMPTION APPROACH

The simplest basic sector estimation procedure, the assumption approach, assigns activities to the basic and nonbasic sectors on the basis of assumed sales patterns for different types of industries.[3] That is, local economic activity in manufacturing, mining, agriculture, and federal and state government is generally assumed to be determined largely by external conditions and is assigned entirely to the basic sector. The remaining activities such as retail, wholesale, transportation, and services are assumed to serve local markets and are assigned totally to the nonbasic sector.[4]

Table 10.1 illustrates the application of the assumption approach to the 1985 employment of Wayne County, Ohio, the study area considered in Part Two. Local employment in the following industries is assigned entirely to the basic sector: agriculture, forestry, and fishing; mining; manufacturing; and state government. Employment in the remaining industries is assigned to the nonbasic sector.

The assumption approach is easily applied and widely used, even for relatively sophisticated applications such as the development and testing of regional econometric models. However, assigning an industry's activity entirely to the basic or nonbasic sector on the basis of assumed sales patterns can generate substantial errors. For example, assigning all manufacturing and agriculture to the basic sector ignores manufacturing industries such as bakeries, printing firms, and brick

Table 10.1

Basic and Nonbasic Employment Estimates, Assumption Approach

SIC Code (i)	Industry	Basic Employment (b_i^{1985})	Nonbasic Employment (n_i^{1985})	Total Employment[a] (e_i^{1985})
(1)	(2)	(3)	(4)	(5)
A	AGRICULTURE, FORESTRY, FISHING	...	...	...
–	Agricultural production[b]	5,240	0	5,240
–	Agricultural services, forestry, fisheries[c]	120	0	120
B	MINING	913	0	913
C	CONSTRUCTION	0	1,378	1,378
D	MANUFACTURING	...	...	...
20	Food products	1,687	0	1,687
24	Lumber and wood products	639	0	639
25	Furniture and fixtures	140	0	140
26	Paper products	1,091	0	1,091
27	Printing and publishing	213	0	213
28	Chemicals	385	0	385
30	Rubber and plastics	2,198	0	2,198
32	Stone, clay, glass	426	0	426
33	Primary metals	882	0	882
34	Fabricated metals	2,398	0	2,398
35	Machinery	1,035	0	1,035
36	Electric equipment	189	0	189
37	Transport equipment	1,022	0	1,022
–	Other manufacturing	972	0	972
E	TRANSPORTATION AND PUBLIC UTILITIES	...	...	...
47	Transport services	0	612	612
48	Communication	0	161	161
49	Electric and gas	0	193	193
F	WHOLESALE TRADE	0	1,572	1,572
G	RETAIL TRADE	0	5,474	5,474
H	FINANCE and INSURANCE	0	1,346	1,346
I	SERVICES	...	...	...
70	Hotels and lodging	124	0	124
72	Personal services	0	317	317
80	Health services	0	1,638	1,638
–	Other services	0	2,996	2,996
–	GOVERNMENT	...	...	...
–	State government	1,390	0	1,390
–	Local government	0	4,060	4,060
Total	...	21,064	19,747	40,811

[a] These data are from Ohio Bureau of Employment Services (1986).
[b] This includes SIC Major Groups 01 and 02. These data are from U.S. Bureau of the Census (1984c, Tables 5 and 9; and 1984d).
[c] This includes SIC Major Groups 07, 08, and 09.

plants and agricultural activities such as truck farms and dairies that serve largely local markets. Service industries such as the home offices of insurance companies and regional financial institutions that serve primarily nonlocal markets would similarly be incorrectly assigned to the nonbasic sector.

In fact, nearly all industries and firms serve both a local and a nonlocal market. In addition, the relative proportion of local and nonlocal sales varies for different industries and different regions and can change over time as the nature of local and external production and demand changes. The size of the local market (and, correspondingly the proportion of a firm's local sales) also increases as the size of the analysis region increases. As a result, industries and firms primarily serving an export market for a single city or county may serve only local markets for states and large, multicounty regions.

Although inadequate as a general basic sector estimation procedure, the assumption technique is appropriate for segments of the economy that clearly serve local and nonlocal markets. For example, activities related to federal and state government, tourism, and temporary community residents such as college students are dependent almost exclusively on nonlocal economic conditions and can be assumed to be basic, by definition. Similarly activities dependent largely on local market conditions such as local government, contract construction, and real estate can similarly be assigned entirely to the nonbasic sector.

Other assignments can be made on the basis of an analyst's knowledge of a local area. For example, local transportation-related employment that is known to consist largely of a regional railroad maintenance facility or an airline reservation phonebank can be assigned to the basic sector. Local knowledge can also be used to allocate an industry's activity between the basic and nonbasic sectors, such as determining the proportions of the regional railroad service center's activity serving local and nonlocal demand.

LOCATION QUOTIENT APPROACH

The location quotient approach was developed in the 1940s by Hildebrand and Mace (1950) and has become the most widely used—and most widely criticized—approach for estimating the basic employment in a local economy.[5] The approach gets its name from the ratio or *location quotient* used to measure the extent to which an area is specialized, relative to another area, in the production of a particular product. For economic base studies, the location quotient is defined as the ratio of an industry's share of the local economy to the industry's share of the national economy.[6] For example, the location quotient for employment can be defined as follows:

$$LQ_i = \frac{e_i^t}{e_T^t} \div \frac{E_i^t}{E_T^t} \tag{10.1}$$

where

e_i^t = regional employment in industry i in year t

e_T^t = total regional employment in year t

E_i^t = national employment in industry i in year t

E_T^t = total national employment in year t

Industries with location quotients equal to 1.0 have a local employment share e_i^t/e_T^t exactly equal to their national share E_i^t/E_T^t. Local production in these industries is assumed to be just sufficient to satisfy local demand, and the industry is assumed to contain no basic employment. Industries with location quotients less than 1.0 have local employment shares e_i^t/e_T^t smaller than their national shares E_i^t/E_T^t. Local production in these industries is assumed to be insufficient to satisfy local demand requiring products to be imported. As a result, local production is assumed to serve only local demand, and there is no basic sector activity.[7]

Industries with location quotients greater than 1.0 have local employment shares e_i^t/e_T^t which are larger than their national shares E_i^t/E_T^t. Local production is specialized in these industries, relative to the nation, and is therefore assumed to exceed local demand, allowing the excess to be exported. As a result, local economic activity in these industries is assumed to include basic sector activity dependent on nonlocal conditions. For example, the proportion of Detroit's employment devoted to automobile production is substantially higher than the national proportion. The location quotient approach assumes that the high concentration of automobile employment does not result from the fact that people in Detroit own more cars but from the fact that Detroit produces cars for export to the rest of the country. As a result, Detroit's automobile production is assumed to include a substantial amount of basic sector activity.

Table 10.2 illustrates the use of the location quotient to identify industries containing basic sector activity. For example, the location

Table 10.2

Location Quotients, 1985

SIC Code (i)	Industry	1985 Employment Local[a] (e_i^{1985})	1985 Employment U.S.[b] (E_i^{1985})	Location Quotient (LQ_i)
(1)	(2)	(3)	(4)	(5)
A	AGRICULTURE, FORESTRY, FISHING	...	...	...
–	Agricultural production[c]	5,240	7,096,533	1.8598
–	Agricultural services, forestry, fisheries[d]	120	569,474	0.5308
B	MINING	913	923,143	2.4911
C	CONSTRUCTION	1,378	4,642,735	0.7476
D	MANUFACTURING	...	...	...
20	Food products	1,687	1,601,466	2.6533
24	Lumber and wood products	639	696,033	2.3124
25	Furniture and fixtures	140	494,241	0.7135
26	Paper products	1,091	677,803	4.0543
27	Printing and publishing	213	1,425,114	0.3765
28	Chemicals	385	1,044,190	0.9287
30	Rubber and plastics	2,198	787,549	7.0298
32	Stone, clay, glass	426	587,891	1.8252
33	Primary metals	882	810,590	2.7407
34	Fabricated metals	2,398	1,471,232	4.1054
35	Machinery	1,035	2,187,912	1.1915
36	Electric equipment	189	2,200,312	0.2164
37	Transport equipment	1,022	1,978,880	1.3008
–	Other manufacturing	972	3,310,151	0.7396
E	TRANSPORTATION AND PUBLIC UTILITIES	...	...	...
47	Transport services	612	272,313	5.6608
48	Communication	161	1,320,958	0.3070
49	Electric and gas	193	902,949	0.5384
F	WHOLESALE TRADE	1,572	5,715,253	0.6928
G	RETAIL TRADE	5,474	17,341,892	0.7951
H	FINANCE and INSURANCE	1,346	5,846,839	0.5799
I	SERVICES	...	...	...
70	Hotels and lodging	124	1,334,210	0.2341
72	Personal services	317	1,055,026	0.7568
80	Health services	1,638	6,249,823	0.6601
–	Other services	2,996	11,804,762	0.6393
–	GOVERNMENT	...	...	...
–	State government	1,390	3,518,253	0.9951
–	Local government	4,060	9,326,667	1.0965
Total	...	40,811	102,794,508[e]	...

[a] These data are from Ohio Bureau of Employment Services (1986).
[b] These data are from U.S. Bureau of Labor Statistics (1987, 3–24).
[c] This includes SIC Major Groups 01 and 02. These data are from U.S. Bureau of the Census (1984c, Tables 5 and 9; and 1984d).
[d] This includes SIC Major Groups 07, 08, and 09.
[e] This total includes industries not shown.

quotient for SIC Major Group 20, Food Products, is computed by applying Eq. (10.1):

$$LQ_{20} = \frac{e_{20}^{1985}}{e_T^{1985}} \div \frac{E_{20}^{1985}}{E_T^{1985}}$$

$$= \frac{1{,}687}{40{,}811} \div \frac{1{,}601{,}466}{102{,}794{,}508}$$

$$= 0.04134 \div 0.01558 = 2.6533$$

The location quotient value for Major Group 20 is greater than 1.0, indicating that the industry's share of the local economy, e_{20}^{1985}/e_T^{1985}, or 0.047134, is larger than the industry's national share, E_{20}^{1985}/E_T^{1985}, or 0.01558. This suggests that the local economy is specialized in food production relative to the nation and that this industry can be assumed to include basic sector activity.

The location quotient for SIC Major Group 25, Furniture and Fixtures, is less than 1.0, indicating that this industry's share of the local economy is smaller than its national share. As a result, it is assumed that this region does not export furniture and fixtures, and SIC Major Division 25 is assumed to contain no basic sector activity.

Location quotients can easily be computed to identify industries in which the local economy is specialized, relative to the nation. Caution must be used, however, in using this indirect measure of export-related activity to identify industries which do, or do not, contain basic sector activity. For example, in Table 10.2, Major Division 70, Hotels and Lodging, is assumed to contain basic sector activity even though the location quotient is less than 1.0 because the local activity is assumed to serve tourists and temporary visitors and thus to be determined largely by nonlocal demand. Local government is similarly assigned to the nonbasic sector, even though the location quotient is greater than 1.0, because local government activity is dependent largely on local economic conditions. Federal and state governments are generally assumed to contain basic activity, regardless of the location quotient, because local activity in these sectors is dependent largely on nonlocal factors such as the condition of the national or state economy.

Similarly, location values larger than 1.0 do not necessary imply the presence of basic sector activity. For example, rapidly growing areas often have higher concentrations of general contractors and real estate agents than the nation as a whole, This does not mean, however, that the construction serves nonlocal demand or that property is being exported. It only means that the region's rapid growth—caused by factors such as a booming economy or an influx of retirees—has been reflected in an unusually high level of activity in growth-related activities such as construction and real estate. As a result, activities clearly associated with local demand should be assigned to the nonbasic sector, regardless of the location quotient value. In all of these cases, the location quotient values cannot be interpreted blindly without a familiarity with the study region and a careful assessment of the resulting basic and nonbasic assignments.

Table 10.3 lists the estimated basic and nonbasic employment for each of the industries shown in Table 10.2. Industries with location quotients less than or equal to 1.0 are assumed to serve only local demand and are assigned entirely to the nonbasic industry. Industries such as local government that have location quotients greater than 1.0 but are assumed to reflect local economic conditions are also assigned entirely to the nonbasic sector.

Basic activities in industries with location quotients greater than 1.0 can be estimated by applying Eq. (10.2) (Isserman 1977, 34–35) as follows:[8]

$$b_i^t = \left(\frac{e_i^t}{E_i^t} - \frac{e_T^t}{E_T^t} \right) E_i^t \tag{10.2}$$

For example, substituting the appropriate values for SIC Major Group 20 into Eq. (10.3) yields

$$b_{20}^{1985} = \left(\frac{e_{20}^{1985}}{E_{20}^{1985}} - \frac{e_T^{1985}}{E_T^{1985}} \right) E_{20}^{1985}$$

$$= \left(\frac{1,687}{1,601,466} - \frac{40,811}{102,794,508} \right) 1,601,466$$

$$= (0.001053 - 0.000397)\, 1,601,466$$

$$= 1,051$$

Nonbasic activity in these industries can be determined by subtracting the estimated basic sector employment from the total employment. For example, the estimated nonbasic employment for SIC Division B in Table 10.3, 367, is equal to the total employment, 913, minus the estimated basic employment, 546.

Equation (10.2) should only be used for industries with location quotients greater than 1.0. Attempts to apply the equation to industries

Table 10.3

Location Quotient Basic and Nonbasic Employment Estimates, 1985

SIC Code (i) (1)	Industry (2)	Location Quotient[a] (LQi) (3)	Local[b] (e_i^{1985}) (4)	U.S.[c] (E_i^{1985}) (5)	Basic Employment (b_i^{1985}) (6)	Nonbasic Employment (n_i^{1985}) (7)
A	AGRICULTURE, FORESTRY, FISHING	...	...	...	...	...
–	Agricultural production[d]	1.8598	5,240	7,096,533	2,423	2,817
–	Agricultural services, forestry, fisheries[e]	0.5308	120	569,474	0	120
B	MINING	2.4911	913	923,143	546	367
C	CONSTRUCTION	0.7476	1,378	4,642,735	0	1,378
D	MANUFACTURING	...	...	...	...	...
20	Food products	2.6533	1,687	1,601,466	1,051	636
24	Lumber and wood products	2.3124	639	696,033	363	276
25	Furniture and fixtures	0.7135	140	494,241	0	140
26	Paper products	4.0543	1,091	677,803	822	269
27	Printing and publishing	0.3765	213	1,425,114	0	213
28	Chemicals	0.9287	385	1,044,190	0	385
30	Rubber and plastics	7.0298	2,198	787,549	1,885	313
32	Stone, clay, glass	1.8252	426	587,891	193	233
33	Primary metals	2.7407	882	810,590	572	310
34	Fabricated metals	4.1054	2,398	1,471,232	1,814	584
35	Machinery	1.1915	1,035	2,187,912	166	869
36	Electric equipment	0.2164	189	2,200,312	0	189
37	Transport equipment	1.3008	1,022	1,978,880	236	786
–	Other manufacturing	0.7396	972	3,310,151	0	972
E	TRANSPORTATION AND PUBLIC UTILITIES	...	...	...	...	...
47	Transport services	5.6608	612	272,313	504	108
48	Communication	0.3070	161	1,320,958	0	161
49	Electric and gas	0.5384	193	902,949	0	193
F	WHOLESALE TRADE	0.6928	1,572	5,715,253	0	1,572
G	RETAIL TRADE	0.7951	5,474	17,341,892	0	5,474
H	FINANCE and INSURANCE	0.5799	1,346	5,846,839	0	1,346
I	SERVICES	...	...	...	...	...
70	Hotels and lodging	0.2341	124	1,334,210	124	0
72	Personal services	0.7568	317	1,055,026	0	317
80	Health services	0.6601	1,638	6,249,823	0	1,638
–	Other services	0.6393	2,996	11,804,762	0	2,996
–	GOVERNMENT	...	...	...	...	...
–	State government	0.9951	1,390	3,518,253	1,390	0
–	Local government	1.0965	4,060	9,326,667	0	4,060
Total	...	...	40,811	102,794,508[f]	12,089	28,722

[a] These data are from Table 10.2, column 5.
[b] These data are from Ohio Bureau of Employment Services (1986).
[c] These data are from U.S. Bureau of Labor Statistics (1987, 3–24).
[d] This includes SIC Major Groups 01 and 02. These data are from U.S. Bureau of the Census (1984c, Tables 5 and 9; and 1984d).
[e] This includes SIC Major Groups 07, 08, and 09.
[f] This total includes industries not shown.

with location quotients less than 1.0 generate negative values, which indicates that an error has been. For example, application of Eq. (10.2) to SIC Major Group 25 in Table 10.3 yields the following:

$$b_{25}^{1985} = \left(\frac{e_{25}^{1985}}{E_{25}^{1985}} - \frac{e_T^{1985}}{E_T^{1985}} \right) E_{25}^{1985}$$

$$= \left(\frac{140}{494,241} - \frac{40,811}{102,794,508} \right) 494,241$$

$$= (0.000283 - 0.000397)\ 494{,}241$$

$$= -56$$

Since it is impossible to have a negative number of employees, the negative employment estimate clearly reflects a computational error. However, the result also serves as an indirect estimate of the additional regional employment required to make the region self-sufficient in furniture and fixtures. That is, the "negative basic employment" estimate is an indirect measure of the nonlocal employment required to satisfy local demand. This deficit represents an opportunity for expanding local production to satisfy demand that is currently being satisfied by imported goods and services.

REFINEMENTS TO THE LOCATION QUOTIENT APPROACH

The underlying rationale for the location quotient approach can be illustrated by examining Eq. (10.2), reproduced below.[9] Given certain assumptions to be discussed in this section, the first term inside the parentheses, the ratio of regional employment in industry i to national employment in i, is a proxy for the region's share of national production in industry i. Given a second set of assumptions, the second term, the ratio of total regional employment to total national employment, is a proxy for the region's share of national consumption in industry i.

$$b_i^t = \left(\frac{e_i^t}{E_i^t} - \frac{e_T^t}{E_T^t} \right) E_i^t \qquad (10.2)$$

The location quotient approach assumes that if the region's production share in an industry is larger than its consumption share (i.e., the first term in Eq. [10.2] is larger than the second), local production exceeds local consumption and the excess is exported. If the local production share equals its consumption share (i.e., the first term is equal to the second), the region is assumed to be self-sufficient with no exports or imports. And if the local production share is smaller than its consumption share (i.e., the first term is smaller than the second), local consumption is assumed to exceed regional production and goods must be imported.

Consider, for example, a region with 4 percent of the national employment in an industry (i.e., the first term in Eq. [10.2], is 0.04) and 2 percent of the national employment in all industries (i.e., the second term in Eq. [10.2] is 0.02). If the industry's total national employment is 100,000, Eq. (10.2) indicates that the basic employment in the industry equals the difference between the proportions, that is, 0.04 minus 0.02, or 0.02, multiplied by 100,000, or 2,000.[10]

While widely used in practice, the location quotient approach has also been severely criticized in the economic literature. Many of the critiques deal with four auxiliary assumptions that underlie the assumed relationship between local production and consumption reflected in Eq. (10.2): (1) equal productivity, (2) equal consumption, (3) no net national exports, and (4) no crosshauling. The following sections examine adjustments that can be introduced to help ensure that these assumptions are valid, minimizing some of the most serious theoretical limitations of the location quotient approach.

Equal Productivity Adjustments. As Eq. (10.2) illustrates, the location quotient approach uses the local share of the national employment in an industry, E_i^t/e_i^t, as a measure of the region's share of national production in the industry. However, this ratio is only appropriate if the industry's regional and national productivity per employee are equal. If regional productivity exceeds national productivity, fewer local employees are required for a given level of production than are required nationally. As a result, the region's employment share will underestimate the region's share of national production in the industry and Eq. (10.2) will underestimate the industry's basic employment. Conversely, if regional productivity per employee is lower than national productivity, the industry's employment share will overstate the region's share of national production and Eq. (10.2) will overestimate the industry's basic sector employment.

National and regional data on employment and value added in manufacturing, mining, and construction can be used to compute the regional and national value added per employee that serves as a measure of regional and national labor productivity. The ratio of regional value added to national value added, v_i, can then be used to modify Eq. (10.2) to account for regional productivity differences (Isserman 1977c, 38; and 1980, 158):

$$b_i^t = \left[v_i \left(\frac{e_i^t}{E_i^t} \right) - \frac{e_T^t}{E_T^t} \right] \frac{E_i^t}{v_i} \qquad (10.3)$$

If the local value added per employee exceeds the national value, v_i will be greater than 1.0, increasing the first term in Eq. (10.3) and increasing the estimated basic employment in an industry. If the regional value added per employee is lower than the national rate, v_i will be less than 1.0, reducing the first term in Eq. (10.3) and decreasing the industry's basic employment estimate.

Table 10.4 reports the estimated basic and nonbasic employment by industry obtained by applying Eq. (10.3) to the employment data considered previously.[11] State and national data on the value added by

Table 10.4

Location Quotient Estimates with Productivity Adjustment

SIC Code (i)	Industry	1985 Employment Local[a] (e_i^{1985})	1985 Employment U.S.[b] (E_i^{1985})	Value Added/ Employee[c] (v_i)	Basic Employment (b_i^{1985})	Nonbasic Employment (n_i^{1985})
(1)	(2)	(3)	(4)	(5)	(6)	(7)
A	AGRICULTURE, FORESTRY, FISHING	...	...	...	...	...
–	Agricultural production[d]	5,240	7,096,533	–	2,423	2,817
–	Agricultural services, forestry, fisheries[e]	120	569,474	–	0	120
B	MINING	913	923,143	0.4764	144	769
C	CONSTRUCTION	1,378	4,642,735	0.8435	0	1,378
D	MANUFACTURING	...	...	...	...	...
20	Food products	1,687	1,601,466	1.3031	1,199	488
24	Lumber and wood products	639	696,033	1.0771	382	257
25	Furniture and fixtures	140	494,241	1.1707	0	140
26	Paper products	1,091	677,803	0.7888	750	341
27	Printing and publishing	213	1,425,114	0.9506	0	213
28	Chemicals	385	1,044,190	1.1219	15	370
30	Rubber and plastics	2,198	787,549	0.9461	1,868	330
32	Stone, clay, glass	426	587,891	1.0183	197	229
33	Primary metals	882	810,590	1.1257	596	286
34	Fabricated metals	2,398	1,471,232	1.1244	1,879	519
35	Machinery	1,035	2,187,912	0.8953	65	970
36	Electric equipment	189	2,200,312	1.2047	0	189
37	Transport equipment	1,022	1,978,880	1.0700	288	734
–	Other manufacturing	972	3,310,151	–	0	972
E	TRANSPORTATION AND PUBLIC UTILITIES	...	...	...	...	...
47	Transport services	612	272,313	–	504	108
48	Communication	161	1,320,958	–	0	161
49	Electric and gas	193	902,949	–	0	193
F	WHOLESALE TRADE	1,572	5,715,253	–	0	1,572
G	RETAIL TRADE	5,474	17,341,892	–	0	5,474
H	FINANCE and INSURANCE	1,346	5,846,839	–	0	1,346
I	SERVICES	...	...	...	...	...
70	Hotels and lodging	124	1,334,210	–	124	0
72	Personal services	317	1,055,026	–	0	317
80	Health services	1,638	6,249,823	–	0	1,638
–	Other services	2,996	11,804,762	–	0	2,996
–	GOVERNMENT	...	...	...	...	...
–	State government	1,390	3,518,253	–	1,390	0
–	Local government	4,060	9,326,667	–	0	4,060
Total	...	40,811	102,794,508[f]	...	11,822	28,989

[a] These data are from Ohio Bureau of Employment Services (1986).
[b] These data are from U.S. Bureau of Labor Statistics (1987, 3–24).
[c] The employment and value added data required to compute the productivity adjustment factors are from the following sources: SIC Division B, Mining: 1982 Census of Mineral Industries (U.S. Bureau of the Census 1985b, Table 2a; 1985c, Table 2a); SIC Division C, Construction: 1982 Census of Construction Industries (U.S. Bureau of the Census 1984e, Table 3; 1984f, Table 3); SIC Division D, Manufacturing: 1982 Census of Manufactures (U.S. Bureau of the Census 1985a, Table 5; 1986c, Table 5). For a more complete discussion of these sources see *Community Analysis and Planning Programs Users Guide*, Chapter 5.
[d] This includes SIC Major Groups 01 and 02. These data are from U.S. Bureau of the Census (1984c, Tables 5 and 9; and 1984d).
[e] This includes SIC Major Groups 07, 08, and 09.
[f] This total includes industries not shown.

SIC Division are divided by the corresponding employment data to compute the value added per employee at the state and national level. The v_i adjustments in column 5 are then computed by dividing the state value added figures by the national figures. Value added data are only available for states and for mining, construction, and manufacturing, which means that state-level productivity adjustments can only be applied to SIC Divisions B, C, and D and used as proxies for local productivity rates.

For example, for Major Group 20, Food Products,

$$b_{20}^{1985} = \left[v_{20} \left(\frac{e_{20}^{1985}}{E_{20}^{1985}} \right) - \frac{e_T^{1985}}{E_T^{1985}} \right] \frac{E_{20}^{1985}}{v_{20}}$$

$$= \left[1.3031 \left(\frac{1,687}{1,601,466} \right) - \frac{40,811}{102,794,508} \right] \frac{1,601,466}{1.303}$$

$$= [1.3031 (0.001053) - 0.000397] \, 1,229,060$$

$$= 1,199$$

A comparison of Tables 10.4 and 10.3 indicates that the productivity adjustments increase the basic employment estimates when the regional productivity per employee exceeds the national productivity per employee and reduces the basic estimates when the regional productivity is less than the national productivity. These results correspond to the assumed effect of regional productivity differences.

Equal Consumption Adjustments. As Eq. (10.2) illustrates, the location quotient approach uses the local total employment share, e_T'/E_T', as a measure of the region's share of national consumption in an industry. However, this ratio is only accurate if the industry's regional consumption and national consumption per employee are equal. If local consumption per employee exceeds national consumption rates, the total employment ratio will underestimate local consumption; that is, the second term in Eq. (10.2) will be too small, and the industry's basic employment will be overestimated.

For example, it is reasonable to assume that the per-employee consumption of ski equipment and down vests is higher in New England and lower in Florida than it is nationally. As a result, the total employment ratio in Eq. (10.2) will underestimate the number of skis and down vests that will be purchased in New England and overstate the proportion of local production that is exported. Conversely, the total employment ratio will overstate the consumption of these goods in Florida and underestimate the size of the basic sector for any winter sports industries located in Florida.

The assumption of identical per-employee consumption could be obviated by using regional and national consumption data to adjust for regional consumption differences. Unfortunately, regional consumption data by industry or commodity group are unavailable. As a result, less direct adjustment procedures must be used to account for regional consumption differences.

The *population ratio adjustment* replaces the regional and national total employment figures in Eq. (10.2) by the corresponding total population values. This technique is particularly appropriate for retirement areas in which local consumption levels are more directly related to the region's total population than to its employed population.[12]

A second procedure, called the *personal income adjustment*, replaces the total employment values in Eq. (10.2) by the total regional and national personal income, y^t and Y^t, as follows:

$$b_i^t = \left(\frac{e_i^t}{E_i^t} - \frac{y^t}{Y^t}\right) E_i^t \qquad (10.4)$$

This procedure is appealing because regional consumption patterns are more closely related to regional personal income than to the number of employed persons or residents in the region, particularly in retirement communities and low-income areas with substantial non–job-related income.

Table 10.5 records the basic and nonbasic employment estimates obtained by applying Eq. (10.4) to the employment data previously considered. Total personal income in 1984 was \$3,016,317.0 million for the United States and \$1,134.0 million for the study area (U.S. Bureau of Economic Analysis 1986). Substituting these values into Eq. (10.4) for SIC Major Group 20 yields the following:

$$b_{20}^{1985} = \left(\frac{e_{20}^{1985}}{E_{20}^{1985}} - \frac{y^{1984}}{Y^{1984}}\right) E_{20}^{1985}$$

$$= \left(\frac{1,687}{1,601,466} - \frac{\$1,134.0}{\$3,016,317.0}\right) 1,601,466$$

$$= (0.001053 - 0.000375)\, 1,601,466$$

$$= 1,085$$

A comparison of the basic employment estimates in Tables 10.5 and

Table 10.5

Location Quotient Estimates with Consumption Adjustment

SIC Code (i) (1)	Industry (2)	1985 Employment Local[a] (e_i^{1985}) (3)	1985 Employment U.S.[b] (E_i^{1985}) (4)	Basic Employment (b_i^{1985}) (5)	Nonbasic Employment (n_i^{1985}) (6)
A	AGRICULTURE, FORESTRY, FISHING	...	...	...	...
–	Agricultural production[c]	5,240	7,096,533	2,572	2,668
–	Agricultural services, forestry, fisheries[d]	120	569,474	0	120
B	MINING	913	923,143	566	347
C	CONSTRUCTION	1,378	4,642,735	0	1,378
D	MANUFACTURING	...	...	...	...
20	Food products	1,687	1,601,466	1,085	602
24	Lumber and wood products	639	696,033	377	262
25	Furniture and fixtures	140	494,241	0	140
26	Paper products	1,091	677,803	836	255
27	Printing and publishing	213	1,425,114	0	213
28	Chemicals	385	1,044,190	0	385
30	Rubber and plastics	2,198	787,549	1,902	296
32	Stone, clay, glass	426	587,891	205	221
33	Primary metals	882	810,590	577	305
34	Fabricated metals	2,398	1,471,232	1,845	553
35	Machinery	1,035	2,187,912	212	823
36	Electric equipment	189	2,200,312	0	189
37	Transport equipment	1,022	1,978,880	278	744
–	Other manufacturing	972	3,310,151	0	972
E	TRANSPORTATION AND PUBLIC UTILITIES	...	...	...	...
47	Transport services	612	272,313	510	102
48	Communication	161	1,320,958	0	161
49	Electric and gas	193	902,949	0	193
F	WHOLESALE TRADE	1,572	5,715,253	0	1,572
G	RETAIL TRADE	5,474.	17,341,892	0	5,474
H	FINANCE and INSURANCE	1,346	5,846,839	0	1,346
I	SERVICES	...	...	...	...
70	Hotels and lodging	124	1,334,210	124	0
72	Personal services	317	1,055,026	0	317
80	Health services	1,638	6,249,823	0	1,638
–	Other services	2,996	11,804,762	0	2,996
–	GOVERNMENT	...	...	...	...
–	State government	1,390	3,518,253	1,390	0
–	Local government	4,060	9,326,667	0	4,060
Total	...	40,811	102,794,508[e]	12,480	28,331

[a] These data are from Ohio Bureau of Employment Services (1986).
[b] These data are from U.S. Bureau of Labor Statistics (1987, 3–24).
[c] This includes SIC Major Groups 01 and 02. These data are from U.S. Bureau of the Census (1984c, Tables 5 and 9; and 1984d).
[d] This includes SIC Major Groups 07, 08, and 09.
[e] This total includes industries not shown.

10.3 reveals that the personal income adjustment increases all of the basic employment estimates. This reflects the fact that the region's personal income share, y^t/Y^t, or 0.000375, is smaller than its employment share, e_T^t/E_T^t, or 0.000397. As a result, the second term in Eq. (10.4) is smaller than the corresponding term in Eq. (10.2), increasing the basic sector estimates for all industries. The personal income adjustment would reduce the basic sector estimates for regions with personal income shares larger than their employment shares.

An adjustment procedure utilizing total personal income data obviously cannot account for regional consumption differences reflecting differences in tastes, relative prices, climate, ethnic and racial composition, and a host of other factors. Nevertheless, given the aggregated nature of available industry data, personal income is probably the most important cause for regional and consumption differences. As a result, the personal income adjustment provides an acceptable procedure, particularly when combined with judgmental adjustments for products known to have unusual regional consumption patterns (Isserman 1977c, 38).

National Exports Adjustments. The location quotient approach estimates an industry's basic employment by relating the local production share to the local consumption share. This approach assumes, however, that national production in all industries equals national consumption in all industries, that is, there are no net national exports (exports minus imports) by any industry at the national level. For example, if the nation produces more than it consumes in an industry (i.e., exports products in the industry), Eq. (10.2) will overstate the region's share of national consumption in the industry and understate the region's basic employment in the industry. Consider a situation in which the nation's net exports in an industry are equal to one-half of the nation's production; that is, the nation consumes only one-half of the industry's production. Other things being equal, a region with 10 percent of the nation's total employment would consume only 5 percent of the nation's production because the remaining 5 percent is exported to satisfy foreign demand.

Similarly, if the nation is a net importer in an industry, the national employment in the industry will not include foreign employment required to satisfy domestic demand. As a result, Eq. (10.2) will understate the region's share of national consumption and overestimate the industry's basic employment. For example, if the nation imports half of the national consumption in an industry, a region with 10 percent of the nation's total employment would consume 20 percent of the nation's production in the industry, because the region's share of domestic production is supplemented by an equal share of the imported foreign production (Isserman 1977c, 38).

The assumption of no net exports or imports could be dealt with by modifying the second term in Eq. (10.2) to account for foreign consumption (positive net exports) and foreign production (negative net exports). Unfortunately, it is impossible to estimate reliably the domestic employment that is replaced by a given level of imports.[13] As a result, data are only available on the domestic employment generated directly or indirectly by exports. These data can be used as follows to modify Eq. (10.2) to account for the effect of national exports

$$b_i^t = \left[\frac{e_i^t}{E_i^t} - d_i \left(\frac{e_T^t}{E_T^t} \right) \right] E_i^t \qquad (10.5)$$

The *proportion domestic, d_i,* is equal to the non–export-related production in an industry divided by the industry's total national employment. This adjustment can never exceed 1.0, because the numerator, total employment minus export-related employment, can never be larger than the denominator, total employment. As a result, the exports adjustment expressed as Eq. (10.5) always reduces the estimated local consumption share and increases the basic employment estimate.

Table 10.6 contains the basic and nonbasic employment estimates obtained by applying Eq. (10.5) to the employment data previously considered. The d_i values in column 5 are derived from the national employment data in column 4 and published data on the contributions of exports to U.S. employment (U.S. International Trade Administration 1986, 26). For example, in 1983, an estimated 126,000 full-time equivalent jobs in SIC Division B, Mining, were related to exports.[14] As a result, the proportion domestic, d_B, 0.864, is equal to the total national employment, 923,143, minus the export-related employment, 126,000, or 797,143, divided by the total national employment, 923,143.

The basic employment estimates are obtained by applying Eq. (10.5). For example, for SIC Division B,

$$b_B^{1985} = \left[\frac{e_B^{1985}}{E_B^{1985}} - d_B \left(\frac{e_T^{1985}}{E_T^{1985}} \right) \right] E_B^{1985}$$

$$= \left[\frac{913}{923,143} - 0.864 \left(\frac{40,811}{102,794,508} \right) \right] 923,143$$

$$= [0.000989 - 0.864 (0.000397)] \, 923,143$$

$$= 597$$

A comparison of Tables 10.6 and 10.3 reveals that the exports adjustment increases the basic employment estimate for all industries with national exports, as the preceding discussion suggests. In several cases Major Groups that have no basic employment with the unadjusted location quotient formula are found to have basic employment when the national exports adjustment is employed.

Table 10.6

Location Quotient Estimates with Exports Adjustment

SIC Code (i)	Industry	1985 Employment Local[a] (e_i^{1985})	1985 Employment U.S.[b] (E_i^{1985})	Prop. Domestic[c] (d_i)	Basic Employment (b_i^{1985})	Nonbasic Employment (n_i^{1985})
(1)	(2)	(3)	(4)	(5)	(6)	(7)
A	AGRICULTURE, FORESTRY, FISHING	...	...	...	...	...
–	Agricultural production[d]	5,240	7,096,533	0.912	2,670	2,570
–	Agricultural services, forestry, fisheries[e]	120	569,474	0.888	0	120
B	MINING	913	923,143	0.864	597	316
C	CONSTRUCTION	1,378	4,642,735	0.975	0	1,378
D	MANUFACTURING	...	...	...	...	...
20	Food products	1,687	1,601,466	1.000	1,051	636
24	Lumber and wood products	639	696,033	0.980	368	271
25	Furniture and fixtures	140	494,241	0.960	0	140
26	Paper products	1,091	677,803	0.938	839	252
27	Printing and publishing	213	1,425,114	0.955	0	213
28	Chemicals	385	1,044,190	0.839	37	348
30	Rubber and plastics	2,198	787,549	0.986	1,890	308
32	Stone, clay, glass	426	587,891	0.973	199	227
33	Primary metals	882	810,590	0.870	602	280
34	Fabricated metals	2,398	1,471,232	0.953	1,841	557
35	Machinery	1,035	2,187,912	0.804	336	699
36	Electric equipment	189	2,200,312	0.155	54	135
37	Transport equipment	1,022	1,978,880	0.880	331	691
–	Other manufacturing	972	3,310,151	1.000	0	972
E	TRANSPORTATION AND PUBLIC UTILITIES	...	...	...	...	...
47	Transport services	612	272,313	1.000	504	108
48	Communication	161	1,320,958	0.963	0	161
49	Electric and gas	193	902,949	0.947	0	193
F	WHOLESALE TRADE	1,572	5,715,253	1.000	0	1,572
G	RETAIL TRADE	5,474	17,341,892	1.000	0	5,474
H	FINANCE and INSURANCE	1,346	5,846,839	0.986	0	1,346
I	SERVICES	...	...	...	...	...
70	Hotels and lodging	124	1,334,210	1.000	124	0
72	Personal services	317	1,055,026	1.000	0	317
80	Health services	1,638	6,249,823	1.000	0	1,638
–	Other services	2,996	11,804,762	1.000	0	2,996
–	GOVERNMENT	...	...	...	...	...
–	State government	1,390	3,518,253	1.000	1,390	0
–	Local government	4,060	9,326,667	1.000	0	4,060
Total	...	40,811	102,794,508[f]	...	12,831	27,980

[a] These data are from Ohio Bureau of Employment Services (1986).
[b] These data are from U.S. Bureau of Labor Statistics (1987, 3–24).
[c] These data are from U.S. International Trade Administration (1986, 26) and U.S. Bureau of Labor Statistics (1987, 3–24).
[d] This includes SIC Major Groups 01 and 02. These data are from U.S. Bureau of the Census (1984c, Tables 5 and 9; and 1984d).
[e] This includes SIC Major Groups 07, 08, and 09.
[f] This total includes industries not shown.

Crosshauling Adjustment. The location quotient approach identifies regional exports and associated basic sector employment by subtracting a region's estimated share of national consumption in an industry (the second term in Eq. [10.2]) from the region's estimated share of national production in the industry (the first term in Eq. [10.2]). However, this procedure is only accurate when there is no *crosshauling,* that is, importing of goods in an export sector.[15] Thus, if local consumption in an export industry is partially satisfied by imports,

Eq. (10.2) overstates local consumption of locally produced products; as a result, the industry's exports and associated basic employment are underestimated.

Consider, for example, a region that consumes 1 percent of the nation's beer and contains a brewery producing 1 percent of the nation's beer. Because the region's production and consumption share are equal, application of Eq. (10.2) suggests that the brewery serves only local demand and has no basic activity. In fact, the brewery undoubtedly produces only one brand of beer and exports substantial quantities of beer to other parts of the country. These exports are replaced by crosshauled imports of other beer brands imported to satisfy local demand.

Crosshauling can also result from *product mix*—the presence of a range of different goods within a product category. For example, a region that produces more than its share of electrical machinery rarely produces all types of electrical machinery. Typically, it exports some types of electrical machinery and imports (or crosshauls) others in the same broad product category. As a result, offsetting crosshauled imports mask regional exports and underestimate the basic sector activity in crosshauling industries.

The effects of crosshauling can be reduced by using more refined industrial categories to reduce the possibility for offsetting exports and imports within a given product category. For example, the location quotient analysis in Table 10.2 indicates that the analysis region has no basic sector activity in SIC Division F, Wholesale Trade. However, Table 10.7 reports a total of 402 basic employees in this SIC Division when Eq. (10.2) is applied at the three-digit SIC level.

The results in Table 10.7 reflect the fact that while the region has less than its share of employment in wholesale trade (i.e., the location quotient for SIC Division F in Table 10.3 is 0.6928), it has more than its share of employment in five three-digit SIC industry groups having location quotients above 1.0: Nonpetroleum Minerals, Miscellaneous Durable Goods, and so on. By revealing export activity masked by crosshauled imports, disaggregated analyses at the three- or four-digit SIC level provide a much more accurate picture of an industry's basic sector activity (Isserman 1977c, 35–38).

Combined Adjustments. The preceding discussion has considered four adjustments to the traditional basic employment estimation formula represented by Eq. (10.2), reproduced below.

$$b_i^t = \left(\frac{e_i^t}{E_i^t} - \frac{e_T^t}{E_T^t} \right) E_i^t \tag{10.2}$$

Table 10.7

Three-Digit Location Quotient Estimates for SIC Division F

SIC Code (i)	Industry	1985 Employment Local^a (e_i^{1985})	1985 Employment U.S.^{b} (E_i^{1985})	Location Quotient (LQ_i)	Basic Employment (b_i^{1985})	Nonbasic Employment (n_i^{1985})
(1)	(2)	(3)	(4)	(5)	(6)	(7)
50	Wholesale — durable goods	...	...	...	...	...
501	Motor vehicles and equipment	23	432,161	0.1341	0	23
503	Lumber and materials	28	216,864	0.3252	0	28
505	Nonpetroleum minerals	90	136,645	1.6590	36	54
506	Electrical goods	11	494,922	0.0560	0	11
508	Machinery and equipment	545	1,444,181	0.9505	0	545
509	Miscellaneous durable goods	85	196,002	1.0923	7	78
51	Wholesale — nondurable goods	...	...	...	...	...
514	Groceries and related	108	733,905	0.3707	0	108
515	Farm products, raw	186	136,745	3.4261	132	54
517	Petroleum and related	264	204,862	3.2459	183	81
519	Miscellaneous nondurable goods	217	434,058	1.2592	45	172
–	Other wholesale goods	15	1,284,908	0.0294	0	15
	Division Total	1,572	5,715,253	...	402	1,170

^{a} These data are from Ohio Bureau of Employment Services (1986).
^{b} These data are from U.S. Bureau of Labor Statistics (1987, 3–24).

The first adjustment, represented by Eq. (10.3), modifies the first and last terms in Eq. (10.2) by the ratio of local to national value added per employee, v_i, to help account for regional productivity differences that distort the region's estimated production share. The second adjustment, represented by Eq. (10.4), replaces the total employment values in Eq. (10.2) by the corresponding personal income values, y^t and Y^t, to help account for regional consumption differences that distort the region's estimated consumption share. The third adjustment, represented by Eq. (10.5), multiplies the second term in Eq. (10.2) by d_i, the proportion of the national production in each industry that serves domestic demand, to help account for national exports that overestimate the region's consumption share. The fourth adjustment uses more disaggregated data to help identify regional exports hidden in more aggregated data for crosshauled industries.

The first three adjustments can be incorporated into a single estimation formula represented by Eq. (10.6),

$$ b_i^t = \left[v_i \left(\frac{e_i^t}{E_i^t} \right) - d_i \left(\frac{y^t}{Y^t} \right) \right] \frac{E_i^t}{v_i} \qquad (10.6) $$

Table 10.8 reports the results of applying Eq. (10.6) to the employment data considered previously. For example, for SIC Major Group 24, Lumber and Wood Products,

Table 10.8

Location Quotient Estimates with Combined Adjustments

SIC Code (i) (1)	Industry (2)	1985 Employment Local[a] (e_i^{1985}) (3)	1985 Employment U.S.[b] (E_i^{1985}) (4)	Basic Employment (b_i^{1985}) (5)	Nonbasic Employment (n_i^{1985}) (6)
A	AGRICULTURE, FORESTRY, FISHING	...	...	...	...
–	Agricultural production[c]	5,240	7,096,533	2,807	2,433
–	Agricultural services, forestry, fisheries[d]	120	569,474	0	120
B	MINING	913	923,143	284	629
C	CONSTRUCTION	1,378	4,642,735	0	1,378
D	MANUFACTURING	...	...	...	...
20	Food products	1,687	1,601,466	1,225	462
24	Lumber and wood products	639	696,033	401	238
25	Furniture and fixtures	140	494,241	0	140
26	Paper products	1,091	677,803	788	303
27	Printing and publishing	213	1,425,114	0	213
28	Chemicals	385	1,044,190	91	294
30	Rubber and plastics	2,198	787,549	1,889	309
32	Stone, clay, glass	426	587,891	215	211
33	Primary metals	882	810,590	646	236
34	Fabricated metals	2,398	1,471,232	1,929	469
35	Machinery	1,035	2,187,912	296	739
36	Electric equipment	189	2,200,312	83	106
37	Transport equipment	1,022	1,978,880	410	612
–	Other manufacturing	972	3,310,151	0	972
E	TRANSPORTATION AND PUBLIC UTILITIES	...	...	...	...
47	Transport services	612	272,313	510	102
48	Communication	161	1,320,958	0	161
49	Electric and gas	193	902,949	0	193
F	WHOLESALE TRADE	1,572	5,715,253	0	1,572
G	RETAIL TRADE	5,474	17,341,892	0	5,474
H	FINANCE and INSURANCE	1,346	5,846,839	0	1,346
I	SERVICES	...	.. .	...	...
70	Hotels and lodging	124	1,334,210	124	0
72	Personal services	317	1,055,026	0	317
80	Health services	1,638	6,249,823	0	1,638
–	Other services	2,996	11,804,762	0	2,996
–	GOVERNMENT	...	...	...	...
–	State government	1,390	3,518,253	1,390	0
–	Local government	4,060	9,326,667	0	4,060
	Total ...	40,811	102,794,508[e]	13,088	27,723

[a] These data are from Ohio Bureau of Employment Services (1986).
[b] These data are from U.S. Bureau of Labor Statistics (1987, 3–24).
[c] This includes SIC Major Groups 01 and 02. These data are from U.S. Bureau of the Census (1984c, Tables 5 and 9; and 1984d).
[d] This includes SIC Major Groups 07, 08, and 09.
[e] This total includes industries not shown.

$$b_{24}^{1985} = \left[v_{24} \left(\frac{e_{24}^{1985}}{E_{24}^{1985}} \right) - d_{24} \left(\frac{y^{1982}}{Y^{1982}} \right) \right] \frac{E_{24}^{1985}}{v_{24}}$$

$$= \left[1.077 \left(\frac{639}{696,033} \right) - 0.980 \left(\frac{\$1,134.0}{\$3,016,317.0} \right) \right] \frac{696,033}{1.077}$$

$$= [1.077 (0.000918) - 0.980 (0.000376)] \, 646,270$$

$$= (0.000989 - 0.000368) \, 646,270$$

$$= 401$$

A comparison of the combined adjustment estimates in Table 10.8 and the unadjusted estimates in Table 10.3 reveals that the three adjustment procedures have increased the total basic employment estimate from 12,089 to 13,088. The crosshauling adjustment can also be included by applying Eq. (10.6) to three-digit SIC employment data. The three adjustments increase three-digit total basic sector estimate from 15,167, using Eq. (10.2), to 16,102, using Eq. (10.6). The alternative basic employment estimates are evaluated at the end of Chapter 11, which reviews another estimation procedure—the minimum requirements approach.

ENDNOTES

1. See Andrews (1954a) and Tiebout (1962, 50–55) for more complete discussions of these direct measurement approaches. See Gibson and Worden (1981, 147–53) for a description of a detailed survey of 20 small communities in Arizona.

2. Alternative indirect measurement approaches using ordinary least squares regression techniques and time series "econometric" techniques to determine local employment multipliers have been proposed in the literature but rarely used in practice. See, for example, Terry (1965), Park (1970), Rosen and Mathur (1973), and Mathur and Rosen (1974).

3. The following discussion of the assumption approach is based largely on similar discussions in Tiebout (1962, 46–47) and Isserman (1980, 164–65).

4. Alternative assignment procedures have also been used. See, for example, Garnick (1970, 42).

5. The following discussion draws heavily on Tiebout (1962, 47–49) and Isserman (1977c).

6. This formulation is only one of a family of related measures developed for various specialized purposes. Other applications of the general concept, the ratio of two ratios, include the coefficient of localization, the coefficient of specialization, the index of diversification, and many others. Location quotients have also been used to compare the local and national population, number of households, and personal income or the number of theater seats to the total population. See, for example, Bendavid-Val (1983, 76–77) and Isard et al. (1960, 124–25).

7. The U.S. Bureau of Economic Analysis OBERS projections for states use location quotients larger than 1.0 as a cutoff value. For example, nonmetal mining is assumed to be basic only if the location quotient is greater than 1.50, and food manufacturing is only basic if the location quotient is larger than 1.20 (see, e.g., U.S. Bureau of Economic Analysis 1985a, xvi). However, these cutoff values are probably inappropriate for smaller areas such as cities and

counties, which generally have smaller proportions of local (i.e., nonbasic) activity.

8. Equation (10.2) is derived as follows: Given Eq. (9.1),

$$e_i^t = b_i^t + n_i^t$$

Rearranging terms yields the following:

$$b_i^t = e_i^t - n_i^t$$

The proportion of the local employment in a basic industry serving local demand can be assumed to equal the industry's share of the nation's total employment. As a result, the nonbasic employment in a basic industry, n_i^t, can be computed as follows:

$$n_i^t = \left(\frac{E_i^t}{E_T^t}\right) e_T^t$$

Substituting the expression for n_i^t from this equation into the previous equation yields the following:

$$b_i^t = e_i^t - \left(\frac{E_i^t}{E_T^t}\right) e_T^t$$

Dividing the expressions on the right-hand side of the equation by E_i^t and rearranging terms yields Eq. (10.2), that is,

$$b_i^t = \left(\frac{e_i^t}{E_i^t} - \frac{e_T^t}{E_T^t}\right) E_i^t$$

The basic employment in industries with location quotients greater than 1.0 can also be estimated from the location quotient by applying the following equation:

$$b_i^t = \left(1 - \frac{1}{LQ_i}\right) e_i^t$$

9. The following section draws heavily on Isserman (1977c); also see Tiebout (1962, 48) and Isserman (1980, 156–59).

10. Isserman (1980) uses a similar simple numerical example to illustrate the implications of the different refinements to the traditional procedure for location quotient estimation.

11. See Table 10.4, footnote c, for a detailed description of the sources used to obtain the value added data in column 5.

12. See, for example, Norcliffe (1983) and Forward (1982) for applications of the population ratio technique within the standard location quotient framework.

13. Estimates for the domestic employment replaced by a given level of imports require auxiliary assumptions concerning the types of domestic production and associated productivity levels that would have occurred in the

absence of foreign competition. Because these assumptions cannot be prepared in an acceptable way, making reliable estimates for import-related employment is impossible.

14. Caution must be used in interpreting and using the employment data reported in Table 8 of the report by the U.S. International Trade Administration (1986, 26). Although the data on each row of the table correspond to the standard SIC categories, some of the data are reported at the SIC Division (one-letter) level and others are reported at the two-, three-, or four-digit level. In addition, goods labeled *manufactures* in this report correspond to Standard International Trade Classification (SITC) classes 5 to 9 and exclude some goods classified as *manufacturing* in SIC classes 19 through 39, such as Food and Kindred Products (SIC 20) and Petroleum Refining and Related Industries (SIC 29). The narrower SITC classification is generally used in international trade analysis (U.S. International Trade Administration 1986, 32).

15. The no crosshauling assumption is often referred to as the *homogeneous product assumption,* that is, the assumption that an industry's local product is identical to its product in the rest of the nation. If this were the case, there would be no need to export and import (i.e., crosshaul) the product in question (Isserman 1977c, 35).

Chapter 11

Minimum Requirements Approach

The minimum requirements approach was first presented by Edward Ullman and Michael Dacey in 1960 (Ullman and Dacey 1960).[1] More recent applications include a major study by Ullman, Dacey, and Brodsky (1969); two important articles, one by Moore (1975) and the other by Moore and Jacobsen (1984); and the use of the technique in a developing country (Brodsky and Sarfaty 1977).

The relationship between the location quotient approach and the minimum requirements approach can be illustrated by examining Eq. (11.1), a modified version of Eq. (10.2).[2]

$$b_i^t = \left(\frac{e_i^t}{e_T^t} - \frac{E_i^t}{E_T^t} \right) e_T^t \qquad (11.1)$$

As before, b_i^t is the basic employment in industry i in year t; e_i^t is the local employment in industry i in year t; e_T^t is the total local employment in year t; E_i^t is the national employment in industry i in year t; and E_T^t is the total national employment in year t.

On this interpretation, the location quotient approach estimates the basic employment in each industry by relating an industry's local employment share (the first term in Eq. [11.1]) to its national employment share (the second term in Eq. [11.1]). If the industry's local employment share exceeds its national share (i.e., the first term in Eq. [8.1] is larger than the second), local production is assumed to exceed local demand and local employment is assumed to include basic activity. If the local employment share is less than or equal to the national share (i.e., the first term is less than or equal to the second),

149

local production is assumed not to exceed local demand and no basic activity is assumed.

The minimum requirements approach compares an industry's local employment patterns to a sample of similarly sized regions, rather than to the nation as a whole. That is, the minimum requirements approach estimates an industry's basic employment by applying Eq. (11.2):

$$b_i^t = \left(\frac{e_i^t}{e_T^t} - \frac{e_{im}^t}{e_m^t} \right) e_T^t \tag{11.2}$$

The e_m^t and e_{im}^t terms refer to the total employment and local employment in industry i in the *minimum shares region, m,* a comparable region with the smallest employment share in industry i, that is, the smallest value for the ratio e_i^t/e_T^t.

The minimum requirements approach assumes that local production in the minimum shares region is just sufficient to satisfy local requirements. As a result, the minimum shares region is assumed to produce no exports in this industry and have no associated basic sector employment. Every other region in the size category has a larger employment share—by definition—and is assumed to export products in industry i. The associated export activity is assumed to equal the difference between the industry's local employment share (the first term in Eq. [11.2]) and the industry's employment share in the minimum shares region (the second term in Eq. [11.2]).

Equations (11.1) and (11.2) both estimate an industry's basic employment by relating the industry's local employment share (the first term in each equation) to the industry's employment share in a second, reference, region. The location quotient approach in Eq. (11.1) assigns to the basic sector all local employment that exceeds the industry's national employment share, E_i^t/E_T^t. The minimum requirements approach in Eq. (11.2) assigns to the basic sector all local employment that exceeds the industry's share for the minimum shares region, e_{im}^t/e_m^t (Isserman 1980, 160).

The minimum requirements approach can be applied by computing the employment shares (e_i^t/e_T^t) for a sample of regions whose population, location, and other characteristics are comparable to the study region. The smallest employment share for the sample cities can be assumed to be the minimum required to satisfy local demand and substituted for the second term in Eq. (11.2). For example, Gibson and Worden (1981) computed employment shares for 178 western towns comparable to the twenty Arizona communities in their study. The observed minimum shares for each industry were then used to estimate the basic employment in their twenty communities.

The minimum requirements approach can also be used by applying the minimum shares estimation parameters developed by Moore and Jacobsen (1984). Their study used data from the 1980 census of population and housing to compute minimum employment shares for fifteen employment sectors and eleven classes of regions based on population. Their sample included all free-standing MSAs in the continental United States and a random sample of thirty-eight cities. The sample excluded regions such as Las Vegas, Detroit, and Washington, D.C., which have extremely high employment concentrations in one sector.

The minimum employment share for each employment category i and each population category j, s_{ij}, was related to the category's median population, P_j, by the following linear equation:

$$s_{ij} = a_i + b_i (\log P_j)$$

The *minimum employment share, s_{ij}*, is expressed as a percentage. Log P_j is the common (or base-ten) logarithm of the median population value for each size category. The a_i and b_i terms are the linear curve parameters that provide the best fit for each set of values for log P_j and s_{ij}.[3] Similar procedures were used to compute minimum shares estimation parameters for 1970 (Moore 1975) and 1940 through 1960 (Ullman and Dacey 1960).

The computed a and b parameters for the 15 employment categories and the total economy in 1980 are shown in Table 11.1. Given these parameters, the minimum employment share, s_i^t, for employment category i in year t for a region with population P^t can be estimated by applying Eq. (11.3)

$$s_i^t = a_i + b_i (\log P^t) \qquad (11.3)$$

where a_i and b_i are the minimum shares estimation parameters in Table 11.1.

The minimum employment share estimate, s_i^t, in Eq. (11.3) is equivalent to the second term in Eq. (11.2), expressed as a percentage. As a result, the basic employment in employment category i in year t, b_i^t, can be estimated by using Eq. (11.3) to estimate s_i^t and then applying Eq. (11.4).

$$b_i^t = \left(\frac{e_i^t}{e_T^t} - \frac{s_i^t}{100} \right) e_T^t \qquad (11.4)$$

Table 11.1

Minimum Shares Estimation Parameters, 1980

Category Number (i) (1)	Category (2)	SIC Code (3)	Minimum Shares Parameters	
			(a_i) (4)	(b_i) (5)
1	MANUFACTURING	D	−13.88699	3.71016
2	Nondurable manufacturing	20–23,26–31	−4.48547	1.30744
3	Durable manufacturing	24–25,32–39	−9.40152	2.40272
4	Transportation	40–42,44–47	−2.36507	0.84862
5	Communications	48	−1.37329	0.57021
6	WHOLESALE TRADE	F	−3.85368	1.15382
7	RETAIL TRADE	G	4.37027	1.61512
8	COMBINED TRADE	F,G	0.51658	2.76894
9	FINANCE, INSURANCE AND REAL ESTATE	H	−5.18366	1.60076
10	Business services	73	−4.47106	1.26062
11	Personal services	72	−0.23893	0.52127
12	Health services	80	−4.16849	1.63897
13	Educational services	82	1.32848	0.84995
14	Professional services	81,89	−2.01782	0.89891
15	PUBLIC ADMINISTRATION	J	−1.19286	0.64891
16	AGGREGATE ACTIVITY	...	−30.40331	15.58022

Source: Moore and Jacobsen (1984, 219). Reprinted by permission.

Table 11.2 records the results of applying Eqs. (11.3) and (11.4) to the employment data considered in the previous chapters for an estimated local population of 100,500. For example, substituting this population into Eq. (11.3) yields the following minimum shares estimate for employment category 2, Nondurable Manufacturing:

$$\begin{aligned} s_2^{1985} &= a_2 + b_2 \, (\log P^{1985}) \\ &= -4.48547 + 1.30744 \, (\log 100{,}500) \\ &= 2.055 \end{aligned}$$

Substituting this value into Eq. (11.4) yields

$$\begin{aligned} b_2^{1985} &= \left(\frac{e_2^{1985}}{e_T^{1985}} - \frac{s_2^{1985}}{100} \right) e_T^{1985} \\ &= \left(\frac{5{,}574}{40{,}811} - \frac{2.055}{100} \right) 40{,}811 \\ &= (0.13658 - 0.02055) \, 40{,}811 \\ &= 4{,}736 \end{aligned}$$

Similar computations yield basic employment estimates for all of the

Table 11.2

Minimum Requirements Basic and Nonbasic Employment Estimates, 1985

Category Number (*i*) (1)	Category (2)	SIC Code (3)	Total Employment[a] (e_T^{1985}) (4)	Basic Employment (b_i^{1985}) (5)	Nonbasic Employment (n_i^{1985}) (6)
–	AGRICULTURE, FORESTRY, FISH	A	5,360[b]	5,360	0
–	MINING	B	913	913	0
–	CONSTRUCTION	C	1,378	0	1,378
1	MANUFACTURING	D	...	...	...
2	Nondurable manufacturing	20–23, 26–31	5,574	4,736	838
3	Durable manufacturing	24–25, 32–39	7,703	6,635	1,068
–	TRANSPORTATION AND PUBLIC UTILITIES	E	...	...	...
4	Transportation	40–42, 44–47	612	0	612
5	Communications	48	161	0	161
–	Electric and gas	49	193	0	193
6	WHOLESALE TRADE	F	1,572	789	783
7	RETAIL TRADE	G	5,474	393	5,081
9	FINANCE, INSURANCE AND REAL ESTATE	H	1,346	194	1,152
–	SERVICES	I	...	...	...
–	Hotels and lodging	70	124	124	0
11	Personal services	72	317	0	317
12	Health services	80	1,638	0	1,638
–	Other services	–	2,996	0	2,996
15	PUBLIC ADMINISTRATION	J	5,450	4,612	838
Total	...	...	40,811	23,756	17,055

1985 Population: 100,500[c]

[a] These data are from Ohio Bureau of Employment Services (1986).
[b] This total includes SIC Major Groups 01, 02, 07, 08, and 09. the data are obtained from Ohio Bureau of Unemployment Services (1986) and U.S. Bureau of the Census (1984, Tables 5 and 9; and 1984d).
[c] This figure is from U.S. Bureau of the Census (1986b, 5).

employment categories for which estimation parameters are provided in Table 11.1.

Table 11.1 does not provide estimation parameters for employment categories in which the minimum employment share was not significantly related to the regional population. For example, construction was excluded because the employment required to support local demand is related more closely to a region's growth rate and economic health than to its population size. Agriculture was also not included because a region's agricultural employment is related more directly to its location and natural resource base than to its population (Moore 1975, 352).

As a result, the assumption approach must be used for industries for which estimation parameters are not provided. For example, in Table 11.2 the local employment in SIC Division A, Agriculture, Forestry, and Fisheries; Division B, Mining; and Major Group 70, Hotels and

Lodging, has been assigned entirely to the basic sector. Similarly, the local employment in Division C, Construction; Major Group 49, Electric and Gas; and the residual service category, Other Services, has been assigned totally to the nonbasic sector.

Total basic and nonbasic employment can also be estimated by applying the Aggregate Activity parameters in Table 11.1. These parameters relate the local employment share required to support local demand, that is, n_T^t/e_T^t, to the local population, P^t. For example, for a local population of 100,500,

$$
\begin{aligned}
s_{16}^{1985} &= a_{16} + b_{16} (\log P^{1985}) \\
&= -30.40331 + 15.58022 (\log 100,500) \\
&= 47.53
\end{aligned}
$$

This indicates that 47.53 percent of the local employment is required to satisfy local demand in all sectors of the local economy. As a result, the total local basic employment, b_T^t, is equal to the total local employment, 40,811, multiplied by one minus the estimated proportion serving local demand, s_{16}^t, divided by 100. That is,

$$
\begin{aligned}
b_T^{1985} &= \left(1 - \frac{s_{16}^{1985}}{100}\right) e_T^{1985} \\
&= \left(1 - \frac{47.53}{100}\right) 40,811 \qquad (11.5) \\
&= 21,413
\end{aligned}
$$

Note that the total basic employment estimate obtained by applying the aggregate activity parameters a_{16} and b_{16} differs from the sum of the individual basic employment estimates in Table 11.2.

As the computations in Table 11.2 illustrate, caution must be used in applying the minimum requirements estimation parameters in Table 11.1. For example, the employment sectors overlap in two cases. That is, Category 1, Manufacturing, subsumes Category 2, Nondurable Manufacturing, and Category 3, Durable Manufacturing. Similarly, Category 8, Combined Trade, includes Categories 6, Wholesale Trade, and 7, Retail Trade. As a result, one set of employment categories or the other must be used to avoid double counting.

Application of Eqs. (11.3) and (11.4) can also yield negative basic employment estimates in some cases. For example, for Category 11, Personal Services,

$$s_{11}^{1985} = a_{11} + b_{11} \, (\log P^{1985})$$
$$= -0.23893 + 0.52127 \, (\log 100,500)$$
$$= 2.369$$

Substituting this value into Eq. (11.4) yields the following:

$$b_{11}^{1985} = \left(\frac{e_{11}^{1985}}{e_T^{1985}} - \frac{s_{11}^{1985}}{100} \right) e_T^{1985}$$

$$= \left(\frac{317}{40,811} - \frac{2.369}{100} \right) 40,811$$

$$= (0.00777 - 0.02369) \, 40,811$$

$$= -650$$

The negative basic employment estimate can be explained by examining the estimated minimum employment share, s_i'. Equation (11.3) indicates that 2.369 percent of the total local employment of 40,811, or 967 employees, is required to satisfy the local demand for personal services. However, the region has only 317 employees in this category, which means that the region's estimated demand for personal services exceeds the local employment by 650. As was true for the location quotient approach, this "negative basic employment" can be interpreted as an estimate for the external employment required to satisfy local demand. In these cases, the negative basic employment value should be ignored and the industry's local employment assigned completely to the nonbasic sector.

REFINEMENTS TO THE MINIMUM REQUIREMENTS APPROACH

The location quotient approach can be interpreted as relating an industry's local production share (the first term in Eq. [10.2], below) to the local consumption share (the second term in Eq. [10.2]).[4]

$$b_i' = \left(\frac{e_i'}{E_i'} - \frac{e_T'}{E_T'} \right) E_i' \tag{10.2}$$

Similarly, the minimum requirements approach can be interpreted as relating an industry's local production share (the first term in Eq. [11.6] below) to the adjusted consumption share for the minimum share region m (the second term in Eq. [11.6]). That is, the local consumption share is assumed to equal the consumption share for minimum share region e^t_{im}/E^t_i, adjusted by the ratio of the total employment for the study region and the minimum shares region, e^t_T/e^t_m.[5]

$$b^t_i = \left[\frac{e^t_i}{E^t_i} - \left(\frac{e^t_{im}}{E^t_i} \right) \left(\frac{e^t_T}{e^t_m} \right) \right] E^t_i \qquad (11.6)$$

As the discussion in Chapter 10 points out, four adjustments can be applied to the standard location quotient estimation formulation, Eq. (10.2). Only the productivity adjustment is required for the minimum requirements approach. The minimum requirements approach does not compare local and national consumption rates and thus does not require an equal consumption adjustment. The minimum requirements consumption term can be interpreted as estimating gross exports and total local consumption, including consumption from imports. As a result, crosshauling, the importing of goods in an export category, causes no problems. And since no assumptions are made concerning net national exports, an exports adjustment is also not required (Pratt 1968 and Isserman 1980, 161–62).

Equal Productivity Adjustment

The minimum requirements approach expressed in Eq. (11.6) uses the local employment share, e^t_i/E^t_i, as a proxy for the region's share of national production in the industry. However, as was true for the location quotient approach, the local employment share will only reflect the region's production share if local productivity per employee is identical to national productivity per employee. If local productivity exceeds national productivity, the employment share will understate local production and Eq. (11.6) will underestimate the industry's basic employment. Conversely, if local productivity is lower than national productivity, the employment ratio will overstate local production and Eq. (11.6) will overestimate an industry's basic employment.

As a result, a productivity adjustment identical to the location quotient adjustment can be used to account for regional productivity differences. National and state value added and employment data can be used to compute the value added per employee that serves as a measure of national and local labor productivity rates. The ratio of local to national value added, v_i, can then be used to modify Eq. (11.6) to account for local productivity differences, as follows:

$$b_i^t = \left[v_i \left(\frac{e_i^t}{E_i^t} \right) - \left(\frac{e_{im}^t}{E_i^t} \right) \left(\frac{e_T^t}{e_m^t} \right) \right] \frac{E_i^t}{v_i}$$

Rearranging terms yields the following estimation equation utilizing the minimum employment share estimates, s_i^t, computed with Eq. (11.3):

$$b_i^t = \left[v_i \left(\frac{e_i^t}{e_T^t} \right) - \frac{s_i^t}{100} \right] \frac{e_T^t}{v_i} \qquad (11.7)$$

Table 11.3 reports the basic and nonbasic employment estimates obtained by applying Eq. (11.7) to the employment data previously considered. The v_i values in column 5 are computed from data from the 1982 Census of Manufactures (U.S. Bureau of the Census 1985a,

Table 11.3

Minimum Requirements Estimates with Productivity Adjustment

Category Number (i)	Category	SIC Code	Total Employment[a] (e_T^{1985})	Value Added/ Employee[b] (v_i)	Basic Employment (b_i^{1985})	Nonbasic Employment (n_i^{1985})
(1)	(2)	(3)	(4)	(5)	(6)	(7)
–	AGRICULTURE, FORESTRY, FISH	A	5,360[c]	...	5,360	0
–	MINING	B	913	...	913	0
–	CONSTRUCTION	C	1,378	...	1,378	...
1	MANUFACTURING	D	...	...	...	...
2	Nondurable manufacturing	20–23,26–31	5,574	1.148	4,844	730
3	Durable manufacturing	24–25,32–39	7,703	1.063	6,698	1,005
–	TRANSPORTATION AND PUBLIC UTILITIES	E	...	...	...	...
4	Transportation	40–42,44–47	612	...	0	612
5	Communications	48	161	...	0	161
–	Electric and gas	49	193	...	0	193
6	WHOLESALE TRADE	F	1,572	...	789	783
7	RETAIL TRADE	G	5,474	...	393	5,081
9	FINANCE, INSURANCE AND REAL ESTATE	H	1,346	...	194	1,152
–	SERVICES	I	...	...	...	...
–	Hotels and lodging	70	124	...	124	0
11	Personal services	72	317	...	0	317
12	Health services	80	1,638	...	0	1,638
–	Other services	–	2,996	...	0	2,996
15	PUBLIC ADMINISTRATION	J	5,697	...	4,612	838
Total		...	40,811	...	23,927	16,884

1985 Population: 100,500[d]

[a] These data are from Ohio Bureau of Employment Services (1986).
[b] These data are computed from data in the 1982 Census of Manufactures (U.S. Bureau of the Census 1985a, Table 5 and 7; 1986c, Table 5) using the procedures for the location quotient productivity adjustment.
[c] This figure is from Table 11.2, column 4.
[d] This figure is from U.S. Bureau of the Census (1986b, 5).

Tables 5 and 7; 1986c, Table 5) using the procedures for the location quotient productivity adjustment. Productivity adjustments can only be applied to Employment Categories 2, Nondurable Manufacturing, and 3, Durable Manufacturing, because value added data are only available for these categories.

For example, for Category 3, Durable Manufacturing, substitution of the appropriate values into Eq. (11.3) yields the following:

$$s_3^{1985} = a_3 + b_3 \, (\log P^{1985})$$
$$= -9.40152 + 2.40272 \, (\log 100{,}500)$$
$$= 2.617$$

Substituting this value into Eq. (11.7) yields the following:

$$b_3^{1985} = \left[v_3 \left(\frac{e_3^{1985}}{e_T^{1985}} \right) - \frac{s_3^{1985}}{100} \right] \frac{e_T^{1985}}{v_3}$$
$$= \left[1.063 \left(\frac{7{,}703}{40{,}811} \right) - \frac{2.617}{100} \right] \frac{40{,}811}{1.063}$$
$$= [1.063(0.18875) - 0.02617] \, 38{,}392$$
$$= 6{,}698$$

A comparison with Table 11.2 indicates that the productivity adjustment has increased the basic employment estimate, which is expected when local productivity per employee exceeds national productivity.

Second Minimum Shares Adjustment

As previously mentioned, the minimum requirements procedure assumes that local production in the minimum shares region is just sufficient to satisfy local consumption with no local exports or imports. That is, the employment share in the minimum shares region, e_{im}^t/e_m^t, is assumed to correspond exactly to local demand in the minimum shares region. However, it is possible that local production in the minimum shares region exceeds local demand and the excess is exported. In this case, e_{im}^t/e_m^t overstates the local consumption share in the minimum shares region because some local employment serves the export market. As a result, the second term in Eq. (11.6) will be too large and the basic employment estimate will be too small.

Local production in the minimum shares region is more likely to be insufficient to satisfy local demand; thus the region will import products in an industry. In this situation, the e_{im}^t/e_m^t term in Eq. (11.6) will understate the local consumption share in the minimum shares region because local employment does not include external employment required to satisfy local demand. As a result, the second term in Eq. (11.6) will be too small and the basic employment estimate will be too large.

Table 11.4 provides a second set of estimation parameters that can be used to reduce the possibility of overestimating an industry's basic employment in this way. These parameters were developed by Moore and Jacobsen (1984, 222) using the same data and procedures employed in deriving the minimum shares parameters in Table 11.1. However, in this case, the median population in each size category is related to the *second smallest* employment share for the size category.

As a result, the parameters in Table 11.4 can be used with Eqs. (11.3) and (11.4) or (11.7) to relate the local consumption share in the analysis region to the adjusted consumption share in a comparable region with the second smallest employment share, e_{im}^t/e_m^t. The use of the second minimum share parameters assumes that the minimum shares region imports products in an industry and the minimum shares parameters overestimate the basic sector employment in the study region. The second minimum shares parameters reduce the basic

Table 11.4

Second Minimum Shares Estimation Parameters, 1980

Category Number (i) (1)	Category (2)	SIC Code (3)	Second Minimum Shares Parameters (a_i) (4)	(b_i) (5)
1	MANUFACTURING	D	−19.67567	5.06861
2	Nondurable manufacturing	20–23,26–31	−7.34193	1.94831
3	Durable manufacturing	24–25,32–39	−12.33375	3.12030
4	Transportation	40–42,44–47	−4.21143	1.23612
5	Communications	48	−0.42186	0.43353
6	WHOLESALE TRADE	F	−4.52424	1.32883
7	RETAIL TRADE	G	7.58024	1.19209
8	COMBINED TRADE	F,G	3.05600	2.52092
9	FINANCE, INSURANCE AND REAL ESTATE	H	−5.87012	1.80141
10	Business services	73	−5.21854	1.44032
11	Personal services	72	0.45512	0.43014
12	Health services	80	−3.60471	1.60455
13	Educational services	82	2.41900	0.70442
14	Professional services	81,89	−2.72897	1.06191
15	PUBLIC ADMINISTRATION	J	−2.13412	0.85484
16	AGGREGATE ACTIVITY	...	−34.19522	17.30088

Source: Moore and Jacobsen (1984, 222). Reprinted by permission.

sector estimates in all industries by increasing the estimated local employment share that serves local demand, that is, by increasing the second term in Eq. (11.6).

There is no way to determine whether the minimum shares regions used to derive the parameters in Tables 11.1 and 11.4 were self-sufficient, exporters, or importers in an employment category. As a result, there is no reliable way to determine whether one should use the minimum shares parameters in Table 11.1, the second minimum shares parameters in Table 11.4, or abandon the minimum requirements approach entirely.[6] These issues are discussed more fully in the following section, which evaluates the alternative basic employment estimation approaches.

SELECTING APPROPRIATE BASIC SECTOR ESTIMATES

Thus far we have examined three basic employment estimation approaches: the assumption approach, the location quotient approach, and the minimum requirements approach. In Chapter 10 we also considered the traditional location quotient approach and alternative formulations incorporating productivity, consumption, and exports adjustments applied at the two- and three-digit SIC level. In this chapter we have also reviewed the traditional minimum shares formulation conducted at an aggregated and disaggregated level, a productivity-adjusted version, and comparable implementations using second minimum shares parameters.

The alternative formulations yield the fourteen basic and nonbasic employment estimates and base multipliers shown in Table 11.5. The base multipliers are derived by applying Eq. (9.6):

$$BM = \frac{e_T^t}{b_T^t} \qquad (9.6)$$

For example, the base multiplier for the unadjusted location quotient formulation, 3.376, is equal to the total local employment, 40,811, divided by the estimated total basic employment, 12,089.

The base multiplier values in Table 11.5 range from 1.706 for the productivity-adjusted first minimum shares formulation to 3.452 for the productivity-adjusted location quotient approach, a difference of more than 100 percent. It is therefore essential to evaluate the alternative

Table 11.5

Alternate Basic and Nonbasic Employment Estimates, 1985

Estimate Number (1)	Estimation Approach (2)	Basic Employment (b_T^{1985}) (3)	Nonbasic Employment (n_T^{1985}) (4)	Base Multiplier (BM) (5)
1	Assumption Approach[a]	21,064	19,747	1.937
	Location Quotient Approach			
2	Unadjusted[b]	12,089	28,722	3.376
3	Productivity Adjustment[c]	11,822	28,989	3.452
4	Consumption Adjustment[d]	12,480	28,331	3.270
5	Exports Adjustment[e]	12,831	27,980	3.181
6	Combined Adjustments, 2-digit[f]	13,088	27,723	3.118
7	Unadjusted, 3-digit[g]	15,167	25,644	2.691
8	Combined Adjustments, 3-digit[h]	16,102	24,709	2.535
	Minimum Requirements Approach			
9	First Minimum (disaggregated)[i]	23,756	17,055	1.718
10	First Minimum (aggregated)[j]	21,413	19,398	1.906
11	First Minimum (adjusted)[k]	23,927	16,884	1.706
12	Second Minimum (disaggregated)[l]	22,927	18,109	1.798
13	Second Minimum (aggregated)[m]	19,448	21,363	2.098
14	Second Minimum (adjusted)[n]	22,908	17,903	1.782

[a] The data in columns 3 and 4 are totals from Table 10.1
[b] The data in columns 3 and 4 are totals from Table 10.3
[c] The data in columns 3 and 4 are totals from Table 10.4
[d] The data in columns 3 and 4 are totals from Table 10.5
[e] The data in columns 3 and 4 are totals from Table 10.6
[f] The data in columns 3 and 4 are totals from Table 10.8
[g] The data in columns 3 and 4 are obtained using Eq. (10.2) to 3-digit SIC data.
[h] The data in columns 3 and 4 are obtained by applying Eq. (10.6) to 3-digit SIC data.
[i] The data in columns 3 and 4 are totals from Table 11.2.
[j] The data in columns 3 and 4 are obtained using Eqs. (11.3) and (11.5) and the parameters in Table 11.1.
[k] The data in columns 3 and 4 are obtained using Eqs. (11.7) and the parameters in Table 11.1.
[l] The data in columns 3 and 4 are obtained using Eqs. (11.3) and (11.4) and the parameters in Table 11.4.
[m] The data in columns 3 and 4 are obtained using Eqs. (11.3) and (11.5) and the parameters in Table 11.4.
[n] The data in columns 3 and 4 are obtained using Eq. (11.7) and parameters in Table 11.4.

estimation approaches on theoretical and empirical grounds to determine which estimate (or set of estimates) provides the most reliable measure of the region's basic and nonbasic sectors.

The evaluation must begin by recognizing that the base multipliers in Table 11.5 are extremely high: generally these values range between 1.0 and 2.0. These results reflect the fact that the study area has largely an agricultural economy and that available county-level employment data do not adequately measure agricultural workers.[7] Since agriculture is primarily a basic sector activity, the area's basic employment is underestimated and the base multiplier estimates are inflated.

Theoretical Evaluation

The alternate basic and nonbasic employment estimates can first be evaluated with respect to their theoretical support. The assumption approach, which assigns the local employment entirely to the basic or nonbasic sector on the basis of assumed market patterns, is perfectly appropriate for sectors such as state and local government and tourism, which are basic or nonbasic by definition. However, it is unacceptable for most industries that can serve local markets, external markets, or both simultaneously. As a result, in the absence of reliable information on local marketing patterns, the assumption approach estimates and base multiplier can be eliminated on theoretical grounds.

Similarly, as Chapter 10 points out, productivity, consumption, national exports, and crosshauling adjustments can be added to the traditional location quotient approach to help counter some of the latter's most serious theoretical limitations. As a result, the estimates of the three-digit location quotient base multiplier (i.e., estimates 7 and 8 in Table 11.5) should be considered to be less theoretically sound than the fully adjusted disaggregated estimate (estimate 8).

Table 11.5 indicates that the three-digit analysis has the most significant impact on the location quotient base multipliers. It must be remembered, however, that even analyses conducted at the three-digit level may still fail to recognize local exports that are offset by cross-hauled imports. As a result, these estimates continue to underestimate the actual basic sector employment and overstate the true base multiplier. As a result, the estimates of the three-digit location quotient base multiplier should be considered the upper bounds for the true multipliers (Isserman 1977b).

The productivity-adjusted minimum requirements estimates (estimates 11 and 14) are similarly superior on theoretical grounds to the unadjusted estimate (estimate 9). An evaluation of the other minimum requirements estimates is less clear, however. The disaggregated estimates (9 and 12) and aggregate estimates (10 and 13) are equally appropriate from a theoretical standpoint. As a result, the aggregate analysis may be preferred because it is easier to implement.

There is also no good theoretical rationale for choosing the first minimum shares estimates (10 or 11) or the second minimum shares estimates (13 or 14). The first minimum shares parameters are appropriate if local production in the minimum shares region exactly matches local demand and there are no imports or exports. The second minimum shares parameters are appropriate if local production in the minimum shares region fails to satisfy local demand and products must be imported. Since there is no way to determine empirically whether either assumption is correct, there is no sound justification for choosing one formulation or the other.

More important, no convincing theoretical argument can be made to support the selection of the location quotient estimates or the minimum requirements estimates. Both procedures are based on rather strong assumptions that are only partially obviated by the adjustments considered above. In the case of the location quotient approach, state-level value added data cannot accurately account for local productivity differences; personal income data cannot adequately recognize local consumption differences; the export adjustment does not deal with national imports; and even a three- or four-digit analysis fails to recognize local exports masked by crosshauled imports.

The minimum requirements approach is similarly weakened in assuming that the consumption rates, per employee, are identical in the study region and the minimum shares region. This assumption is implicit in the second term in Eq. (11.6), which implies that the study region's consumption share is equal to the consumption share in the minimum shares region, adjusted by their total employment ratios, e_T^t/e_m^t. This adjustment is only acceptable if consumption rates, per employee, are identical.

Unfortunately, there is no reason to believe that the local employment share that serves local demand will be identical for all regions in a given size category. Regions with relatively large and diverse manufacturing sectors generally consume a larger share of their production than smaller, more specialized regions because a greater variety of goods is produced locally. As a result, consumption rates, per employee, may differ substantially within a broad population category (Isserman 1980, 163). More important, there is no way to determine whether the minimum shares region in each size category is self-sufficient, an importer, or an exporter for a particular employment category. As a result, there is no theoretical ground for using the minimum shares parameters, or the second minimum shares parameters, or for avoiding the minimum shares approach entirely.

As Isserman concludes in his comprehensive review of export estimation techniques, "The main impression may well be the disquieting, problematic nature of every technique. Each has its serious conceptual flaws" (1980, 167). The assumption technique has little theoretical justification at all. The location quotient is flawed by the fact that it seriously underestimates exports, even when applied at a disaggregated level. And the minimum requirements approach measures the correct thing—gross regional exports—but does so by relating local consumption to the potentially "false minimum" of the minimum shares region.

Empirical Evidence

The preceding theoretical considerations undermine the assumption approach but do not eliminate the location quotient or the minimum requirements approaches. Several studies have used empirical data to evaluate the accuracy of the alternative estimation procedures. For example, Gibson and Worden (1981) employed a complete census of 6,555 employers in twenty small Arizona communities to compute local employment multipliers that served as a benchmark for assessing the accuracy of alternative estimation procedures. Other studies have used regional input-output tables, special census tabulations, and other data to develop benchmarks for evaluating these procedures.[8]

Empirical evaluations of the location quotient approach (e.g., Tiebout 1962; Greytak 1969; and Isserman 1977b) uniformly reveal that this method systematically underestimates exports, as the preceding theoretical discussion suggests. For example, three studies that examined manufacturing found average underestimation errors of 13 percent or more. Thus, theory and the available empirical evidence suggest that the estimates of the location quotient base multiplier are upper bounds for the true multipliers and that methods generating higher base multiplier estimates should be avoided (Isserman 1977b and 1980, 172.

These studies also affirm the value of using disaggregated data to reveal local exports hidden in more aggregated data. In all cases the estimation errors for analyses conducted at the three- or four-digit SIC level were dramatically lower than those for more aggregated analyses. For example, Isserman (1980, 168) found that the total export shares estimates using four-digit SIC data are 45 percent higher on average than equivalent analyses conducted at the two-digit level.

Gibson and Worden (1981) found that the location quotient multipliers were often more than two or three times larger than those produced by any other procedure. Thus, they concluded, "The location quotient approach has absolutely no utility for estimating basic and nonbasic employment shares in relatively small regional economies" (1981, 156). Their analysis also found that an earlier version of the Moore and Jacobsen parameters (Moore 1975) applied at the aggregate level outperformed all other methods and came "fairly close to producing results comparable to those produced with survey data" (Gibson and Worden 1981, 158).

Two considerations qualify Gibson and Worden's endorsement of the minimum requirements approach, however. First, they found that even the minimum requirements approach was not completely satisfactory, producing multipliers that were within 15 percent of the benchmark multipliers in only sixteen of the twenty communities investigated. In addition, their location quotient analysis was conducted at the two-digit SIC level, a level of aggregation that is disadvantageous to this approach.

Two other studies cast further doubt on the minimum requirements approach. Greytak (1969) calculated location quotient and minimum requirements export estimates for a sample of seven state or multistate regions and found average errors of 58.3 percent for the minimum requirements estimates. Linear transformation adjustments reduced the average error for the minimum requirements estimates to 20 percent, compared with 8 percent for the location quotient estimates (Isserman 1980, 171).

Isserman (1980) found that the minimum requirements base multipliers were lower than the location quotient multipliers in 79 of the 101 SMSAs in his sample, as one would expect. However, in the remaining 22 cases, the minimum requirements multipliers were higher than the location quotient multipliers, that is, higher than the acceptable upper bound. His analysis also suggests that this approach is impervious to the export implications of economic structure that are not related to the region's size. As a result, it is particularly inappropriate for cities with specialized economies such as government administrative centers, manufacturing regions, and trade, service, or tourist areas.

No studies have directly assessed the accuracy of the assumption approach. However, Isserman (1980, 171) uses data from three previous studies to evaluate the common strategy of assigning all manufacturing employment to the basic sector. The results are remarkably inconclusive. In one case, the assumption approach is superior to the location quotient approach. In the second, the location quotient approach is superior. In the third, the assumption approach is superior to the minimum requirements approach and the two-digit SIC location quotient analysis but inferior to the four-digit location quotient estimate.

EVALUATION OF THE ALTERNATIVES

The preceding theoretical considerations and empirical evidence provide limited guidance in choosing between the three estimation procedures considered in Chapter 10 and in this chapter. The assumption approach is clearly inadequate for most applications due to its lack of a theoretical base and an explicitly defined assignment procedure. The traditional location quotient and minimum requirements formulations are similarly inferior to the adjusted versions of each. This is particularly true for the location quotient approach, for which the productivity, consumption, and exports adjustments, and the use of disaggregated data directly address obvious limitations of the traditional formulation.

The preceding analysis also indicates that the location quotient and minimum requirements approaches are theoretically flawed and are better suited for some applications than for others. The minimum requirements approach has an obvious practical advantage in requiring only a single piece of readily available information—the local population in the analysis year. Gibson and Worden's (1981) study also indicates that the minimum requirements approach is preferable to the location quotient approach, particularly for small cities and subcounty regions for which disaggregated data are unavailable.

Theoretical considerations and the available evidence suggest that the location quotient approach is better suited for larger regions for which disaggregated data are more readily available. The location quotient approach is also more appropriate for specialized regions such as government administrative centers in which local exports are not related to the local population.

In most situations, analysts lacking the resources required to utilize more sophisticated techniques such as input-output analysis may choose to rely on both techniques. The fully adjusted location quotient approach applied at the three- or four-digit SIC level can be used to compute an upper bound for the region's base multiplier. Minimum requirements estimates that exceed this value can be rejected. Otherwise, the location quotient estimate, the minimum requirements estimate, or an average of both estimates may be used. Neither theory nor empirical evidence can indicate which approach works best in a particular application.

ENDNOTES

1. The following discussion draws heavily on Isserman (1980, 159–164).

2. Equation (11.1) can be derived from Eq. (10.2) as follows: Given Eq. (10.2),

$$b_i^t = \left(\frac{e_i^t}{E_i^t} - \frac{e_T^t}{E_T^t} \right) E_i^t \tag{10.2}$$

removing e_T^t from the expressions inside the parentheses and multiplying both terms by E_i^t yields Eq. (11.1), that is,

$$b_i^t = \left(\frac{e_i^t}{e_T^t} - \frac{E_i^t}{E_T^t} \right) e_T^t \tag{11.1}$$

3. See Chapter 2 for a discussion of the linear curve and Appendix B for a discussion of logarithms.

4. The discussion in the following section draws heavily on Isserman (1980, 159–164).

5. Equation (11.6) can be derived from Equation (11.2) as follows: Given Eq. (11.2),

$$b_i^t = \left(\frac{e_i^t}{e_T^t} - \frac{e_{im}^t}{e_m^t} \right) e_T^t \tag{11.2}$$

dividing both expressions inside the parentheses by E_i^t and multiplying both terms by e_T^t yields Eq. (11.6):

$$b_i^t = \left[\frac{e_i^t}{E_i^t} - \left(\frac{e_{im}^t}{E_i^t} \right) \left(\frac{e_T^t}{e_m^t} \right) \right] E_i^t \tag{11.6}$$

6. Limited support for the second minimum shares parameters is given by data provided by Moore and Jacobsen (1984, 219, 222), which indicate that the logarithms of the median population are more closely related to the second minimum values than they are to the first minimum values for 12 of the 16 employment categories considered.

7. For example, the Census of Agriculture employment data used in these examples do not include unpaid agricultural workers, such as family members, and farm contract laborers and agricultural service workers (Daberkow and Whitener 1986, 2–6). Other estimates for the county's total employment in 1985 are as high as 49,000, over 25 percent higher than the totals in these examples.

8. See, for example, Greytak (1969), Isserman (1977b), and Mulligan and Gibson (1984). The following discussion is based largely on Isserman's (1980, 168–72) comprehensive review of studies assessing the accuracy of these estimation methods.

Chapter 12

Constant-Share and Shift-Share Approaches

Chapters 10 and 11 describe three approaches for estimating the basic and nonbasic employment in a local economy. Several procedures can then be used to project this employment into the future. Detailed analyses can be prepared to assess the basic industries long-term prospects. Industry executives and local economists can be consulted for their assessment of the region's economic future. The community's resource and locational advantages and limitations can also be evaluated to determine the region's suitability for retaining existing firms and attracting new ones (Tiebout 1962, 78–79).

Two strategies can also be used to employ information about the past to project the future (Hellman 1976, 3). The first strategy assumes that the region differs so substantially from the nation and other regions that it must be treated as an isolated, unique entity. Given this assumption, the curve-fitting/extrapolation procedures described in Part One can be used to project the region's historical trends without relating these trends to those of other regions.

The second strategy assumes that the region's growth is closely related to the growth of the nation and other regions of which it is a part. This approach derives local projections from projections for the nation or other regions containing the study area and from historical data relating past growth trends for the two regions. The strategy takes advantage of the fact that large-area projections are generally more detailed and more reliable than small-area forecasts and is particularly useful when large-area projections are available and small-area projections are not.

This chapter examines two approaches based on the second strategy: the constant-share approach and the shift-share approach. Chapter 13 examines techniques that can be used to convert basic employment projections into projections for the total local employment and for other variables of interest.

CONSTANT-SHARE APPROACH

The constant-share projection approach assumes that the local share of a larger region's activity remains constant. For example, the technique may assume that the local share of an industry's employment in a larger reference region (e.g., a state or the nation) is constant.[1] That is, it is assumed that

$$\frac{e_i^t}{E_i^t} = \text{constant for all } t \tag{12.1}$$

where

e_i^t = local employment in industry i at time t

E_i^t = reference region employment in industry i at time t

The local employment share can only remain constant if the industry's local employment and reference region employment grow at the same rate. That is, for Eq. (12.1) to be true, it must also be true that

$$e_i^{t'} = (1 + R_i^{t-t'}) \, e_i^t \tag{12.2}$$

where

e_i^t = local employment in industry i in year t

$e_i^{t'}$ = projected local employment in industry i in year t'

$R_i^{t-t'}$ = projected growth rate for industry i in the reference region for time period t to t'.[2]

Equation (12.2), the constant-share projection formula, suggests that the local employment in an industry can be projected by multiplying its current employment, e_i^t, by one plus the projected growth rate for the reference region, $R_i^{t-t'}$. The reference region's growth rate, $R_i^{t-t'}$, is defined as the change in the reference region's employment in industry i over the time period t to t', divided by the reference region's employment in industry i in year t:

$$R_i^{t-t'} = \frac{E_i^{t'} - E_i^t}{E_i^t} \qquad (12.3)$$

The local growth rate, $r_i^{t-t'}$, is similarly defined as the local employment change in industry i over the time period t to t', divided by the local employment in industry i in year t:

$$r_i^{t-t'} = \frac{e_i^{t'} - e_i^t}{e_i^t} \qquad (12.4)$$

OBERS Employment Projections

National and regional employment and personal income projections are available from the OBERS report series prepared approximately every five years by the U.S. Department of Commerce, Bureau of Economic Analysis (BEA) (see, e.g., U.S. Bureau of Economic Analysis 1985a and 1985b). The projections are called the OBERS projections because they were initially produced jointly by the U.S. Bureau of the Census, Office of Business Economics (OBE, now the BEA), and the U.S. Department of Agriculture, Economic Research Service (ERS). The OBERS name has been retained for continuity, even though the projections are now produced solely by the BEA.

The OBERS projections provide economic and demographic projections for the nation, states, BEA economic areas, metropolitan statistical areas (MSAs), and other substate areas. The 1985 projections for the U.S. and states include the following: (1) population aged 0 to 14, 15 to 64, and 65 and above; (2) personal income by major income component; and (3) employment and earnings (wages and salaries, other labor income, and proprietors' income) for fifty-seven industrial groups. Projections provided for MSAs and other substate areas include the following: (1) total population; (2) total personal income; and (3) earnings and employment for fourteen major industrial groups. The 1985 reports include projections for 1990, 1995, 2000, 2005, 2015, and 2035 and historical data for 1969, 1973, 1978, and 1983.

The OBERS employment projections are prepared with a step-down procedure that first projects the national employment and then allocates these projections to states and to substate areas. The national employment projections are derived from projections for approximately 150 industries prepared with the U.S. Bureau of Labor Statistics' input-output and econometric models. Preliminary state-level projections are based on the national employment projections and projections for the portion of each state's employment in an industry required to meet intrastate demand.

The preliminary state-level projections are adjusted, as appropriate, by applying a modified economic base procedure. The fifty-seven OBERS industrial groups in each state either are assumed to be basic or nonbasic in all states or are allocated to the basic and nonbasic sectors by applying a modified location quotient analysis. The preliminary state projections for the basic industries are adjusted, if necessary, so that the factors determining the state's past employment share (e.g., its relative wage rates and access to markets) affect its share to a lesser degree in the future. Preliminary state projections for the nonbasic industries are modified, as necessary, to correspond to projections derived from the basic industry projections by applying a location quotient multiplier. MSA projections are based on dampened extensions of the historical average annual growth rate in each area's share, adjusted as necessary to account for extreme growth rates and for local factors not reflected in the historical employment estimates (U.S. Bureau of Economic Analysis 1985a, x–xv, and 1985b, vii–viii).

Appendix C lists the fifty-seven industrial groups for which OBERS employment and earnings projections are available at the national and state level and the fourteen industrial groups for which projections are available at the substate level. Industrial groups projected at the national and state level are indicated by number; industrial groups projected at the substate level are identified by letter. Appendix C also lists the corresponding 1972 Standard Industrial Classification (SIC) codes for each OBERS industrial group.

Projections based on the OBERS data must use either the relatively disaggregated national- and state-level data or the more aggregated substate data. The state projections are generally used because they provide disaggregated employment data at the lowest geographic level. Their use for constant-share projections assumes that each local industry will maintain a constant share of the state employment in the industry, that is, that the local and state employment in each industry will grow by the same rate.

Growth Rate Adjustment Procedures

As Eq. (12.2) indicates, constant-share projections are prepared by multiplying the current employment in each local industry by one plus the industry's projected growth rate in the reference region. For example, Table 12.1 reports the state-level data from the 1985 OBERS

Table 12.1

OBERS Growth Rate Projections, Ohio: 1983 to 2000

SIC Code (i) (1)	Industry (2)	OBERS Group (g) (3)	Employment[a] 1983 (E_g^{1983}) (4)	2000 (E_g^{2000}) (5)	Growth Rate 1983–2000 ($R_g^{1983-2000}$) (6)
A	AGRICULTURE, FORESTRY, FISHERIES	...	...	...	...
–	Agricultural Production[b]	A	133.4	125.4	–0.0600
–	Agricultural service, forestry, fisheries[c]	B	19.7	30.9	0.5685
B	MINING	C	27.5	37.2	0.3527
C	CONSTRUCTION	D	179.2	239.4	0.3359
D	MANUFACTURING	...	...	...	...
20	Food products	8	64.2	59.5	–0.0732
24	Lumber and wood products	18	15.6	21.2	0.3590
25	Furniture and fixtures	19	13.6	12.4	–0.0882
26	Paper products	12	35.0	33.2	–0.0514
27	Printing and publishing	13	65.6	75.6	0.1524
28	Chemicals	14	63.7	67.3	0.0565
30	Rubber and plastics	16	82.6	96.1	0.1634
32	Stone, clay, glass	20	52.5	59.5	0.1333
33	Primary metals	21	104.4	112.4	0.0766
34	Fabricated metals	22	130.9	158.4	0.2101
35	Machinery	23	155.0	158.5	0.0226
36	Electric equipment	24	90.4	83.2	–0.0796
37	Transport equipment	25	44.6	52.5	0.1771
–	Other manufacturing	–	158.0	182.7	0.1563
E	TRANSPORTATION AND PUBLIC UTILITIES	...	...	...	...
42	Trucking and warehouse	32	74.6	87.7	0.1756
48	Communication	37	52.8	73.2	0.3864
49	Electric and gas	38	40.6	45.9	0.1305
–	Other transportation	–	44.0	45.5	0.0341
F	WHOLESALE TRADE	H	226.1	269.1	0.1902
G	RETAIL TRADE	I	787.1	955.1	0.2134
H	FINANCE AND INSURANCE	J	234.0	311.9	0.3329
I	SERVICES	...	...	...	...
70	Hotels and lodging	45	36.1	42.4	0.1745
72	Personal services	46	226.4	335.9	0.4837
80	Health services	50·	336.8	513.5	0.5246
–	Other services	–	424.0	524.6	0.2373
–	GOVERNMENT	...	...	...	...
–	State and local	N	559.6	548.8	–0.0193

[a] These data are from U.S. Bureau of Economic Analysis (1985a, 75). Employment figures reported in 1,000s.
[b] This includes SIC Major Groups 01 and 02.
[c] This includes SIC Major Groups 07, 08, and 09.

reports required to project the local employment data considered in the previous chapters to the year 2000.[3] The growth rates in column 6 were computed by applying Eq. (12.3) to the employment data in columns 4 and 5. For example, for SIC Code B, Mining,

$$R_B^{1983-2000} = \frac{E_B^{2000} - E_B^{1983}}{E_B^{1983}}$$

$$= \frac{37.2 - 27.5}{27.5}$$

$$= 0.3527$$

The OBERS growth rate projections in Table 12.1 cannot be used directly to project the employment data in the preceding chapters because the projection periods are different. The employment data given in Chapters 10 and 11 are for the year 1985, which means that a 15-year period is required for projections to the year 2000. The OBERS data in column 4 of Table 12.1 are for 1983, which means that the projected growth rates in column 6 are for a seventeen-year period. Since the growth rate is equal to the change over a time period, divided by the initial value, the growth rates in Table 12.1 will overstate the projected growth rate for 1985 to 2000 because they are based on a longer time period.

As a result, the seventeen-year growth rates in Table 12.1 must be converted to equivalent fifteen-year growth rates. The constant-share formula Eq. (12.2) assumes that the future employment will grow by a constant rate, $R_i^{t-t'}$. As a result, Eq. (12.2) corresponds to the geometric curve $Y_c = ab^x$, where the a parameter is equal to e_i^t, the b parameter is equal to one plus the projected reference region growth rate, $R_i^{t-t'}$, and X equals one. Growth rates for two time periods are therefore related by the ratio of the exponents on the geometric curve parameter $1 + R_i^{t-t'}$:

$$R_i^m = (1 + R_i^n)^{m/n} - 1 \qquad (12.5)$$

where

R_i^m = growth rate for time period of m years
R_i^n = growth rate for time period of n years

For example, a ten-year growth rate of 0.20 (i.e., $n = 10$) can be converted into an equivalent five-year growth rate ($m = 5$) as follows:

$$R_i^5 = (1 + R_i^{10})^{5/10} - 1$$
$$= (1 + 0.20)^{1/2} - 1$$
$$= 0.095$$

The five-year growth rate is less than one-half of the ten-year growth rate to account for the compounding effect of applying the rate twice in a ten-year period.

Table 12.2 illustrates the use of Eq. (12.5) to convert the seventeen-year OBERS growth rate projections in Table 12.1 into equivalent fifteen-year growth rates. For example, the seventeen-year growth rate projection for mining, SIC Major Division B, is equal to 0.3527. Substituting this value into Eq. (12.5) yields the equivalent fifteen-year growth rate, as follows:

$$R_B^{15} = (1 + R_B^{17})^{15/17} - 1$$
$$= (1 + 0.3527)^{15/17} - 1$$
$$= (1.3527)^{0.8824} - 1$$
$$= 0.3055$$

Constant-Share Projections

Given the projected fifteen-year growth rates in Table 12.2, the local employment in each industry can be projected by applying Eq. (12.2) to the current employment in each industry. Table 12.3 records the 1985 employment, the growth rate projections derived in Table 12.2, and the corresponding constant-share projections for the year 2000. For example, for SIC B, Mining,

$$e_B^{2000} = (1 + R_B^{1985-2000}) \, e_B^{1985}$$
$$= (1 + 0.3055) \, 913$$
$$= 1,192$$

Employment projections for all local industries can be generated in a similar way. Basic sector projections can also be prepared by applying Eq. (12.2) and the projected growth rates to the estimated basic employment in each industry. Because the OBERS projections are only prepared at a two-digit SIC level, more disaggregated projections must assume that the future growth rate for each three- or four-digit employment group is equal to the projected growth rate for the two-digit SIC Major Group in which it is found.

SHIFT-SHARE APPROACH

The constant-share projection approach assumes that the local economy will maintain a constant share of the reference region's employment in all industries. The shift-share projection technique introduced in 1960 by Edgar Dunn and others (Dunn 1960; Perloff et al. 1960) recognizes that this assumption is rarely correct.[4] In some cases, an

Table 12.2

Projected Growth Rates, Ohio: 1985 to 2000

SIC Code (i) (1)	Industry (2)	OBERS Group (g) (3)	Growth Rate 1983–2000[a] $(R_g^{1983-2000})$ (4)	Growth Rate 1985–2000 $(R_g^{1985-2000})$ (5)
A	AGRICULTURE, FORESTRY, FISHERIES	...	...	...
–	Agricultural Production[b]	A	–0.0600	–0.0531
–	Agricultural service, forestry, fisheries[c]	B	0.5685	0.4876
B	MINING	C	0.3527	0.3055
C	CONSTRUCTION	D	0.3359	0.2912
D	MANUFACTURING	...	...	...
20	Food products	8	–0.0732	–0.0649
24	Lumber and wood products	18	0.3590	0.3108
25	Furniture and fixtures	19	–0.0882	–0.0783
26	Paper products	12	–0.0514	–0.0455
27	Printing and publishing	13	0.1524	0.1334
28	Chemicals	14	0.0565	0.0497
30	Rubber and plastics	16	0.1634	0.1429
32	Stone, clay, glass	20	0.1333	0.1168
33	Primary metals	21	0.0766	0.0673
34	Fabricated metals	22	0.2101	0.1832
35	Machinery	23	0.0226	0.0199
36	Electric equipment	24	–0.0796	–0.0706
37	Transport equipment	25	0.1771	0.1548
–	Other manufacturing	–	0.1563	0.1367
E	TRANSPORTATION AND PUBLIC UTILITIES	...	...	...
42	Trucking and warehouse	32	0.1756	0.1534
48	Communication	37	0.3864	0.3341
49	Electric and gas	38	0.1305	0.1143
–	Other transportation	–	0.0341	0.0300
F	WHOLESALE TRADE	H	0.1902	0.1661
G	RETAIL TRADE	I	0.2134	0.1861
H	FINANCE AND INSURANCE	J	0.3329	0.2886
I	SERVICES	...	...	...
70	Hotels and lodging	45	0.1745	0.1525
72	Personal services	46	0.4837	0.4164
80	Health services	50	0.5246	0.4508
...	Other services	–	0.2373	0.2067
–	GOVERNMENT	...	...	...
–	State and local	N	–0.0193	–0.0170

[a] These data are obtained from Table 12.1, column 6.
[c] This includes SIC Major Groups 01 and 02.
[d] This includes SIC Major Groups 07, 08, and 09.

industry's local employment grows more rapidly than the reference region's employment, causing the region's share to increase. In other cases, the local employment grows more slowly, causing the region's share to decline. Rarely do the two areas grow by exactly the same rate as the constant-share projection technique assumes.

The shift-share projection technique modifies the constant-share projection formula by adding a *shift term* to account for differences

Table 12.3

Constant Share Employment Projections, 2000

SIC Code (i)	Industry	Total Employment[a] (e_i^{1985})	Projected Growth Rate[b] ($R_g^{1985-2000}$)	Projected Employment (e_i^{2000})
(1)	(2)	(3)	(4)	(5)
A	AGRICULTURE, FORESTRY, FISHERIES	...	...	...
–	Agricultural Production[c]	5,240	–0.0531	4,962
–	Agricultural service, forestry, fisheries[d]	120	0.4876	179
B	MINING	913	0.3055	1,192
C	CONSTRUCTION	1,378	0.2912	1,779
D	MANUFACTURING	...	...	...
20	Food products	1,687	–0.0649	1,578
24	Lumber and wood products	639	0.3108	838
25	Furniture and fixtures	140	–0.0783	129
26	Paper products	1,091	–0.0455	1,041
27	Printing and publishing	213	0.1334	241
28	Chemicals	385	0.0497	404
30	Rubber and plastics	2,198	0.1429	2,512
32	Stone, clay, glass	426	0.1168	476
33	Primary metals	882	0.0673	941
34	Fabricated metals	2,398	0.1832	2,837
35	Machinery	1,035	0.0199	1,056
36	Electric equipment	189	–0.0706	176
37	Transport equipment	1,022	0.1548	1,180
–	Other manufacturing	972	0.1367	1,105
E	TRANSPORTATION AND PUBLIC UTILITIES	...	...	...
42	Trucking and warehouse	612	0.1534	706
48	Communication	161	0.3341	215
49	Electric and gas	193	0.1143	215
–	Other transportation	0	0.0300	0
F	WHOLESALE TRADE	1,572	0.1661	1,833
G	RETAIL TRADE	5,474	0.1861	6,493
H	FINANCE and INSURANCE	1,346	0.2886	1,734
I	SERVICES	...	...	...
70	Hotels and lodging	124	0.1525	143
72	Personal services	317	0.4164	449
80	Health services	1,638	0.4508	2,376
...	Other services	2,996	0.2067	3,615
–	GOVERNMENT	...	...	...
–	State government	1,390	–0.0170	1,366
–	Local government	4,060	–0.0170	3,991
Total	...	40,811	...	45,762

[a] These data are from Table 10.1, column 5.
[b] These data are from Table 12.2, column 5.
[c] This includes SIC Major Groups 01 and 02.
[d] This includes SIC Major Groups 07, 08, and 09.

between local and reference region growth rates that cause an industry's employment to shift into or out of a region:[5]

$$e_i^{t'} = (1 + R_i^{t-t'} + s_i^{t-t'}) e_i^t \qquad (12.6)$$

where

e_i^t = local employment in industry i in year t

$e_i^{t'}$ = projected local employment in industry i in year t'

$R_i^{t-t'}$ = projected growth rate for industry i in the reference region for the period t to t'

$s_i^{t-t'}$ = projected local employment shift for industry i for the period t to t'

The shift term, $s_i^{t-t'}$, is equal to the difference between an industry's local growth rate, $r_i^{t-t'}$, and its growth rate in the reference region, $R_i^{t-t'}$, for the period t to t':

$$s_i^{t-t'} = r_i^{t-t'} - R_i^{t-t'} \qquad (12.7)$$

The projected employment shift is unknown because the projected local employment, $e_i^{t'}$, and thus the projected local growth rate, $r_i^{t-t'}$, are unknown. As a result, the projected employment shift must be assumed to equal the observed employment shift for a past period for which local and reference region employment data are available. The shift term is therefore commonly referred to as the *constant shift term* to reflect the assumption that observed differences between the local and reference region growth rates are constant over time. This assumption is examined in the next section.

The first term in Eq. (12.6), $1 + R_i^{t-t'}$, is identical to the constant-share formula, Eq. (12.2), and projects the local employment change that would occur if the local industry grew by the projected rate for the reference region. The constant shift term, $s_i^{t-t'}$, adjusts the constant-share growth rate by the observed difference between the local and reference region growth rates. If the local employment grew faster than that of the reference region in the past, the shift term is positive, inflating the combined growth rate and the projected employment. If the local employment grew more slowly than that of the reference region, the shift term is negative, reducing the combined growth rate and the projected employment.

The shift-share projection technique can be illustrated with the employment data previously considered. The required information for the constant-share term—the projected state growth rate for each basic industry—is identical to that for the constant-share technique. Table 12.4 contains the information required to compute the constant shift

Table 12.4

Observed State and Local Employment, 1978, 1983, and 1985

SIC Code (i) (1)	Industry (2)	Local Employment 1978[a] (e_i^{1978}) (3)	1985[b] (e_i^{1985}) (4)	OBERS Employment[c] 1978 (E_g^{1978}) (5)	1983 (E_g^{1983}) (6)
A	AGRICULTURE, FORESTRY, FISHERIES	...	...	...	...
–	Agricultural Production[d]	4,932	5,240	143.5	133.4
–	Agricultural service, forestry, fisheries[e]	126	120	16.8	19.7
B	MINING	630	913	29.7	27.5
C	CONSTRUCTION	1,529	1,378	227.2	179.2
D	MANUFACTURING	...	...	...	...
20	Food products	1,584	1,687	75.7	64.2
24	Lumber and wood products	597	639	16.9	15.6
25	Furniture and fixtures	0	140	17.9	13.6
26	Paper products	1,405	1,091	30.9	35.0
27	Printing and publishing	316	213	68.4	65.6
28	Chemicals	475	385	69.4	63.7
30	Rubber and plastics	1,934	2,198	107.6	82.6
32	Stone, clay, glass	427	426	69.2	52.5
33	Primary metals	1,100	882	156.1	104.4
34	Fabricated metals	1,664	2,398	172.0	130.9
35	Machinery	1,547	1,035	221.9	155.0
36	Electric equipment	194	189	123.0	90.4
37	Transport equipment	800	1,022	38.3	44.6
–	Other manufacturing	1,435	972	220.9	158.0
E	TRANSPORTATION AND PUBLIC UTILITIES	...	...	...	...
42	Trucking and warehouse	0	612	92.9	74.6
48	Communication	227	161	52.4	52.8
49	Electric and gas	182	193	38.1	40.6
–	Other transportation	500	0	55.5	44.0
F	WHOLESALE TRADE	1,440	1,572	229.4	226.1
G	RETAIL TRADE	4,916	5,474	803.2	787.1
H	FINANCE AND INSURANCE	1,110	1,346	213.0	234.0
I	SERVICES	...	...	...	...
70	Hotels and lodging	149	124	38.2	36.1
72	Personal services	232	317	202.5	226.4
80	Health services	0	1,638	272.0	336.8
...	Other services	3,469	2,996	400.5	424.0
–	GOVERNMENT	...	...	...	...
–	State government	2,086	1,390	554.2	559.6
–	Local government	3,648	4,060	554.2	559.6
Total	...	33,654	40,811	...	...

[a] These data are from Ohio Bureau of Employment Services (1979).
[b] These data are from Ohio Bureau of Employment Services (1986).
[c] These data are from U.S. Bureau of Economic Analysis (1986a, 75).
[d] These data are from U.S. Bureau of the Census (1981, Tables 4 and 8; U.S. Bureau of the Census 1984, Tables 5 and 9). This includes SIC Major Groups 01 and 02.
[e] This includes SIC Major Groups 07, 08, and 09.

term—the local and state employment in each basic industry for two points in time. In this case, the observed local growth between 1978 and 1985 is compared with the OBERS employment growth between 1978 and 1983. The year 1978 is used to compute both rates because the OBERS employment data are provided for this year.

Table 12.5 contains the computed local and state growth rates for the 1978 to 1985 period and the corresponding observed and projected

Table 12.5

Computing Projected Employment Shift, 1985 to 2000

SIC Code (i)	Industry	Observed Growth Rates		Observed Shift	Projected Shift
		Local[a] ($r_i^{1978-1985}$)	State[b] ($R_i^{1978-1985}$)	($s_i^{1978-1985}$)	($s_i^{1985-2000}$)
(1)	(2)	(3)	(4)	(5)	(6)
A	AGRICULTURE, FORESTRY, FISHERIES	...	...	...	...
–	Agricultural Production[c]	0.0624	–0.0971	0.1595	0.3734
–	Agricultural service, forestry, fisheries[d]	–0.0476	0.2497	–0.2973	–0.5306
B	MINING	0.4492	–0.1021	0.5513	1.5625
C	CONSTRUCTION	–0.0988	–0.2827	0.1839	0.4359
D	MANUFACTURING	...	...	...	...
20	Food products	0.0650	–0.2060	0.2710	0.6718
24	Lumber and wood products	0.0704	–0.1060	0.1764	0.4163
25	Furniture and fixtures	Undef.	–0.3193	0.0000	0.0000
26	Paper products	–0.2235	0.1906	–0.4141	–0.6819
27	Printing and publishing	–0.3259	–0.0568	–0.2691	–0.4892
28	Chemicals	–0.1895	–0.1131	–0.0764	–0.1566
30	Rubber and plastics	0.1365	–0.3094	0.4459	1.2037
32	Stone, clay, glass	–0.0023	–0.3207	0.3184	0.8080
33	Primary metals	–0.1982	–0.4306	0.2324	0.5649
34	Fabricated metals	0.4411	–0.3177	0.7588	2.3533
35	Machinery	–0.3310	–0.3949	0.0639	0.1420
36	Electric equipment	–0.0258	–0.3502	0.3244	0.8260
37	Transport equipment	0.2775	0.2376	0.0399	0.0874
–	Other manufacturing	–0.3226	–0.3745	0.0519	0.1144
E	TRANSPORTATION AND PUBLIC UTILITIES	...	...	...	...
42	Trucking and warehouse	Undef.	–0.2644	0.0000	0.0000
48	Communication	–0.2907	0.0107	–0.3014	–0.5364
49	Electric and gas	0.0604	0.0931	–0.0327	–0.0686
–	Other transportation	–1.0000	–0.2775	0.0000	0.0000
F	WHOLESALE TRADE	0.0917	–0.0201	0.1118	0.2548
G	RETAIL TRADE	0.1135	–0.0279	0.1414	0.3278
H	FINANCE AND INSURANCE	0.2126	0.1407	0.0719	0.1605
I	SERVICES	...	...	...	...
70	Hotels and lodging	–0.1678	–0.0761	–0.0917	–0.1862
72	Personal services	0.3664	0.1690	0.1974	0.4710
80	Health services	Undef.	0.3487	–0.3487	–0.6010
...	Other services	–0.1364	0.0831	–0.2195	–0.4119
–	GOVERNMENT	...	...	...	...
–	State government	–0.3337	0.0137	–0.3474	–0.5992
–	Local government	0.1129	0.0137	0.0992	0.2248

[a] These data are computed by applying Eq. (12.4) to the data in Table 12.4, columns 3 and 4.
[b] These data are computed by applying Eq. (12.3) and Eq. (12.5) to the data in Table 12.4, columns 5 and 6.
[c] This includes SIC Major Groups 01 and 02.
[d] This includes SIC Major Groups 07, 08, and 09.

employment shifts. The local growth rates in column 3 of Table 12.5 are computed by applying Eq. (12.4) to the local employment data in columns 3 and 4 in Table 12.4. For example, for SIC Division B, Mining,

$$r_B^{1978-1985} = \frac{e_B^{1985} - e_B^{1978}}{e_B^{1978}}$$

$$= \frac{913 - 630}{630}$$

$$= 0.4492$$

The local growth rate is undefined for industries such as SIC Major Groups 25 and 42, for which local employment is not reported for either 1978 or 1985. In these cases, the observed and projected shifts are assumed to be zero, which means that the local employment in these industries is assumed to grow by the constant-share rate.

The OBERS employment data in Table 12.4 are for 1978 and 1983. As a result, the state growth rates for the 1978 to 1983 period must first be computed by applying Eq. (12.3). Equation (12.5) must then be used to convert the five-year growth rates into equivalent seven-year growth rates consistent with the local growth rates. For example, for SIC Division B,

$$R_B^{1978-1983} = \frac{E_B^{1983} - E_B^{1978}}{E_B^{1978}}$$

$$= \frac{27.5 - 29.7}{29.7}$$

$$= -0.0741$$

$$R_B^{1978-1985} = (1 + R_B^{1978-1983})^{7/5} - 1$$

$$= [1 + (-0.0741)]^{7/5} - 1$$

$$= (0.9259)^{1.4} - 1$$

$$= -0.1021$$

The observed shift values for 1978 to 1985 in column 5 are computed by applying Eq. (12.7). For example, for SIC Division B,

$$s_B^{1978-1985} = r_B^{1978-1985} - R_B^{1978-1985}$$

$$= 0.4492 - (-0.1021)$$

$$= 0.5513$$

The seven-year observed employment shifts in column 5 were then converted into the equivalent fifteen-year shift projections in column 6 by applying Eq. (12.5). Thus, for SIC Division B,

$$s_B^{1985-2000} = (1 + s_B^{1978-1985})^{15/7} - 1$$
$$= (1 + 0.5513)^{15/7} - 1$$
$$= 1.5625$$

Table 12.6 reports the results of using the shift-share technique to project the local employment in the year 2000. The projected constant-share growth rates in column 4 are taken from Table 12.2; the projected employment shifts in column 5 are taken from Table 12.5. The employment projections for 2000 are computed by applying the shift-share projection formula, Eq. (12.6), to the observed employment in 1985. For example, for SIC Division B,

$$e_B^{2000} = [(1 + R_B^{1985-2000}) + s_B^{1985-2000}] \, e_B^{1985}$$
$$= [(1 + 0.3055) + 1.5625] \, 913$$
$$= 2,618$$

Similar computations yield the projected employment in each industry for the year 2000. Shift-share basic employment projections can be prepared in a similar way by applying Eq. (12.6) to the estimated basic employment in each local industry.

A comparison of Tables 12.3 and 12.6 reveals that the constant-share technique projects a total employment of 45,762 and the shift-share technique projects a total employment of 60,107—a difference of over 30 percent. The difference reflects relatively small constant-share employment changes in industries such as mining and fabricated metals, which are amplified by substantial constant-shift growth changes. The large shift terms result, in turn, from large differences between the local and state growth rates between 1978 and 1985. Even larger employment shifts may be encountered in regions experiencing particularly large employment changes in selected industries in the past.

Neither set of projections can be accepted without a careful evaluation of the study region. In some situations, the constant-share projections may be more appropriate; in others, the shift-share projections may be preferred. In many situations, the constant-share projections may be appropriate for some industries and the shift-share projections appropriate for others. In these cases the constant-share growth rates may be assumed for some industries and the shift-share rates assumed for others. Alternative projections can also be prepared by assuming a

Table 12.6

Shift-Share Employment Projections, 2000

SIC Code (i)	Industry	Total Employment[a] (e_i^{1985})	Projected Growth Rate[b] $(R_g^{1985-2000})$	Projected Shift[c] $(s_i^{1985-2000})$	Projected Employment (e_i^{2000})
(1)	(2)	(3)	(4)	(5)	(6)
A	AGRICULTURE, FORESTRY, FISHERIES	...	...	...	...
–	Agricultural Production[d]	5,240	–0.0531	0.3734	6,918
–	Agricultural service, forestry, fisheries[e]	120	0.4876	–0.5306	115
B	MINING	913	0.3055	1.5625	2,618
C	CONSTRUCTION	1,378	0.2912	0.4359	2,380
D	MANUFACTURING	...	...	...	...
20	Food products	1,687	–0.0649	0.6718	2,711
24	Lumber and wood products	639	0.3108	0.4163	1,104
25	Furniture and fixtures	140	–0.0783	0.0000	129
26	Paper products	1,091	–0.0455	–0.6819	297
27	Printing and publishing	213	0.1334	–0.4892	137
28	Chemicals	385	0.0497	–0.1566	344
30	Rubber and plastics	2,198	0.1429	1.2037	5,158
32	Stone, clay, glass	426	0.1168	0.8080	820
33	Primary metals	882	0.0673	0.5649	1,440
34	Fabricated metals	2,398	0.1832	2.3533	8,481
35	Machinery	1,035	0.0199	0.1420	1,203
36	Electric equipment	189	–0.0706	0.8260	332
37	Transport equipment	1,022	0.1548	0.0874	1,269
...	Other manufacturing	972	0.1367	0.1144	1,216
E	TRANSPORTATION AND PUBLIC UTILITIES	...	...	...	...
42	Trucking and warehouse	612	0.1534	0.0000	706
48	Communication	161	0.3341	–0.5364	128
49	Electric and gas	193	0.1143	–0.0686	202
	Other transportation	0	0.0300	0.0000	0
F	WHOLESALE TRADE	1,572	0.1661	0.2548	2,234
G	RETAIL TRADE	5,474	0.1861	0.3278	8,287
H	FINANCE AND INSURANCE	1,346	0.2886	0.1605	1,950
I	SERVICES	...	...	...	...
70	Hotels and lodging	124	0.1525	–0.1862	120
72	Personal services	317	0.4164	0.4710	598
80	Health services	1,638	0.4508	–0.6010	1,392
...	Other services	2,996	0.2067	–0.4119	2,381
–	GOVERNMENT	...	...	...	...
–	State government	1,390	–0.0170	–0.5992	533
–	Local government	4,060	–0.0170	0.2248	4,904
Total	...	40,811	...	...	60,107

[a] These data are from Ohio Bureau of Employment Services (1986).
[b] These data are from Table 12.2, column 5.
[c] These data are from Table 12.5, column 6.
[d] This includes SIC Major Groups 01 and 02.
[e] This includes SIC Major Groups 07, 08, and 09.

constant ratio of past growth rates or by using the curve-fitting/ extrapolation techniques described in Part One to project past trends in the region's employment share. In all of these cases, informed choices between a range of alternative forecasts is preferable to the blind acceptance of a single set of projections.

EVALUATION

The constant-share and shift-share projection techniques have been shrouded in controversy almost since their introduction.[6] However, they continue to be widely used because they are conceptually and computationally straightforward, require only easily accessible data, and provide fast and reasonably accurate projections, given their costs. Theoretically more appealing techniques such as regional input-output and econometric forecasting models are difficult to understand, much harder to implement, and generally require data that are difficult or even impossible to obtain.

Several studies have evaluated the relative accuracy of alternative constant-share/shift-share projection models.[7] For example, Brown's (1969) pioneering study compares three variations of the constant-share/shift-share technique: (1) a shift-share model equivalent to Eq. (12.6); (2) a constant-share model equivalent to Eq. (12.2) that assumes that local industries will grow by the national growth rate in the preceding period; and (3) a constant-share model that assumes local industries will grow by the observed national growth rate in the projection period.

The models were evaluated with a sample of sixteen metropolitan areas and ten industries reported at the two-, three-, and four-digit SIC levels. Employment projections based on data from the Census of Manufactures were compared with observed employment values in the projection year. For example, projections based on data for 1958 and 1963 were compared with actual employment figures for 1963. The constant-share model based on national growth rates for the projection period yielded the most precise projections in all cases. The constant-share projections utilizing national growth rates in the preceding period were second in accuracy. The shift-share model finished a distant third. The results are distorted, however, by the fact that the preferred model utilizes national-level employment data for the projection period that are unavailable in practice.

The results of the other comparative tests are inconclusive because the tests examined different projection models, data sets, geographic areas, and levels of industrial aggregation. However, they generally support the constant-share model, particularly for county-level projections with small industrial sectors and limited data which preclude systematic modeling of a region's locational advantage (Stevens and Moore 1980, 427–28).

These findings are supported by an evaluation of the theoretical justification for each approach. Application of the constant-shift model assumes that a region that grows faster (or slower) than the nation does so because it has a comparative advantage (or disadvantage) as a production location for a particular industry. Given this assumption, the model further assumes that this advantage (or disadvantage) will continue for the forecast period. Together these assumptions imply that employment shifts that occurred in the past will continue without change in the future.

The first assumption is reasonable because an industry's local growth will differ from national growth rates at least in part because local economic conditions have encouraged (or discouraged) its growth. The second assumption is questionable, however. In some cases positive employment shifts reduce a region's locational advantage by bidding up prices for an industry's regional inputs. In these situations, positive regional shifts in the past can be expected to become smaller in the future.

However, in other cases, past growth, resulting in part from positive employment shifts, promotes regional scale and agglomeration economies that increase a region's locational advantage for an industry. In these situations, positive employment shifts in the past can be expected to become larger in the future. In both cases, there is no reason to assume a constant employment shift for even a five-year forecast horizon. In fact, there is substantial evidence in the literature that employment shifts for a given industry in a particular location are often positive in one five-year period and negative in the following period.

The constant-share technique avoids these problems but encounters others. For example, if national growth in an industry takes place over a relatively short time period, it is unlikely that the production increases will be evenly distributed. Regional demand will vary, at least in the short run. Regional differences such as the availability of skilled labor and slack productive capacity will also affect the regions' ability to expand their production. Regions with firms at or near their optimal size may also respond more slowly than regions with firms below their optimum size. Thus there is no convincing reason to assume that a region's share of national growth (or decline) in an industry will remain constant for even the short run.

As a result, neither the constant-shift nor the constant-share projection technique can be justified on theoretical grounds. Nevertheless, the computational simplicity of these projection models, relative to more sophisticated techniques, provides a pragmatic justification for using them to prepare quick and reasonably accurate short-run projections. They are also appropriate for preparing long-term "baseline" forecasts examining the implications of continuing past employment trends into the future. Their use in both cases is justified largely by the lack of other readily accessible small-area employment projection techniques (Stevens and Moore 1980, 428–30).

ENDNOTES

1. Although this chapter considers the constant-share and shift-share techniques only as economic projection methods, they are also widely used for small-area population projections. See, for example, Pittenger (1976, 79–102) and Isserman (1977b).

2. Equation (12.2) can be derived from Eq. (12.1) as follows: Given Eq. (12.1), the local economy's future employment share must equal its current employment share:

$$\frac{e_i^{t'}}{E_i^{t'}} = \frac{e_i^t}{E_i^t}$$

Multiplying both sides of the equation by $E_i^{t'}$ yields

$$e_i^{t'} = \left(\frac{E_i^{t'}}{E_i^t}\right) e_i^t$$

The future employment in industry i in the reference region, $E_i^{t'}$, is equal to the present reference region employment, E_i^t, plus the employment change over the projection period, $\Delta E_i^{t-t'}$, as follows:

$$E_i^{t'} = E_i^t + \Delta E_i^{t-t'}$$

As a result, by substitution,

$$e_i^{t'} = \left(\frac{E_i^t + \Delta E_i^{t-t'}}{E_i^t}\right) e_i^t$$

Rearranging terms on the right hand side of the equation yields

$$e_i^{t'} = \left(1 + \frac{\Delta E_i^{t-t'}}{E_i^t}\right) e_i^t$$

The term inside the parentheses is equal to one plus the reference region's projected growth rate, R_i^{t-r}. Therefore, direct substitution yields Eq. (12.2),

$$e_i^{t'} = (1 + R_i^{t-r}) e_i^t \tag{12.2}$$

3. The employment in Other Manufacturing, Other Transportation, and Other Services is the residual employment in each Division not included in the Major Groups listed. For example, Other Transportation includes all employment in Division D that is not in Major Groups 42, 48, and 49.

4. The shift-share (or "mix and share") technique can be used both as a predictive tool for projecting future employment trends and as a descriptive device for analyzing historical trends. The discussion here deals only with its use as a predictive tool. For an introduction to its use as an analysis tool, see Bendavid-Val (1983, 67–74). Applications of the shift-share technique as an analysis tool include Dunn (1960); Perloff et al. (1960); Lausen (1971); Edwards (1976); and Lever (1981). For critiques and assessments of its use as an analytic technique, see Houston (1967) and Richardson (1978b, 18–20). Richardson concludes that shift-share is "a harmless pastime for small boys with calculators" (1978a, 202), which "can be far from harmless if used for policy (mis)guidance" (1978b, 18).

5. Only the "classic" shift-share projection model is presented in this chapter. For other formulations, see Greenberg (1972); Emmerson, Ramanathan, and Ramm (1975); Zimmerman (1975); Hellman (1976); and Stevens and Moore (1980, 430–35).

6. The discussion in the following section draws heavily on Stevens and Moore (1980, 422–35).

7. See, for example, Greenberg (1972); Hellman (1976); and Hewings (1976). See Stevens and Moore (1980, 422–28) for a review and assessment of these and other studies.

Chapter 13

Economic Base Projection Model

The economic base technique divides an economy into a basic sector dependent largely on factors external to the local economy and a nonbasic sector dependent primarily on local market conditions. Given this fundamental division, the economic base technique assumes that the basic sector is the prime cause of local economic growth, that is, that the growth or decline of the basic sector causes a corresponding change in the nonbasic sector and the total economy.

The economic base technique further assumes that projected changes in the basic sector can be converted into projections for the total economy by applying a base multiplier, *BM,* defined as the ratio of the total employment in year *t,* e^t_T, to the total basic employment, b^t_T, as follows:

$$BM = \frac{e^t_T}{b^t_T} \qquad (9.6)$$

Equation (9.6) indicates that the base multiplier is invariant over time, that is, if the basic employment increases or decreases by a given amount, the total local employment also changes by this amount. Given this assumption, the base multiplier can be computed from historical data and used to project changes in the total local economy.

LONG-TERM ECONOMIC PROJECTIONS

The economic base technique can be used for long-term economic projections by multiplying the projected total basic sector employment by a base multiplier computed from historical data, as follows:

$$e_T^{t'} = b_T^{t'} \times BM \qquad (13.1)$$

where

$e_T^{t'}$ = projected total local employment in year t'

$b_T^{t'}$ = projected basic employment in year t'

For example, Table 13.1 illustrates the use of Equation (13.1) to project the sample data considered in Chapters 10 through 12 to the year 2000. The basic employment estimates in column four are obtained by applying the fully adjusted location quotient estimation technique at the two-digit SIC level. The basic employment projections in column 7 are obtained by applying the constant-share projection formula, Eq. (12.2) and the projected constant-share growth rates in column 6. For example, for SIC Division B, Mining,

$$b_B^{2000} = (1 + R_B^{1985-2000}) \, b_B^{1985}$$
$$= (1 + 0.3055) \, 284$$
$$= 371$$

The base multiplier can be computed by dividing the total local employment in 1985 by the estimated total basic employment in 1985:

$$BM = \frac{e_T^{1985}}{b_T^{1985}}$$

$$BM = \frac{40,811}{13,088}$$

$$= 3.118$$

The projected total employment in the year 2000 can then be computed by applying Eq. (13.1), as follows:[1]

$$e_T^{2000} = b_T^{2000} \times BM$$
$$= 13,868 \times 3.118$$
$$= 43,240$$

That is, given the basic employment estimates and projections in Table 13.1, the projected total employment in the year 2000 is 43,240.

SHORT-TERM IMPACT ANALYSIS

The economic base technique is also widely used to predict the impact of new manufacturing plants (e.g., Greig 1971), tourism (e.g.,

Table 13.1

Constant-Share Basic Employment Projections, 2000

SIC Code (i)	Industry	Total Employment[a] (e_i^{1985})	Basic Employment[b] (b_i^{1985})	Proportion Basic (p_i^{1985})	Growth Rate[c] ($R_g^{1985-2000}$)	Projected Basic (b_i^{2000})
(1)	(2)	(3)	(4)	(5)	(6)	(7)
A	AGRICULTURE, FORESTRY, FISHERIES	...	...	...	...	...
–	Agricultural Production[d]	5,240	2,807	0.5357	–0.0531	2,658
–	Agricultural service, forestry, fisheries[e]	120	0	0.0000	0.4876	0
B	MINING	913	284	0.3111	0.3055	371
C	CONSTRUCTION	1,378	0	0.0000	0.2912	0
D	MANUFACTURING	...	...	...	...	...
20	Food products	1,687	1,225	0.7261	–0.0649	1,145
24	Lumber and wood products	639	401	0.6275	0.3108	526
25	Furniture and fixtures	140	0	0.0000	–0.0783	0
26	Paper products	1,091	788	0.7223	–0.0455	752
27	Printing and publishing	213	0	0.0000	0.1334	0
28	Chemicals	385	91	0.2364	0.0497	96
30	Rubber and plastics	2,198	1,889	0.8594	0.1429	2,159
32	Stone, clay, glass	426	215	0.5047	0.1168	240
33	Primary metals	882	646	0.7324	0.0673	689
34	Fabricated metals	2,398	1,929	0.8044	0.1832	2,282
35	Machinery	1,035	296	0.2860	0.0199	302
36	Electric equipment	189	83	0.4392	–0.0706	77
37	Transport equipment	1,022	410	0.4012	0.1548	473
–	Other manufacturing	972	0	0.0000	0.1367	0
E	TRANSPORTATION AND PUBLIC UTILITIES	...	...	...	...	...
42	Trucking and warehouse	612	510	0.8333	0.1534	588
48	Communication	161	0	0.0000	0.3341	0
49	Electric and gas	193	0	0.0000	0.1143	0
–	Other transportation	0	0	0.0000	0.0300	0
F	WHOLESALE TRADE	1,572	0	0.0000	0.1661	0
G	RETAIL TRADE	5,474	0	0.0000	0.1861	0
H	FINANCE AND INSURANCE	1,346	0	0.0000	0.2886	0
I	SERVICES	...	...	...	...	...
70	Hotels and lodging	124	124	1.0000	0.1525	143
72	Personal services	317	0	0.0000	0.4164	0
80	Health services	1,638	0	0.0000	0.4508	0
...	Other services	2,996	0	0.0000	0.2067	0
–	GOVERNMENT	...	...	...	...	...
–	State government	1,390	1,390	1.0000	–0.0170	1,366
–	Local government	4,060	0	0.0000	–0.0170	0
Total	...	40,811	13,088	...	...	13,868

[a] These data are from Table 10.8, column 3.
[b] These data are from Table 10.8, column 5.
[c] These data are from Table 10.8, column 4.
[d] This includes SIC Major Groups 01 and 02.
[e] This includes SIC Major Groups 07, 08, and 09.

Archer 1976), and plant expansions or closings (e.g., Brownrigg 1980).[2] The total effect, $\Delta t_i^{t-t'}$, of a projected local employment change is equal to the projected employment change, $\Delta e_i^{t-t'}$, plus the induced effect caused by the change in the basic employment, as follows:

$$\Delta t_i^{t-t'} = \Delta e_i^{t-t'} + (\Delta b_i^{t-t'} \times BM) - \Delta b_i^{t-t'} \qquad (13.2)$$

where

$\Delta t_i^{t-t'}$ = total impact of a projected employment change
in industry i for the period t to t'
$\Delta e_i^{t-t'}$ = projected employment change in industry i
for the period t to t'
$\Delta b_i^{t-t'}$ = projected basic employment change in industry i
for the period t to t'

The projected basic employment change, $\Delta b_i^{t-t'}$, is subtracted from the other terms because it is included in both. It can be computed by multiplying the projected employment change, $\Delta e_i^{t-t'}$, by the proportion of basic employment, p_i':

$$\Delta b_i^{t-t'} = \Delta e_i^{t-t'} \times p_i' \qquad (13.3)$$

The proportion basic is estimated by dividing an industry's estimated basic employment in the past by its total employment in that year. For example, in Table 13.1 the proportion basic for SIC Major Group 34, Fabricated Metals, 0.8044, is equal to the estimated basic employment in 1985, 1,929, divided by the total employment in 1985, 2,398.

Given the employment data in Table 13.1, Eqs (13.2) and (13.3) can be used to predict the total employment impact of adding 200 additional workers to a local fabricated metals plant. The associated basic employment change is computed by applying Eq. (13.3):

$$\begin{aligned}
\Delta b_{34}^{1985-1986} &= \Delta e_{34}^{1985-1986} \times p_{34}^{1985} \\
&= 200 \times 0.8044 \\
&= 161
\end{aligned}$$

The facility's total impact on local employment can then be projected by applying Eq. (13.2):

$$\begin{aligned}
\Delta t_{34}^{1985-1986} &= \Delta e_{34}^{1985-1986} + (\Delta b_{34}^{1985-1986} \times BM) - \Delta b_{34}^{1985-1986} \\
&= 200 + (161 \times 3.118) - 161 \\
&= 541
\end{aligned}$$

That is, the addition of 200 jobs in SIC Major Group 34 is projected to generate a total of 541 additional jobs in the local economy. Similar procedures using personal income or salary data can be used to project the financial impacts of short-term economic changes.

This procedure implies that economic changes in different sectors of the economy have different impacts on the local economy. For example, the impact of 200 additional jobs in SIC Major Group 28, Chemicals, can be determined as follows:

$$\Delta b_{28}^{1985-1986} = \Delta e_{28}^{1985-1986} \times p_{28}^{1985}$$
$$= 200 \times 0.2364$$
$$= 47$$
$$\Delta t_{28}^{1985-1986} = \Delta e_{28}^{1985-1986} + (\Delta b_{28}^{1985-1986} \times BM) - \Delta b_{28}^{1985-1986}$$
$$= 200 + (47 \times 3.118) - 47$$
$$= 300$$

The differential impact of adding the same number of jobs to two different industries is a result of differences in the proportion of basic employment in these sectors. Less than one-quarter of the jobs added to SIC 28 serve external demand and, by hypothesis, generate other local jobs. Over 80 percent of the added jobs in SIC 34 are in the basic sector, generating many more local jobs. The economic base projection model and Eq. (13.2) indicate that jobs added to industries with no basic employment generate no additional local employment. This assumption is examined later in this chapter.

PROJECTING OTHER VARIABLES

Population projections can be easily derived from the total employment projections by applying a dependency ratio, DR, defined as the ratio of the total population in a year, P^t, to the total employed population in that year, e_T^t:

$$DR = \frac{P^t}{e_T^t} \tag{13.4}$$

Like the base multiplier, the dependency ratio assumes a constant ratio between the total population and the total employed population. Given this assumption, the dependency ratio can be computed from historical data and used to convert total employment projections into equivalent population projections:

$$P^{t'} = e_T^{t'} \times DR \qquad (13.5)$$

where $P^{t'}$ is the projected population in year t' and $e_T^{t'}$ is the projected total employment in year t'. For example, given a total population in 1985 of 100,500 and a total employment of 40,811, application of Eq. (13.4) yields the following:

$$
\begin{aligned}
DR &= \frac{P^{1985}}{e_T^{1985}} \\
&= \frac{100,500}{40,811} \\
&= 2.463
\end{aligned}
$$

Given this value, the projected population in 2000 can be computed from the projected employment for that year by applying Eq. (13.5), as follows:

$$
\begin{aligned}
P^{2000} &= e_T^{2000} \times DR \\
&= 43,240 \times 2.463 \\
&= 106,500
\end{aligned}
$$

Thus, given the basic sector estimates and projections in Table 13.1, the region's total population is projected to be 106,500 in the year 2000.

Employment and population projections generated by the economic base technique can also be used to project a community's future land-use requirements. Industrial space requirements can be projected by applying industrial density standards, such as the number of manufacturing workers per acre of industrially used land, to the projected number of industrial workers. Wholesale, retail, and residential space requirements can be derived in a similar way by applying space standards appropriate to the land use being considered.[3]

Forecast accuracy is less crucial for these purposes than for other applications because the density standards generally include a reserve or safety factor, providing additional capacity in excess of that projected to satisfy normal growth and expansion. The effects of forecast variations also tend to be insignificant when compared with the effect of slight differences in the density standards. As a result, the selection of appropriate density standards and related conversion factors is generally more important than the accuracy of the employment and population projections (Chapin and Kaiser 1979, 156–57).

STABILITY OF THE MULTIPLIERS

The stability of the base multiplier over time underlies economic base theory and application. Given this assumption, the base multiplier can be computed from historical data and used to convert basic sector projections into projections for the total economy. If this assumption is incorrect and no reliable procedure exists for projecting base multiplier values, the validity of the entire technique is seriously questioned.[4]

This issue can be examined by considering a simplified model for regional income made up of three sectors: exports, local investment, and local consumption.[5] Export income *(E)* is comprised of wages and salaries paid by exporting firms and sales receipts from temporary community residents. Local investment income *(I)* consists of profits earned by local firms and wages and salaries paid by firms serving exclusively local markets. Local consumption income *(C)* includes revenue received by local nonbasic services such as barbershops and dentists.

The level of income in the export sector is determined largely by external demand independent of local market conditions. In the short term, that is, for periods of a few months to two years corresponding to normal business cycles, the level of local investment can also be assumed to depend on nonlocal factors such as prevailing interest rates and the state of the national economy. As a result, in the short term, only local consumption income is dependent on local conditions.

Local consumption income is derived from the other two sectors by a two-stage process. External sales and local investment income increase the income of local residents. Some of this income is spent locally in the form of additional local consumption purchases. For example, if local residents spend half of their income on local goods and services, that is, if the *propensity to consume locally, p_c,* is 0.5, each additional dollar of export or local investment income generates a 50¢ increase in local consumer purchases.

Part of the 50¢ remains in the local economy as local income in the form of wages and salaries, profits, rents, and so on. However, part of it leaves the community to purchase imported goods and pay wages and salaries to nonresidents. If 40 percent of the income generated by consumer purchases remains in the local economy, the *income propensity of the local sales dollar, p_s,* equals 0.4.

If p_c equals 0.5 and p_s equals 0.4, every dollar added to the export and local investment sectors generates an additional 50¢ in local consumption purchases. Forty percent of this 50¢, or 20¢, remains in the local economy as additional local consumption income. Fifty percent of this additional local income, or 10¢, can then be spent on local consumer purchases. Forty percent of this additional sales revenue, or 4¢, remains in the economy as local consumer income. Fifty percent of this income is then spent locally, and so on.

Fortunately, it is not necessary to trace out each round of increased income, consumer spending, and induced income to determine the total impact of a dollar increase in local income. The multiplier formula in Eq. (13.6) computes the total impact directly:

$$\Delta Y = \Delta(E + I) \left[\frac{1}{1 - (p_c \times p_s)} \right] \qquad (13.6)$$

where

$$\Delta Y = \text{total short-term increase in local income}$$
$$\Delta(E + I) = \text{short-term increase in export and local investment income}$$
$$p_c = \text{propensity to consume locally}$$
$$p_s = \text{income propensity of local sales dollar[6]}$$

For example, if p_c equals 0.5 and p_s equals 0.4, the total short-term impact of an additional dollar in exports or and local investment income can be computed as follows:

$$\Delta Y = \$1.00 \left[\frac{1}{1 - (0.5 \times 0.4)} \right]$$

$$= \$1.00 \left[\frac{1}{1 - 0.2} \right]$$

$$= \$1.25$$

That is, every dollar added to the export or local investment sector stimulates a total local income increase of $1.25.

The traditional base multiplier can also be stated in terms of these two propensities:

$$BM = \frac{1}{1 - (p_c \times p_s)} \qquad (13.7)$$

where p_c and p_s are defined as previously. Equation (13.7) is particularly helpful for revealing assumptions underlying the economic base technique. These assumptions are examined in the next section.

Stability of the Base Multiplier

Equation (13.7) suggests that the base multiplier is directly related to p_c, the propensity to consume locally, and p_s, the income propensity of the local sales dollar. If either propensity increases, the denominator is reduced and the base multiplier is increased. If either propensity decreases, the denominator increases and the base multiplier decreases.

As a result, the stability of the base multiplier turns on whether these two propensities are stable over time. Four factors are frequently assumed to cause changes in these propensities and thus in the base multiplier: (1) aggregate income, (2) population size, (3) per capita income, and (4) the community's economic structure. The role of each factor is considered below.[7]

Changes in a region's aggregate income are important because they affect both propensities. As aggregate demand increases, a local market develops for specialty items such as a legitimate theater and gourmet shops. As a result, consumers tend to purchase a larger proportion of their goods and services locally, increasing the propensity to consume locally. Increases in local demand also promote regional economies of scale, making local production possible where imports were previously required, increasing the proportion of the local sales dollar that remains in the local economy. As a result, changes in regional aggregate income are directly related to changes in the base multiplier.

Changes in a region's aggregate income can reflect changes in the number of community residents or changes in the per capita income of these residents. Population increases tend to expand the local demand for specialty items and create regional economies of scale, increasing both propensities and the base multiplier. Per capita income increases also inflate local aggregate demand and the base multiplier. They also tend to enlarge the market for local services such as health and entertainment with a high proportion of local income per sales dollar, further increasing the base multiplier. However, they also tend to enlarge the income portion that is saved, paid in taxes, spent on vacations, or used to purchase imported luxury goods, reducing the propensity to consume locally and the base multiplier. As a result, the net impact of per capita income changes is not clear.

Changes in the local economic structure can also affect the base multiplier. As the local economy grows and becomes more diverse, locally produced goods and services replace imports, increasing p_s, p_c, and the base multiplier. If the local economy becomes less dependent on manufacturing, the expansion in local services also tends to increase both propensities and the base multiplier (Martin and Miley 1983, 20).

More important, community growth or decline does not mean that the components of the basic sector will change in the same proportion. Some basic industries will expand while others remain static or even decline; some may leave the region entirely and be replaced by new industries. In addition, each basic industry can be expected to support a different amount of nonbasic activity, that is, to have its own base multiplier. Some nonbasic industries respond to all changes in the basic sector; others only change when particular industries change; and others are largely independent of the basic sector. As a result, the differential expansion of a region's basic and nonbasic activities is reflected in changing values for the base multiplier (Gilles and Grigsby 1960, 224–25).

The presumed instability of the base multiplier is supported by a relatively small amount of inconclusive empirical evidence. For example, pioneering studies by Hildebrand and Mace (1950) and the Kansas City Federal Reserve Bank (1952) found that the base multipliers for Los Angeles and Wichita varied dramatically. Martin and Miley (1983) found that personal income multipliers for the eight BEA regions were unstable in all regions between 1959 and 1979 and tended to increase as an area matures, as the preceding theoretical analysis suggests. On the other hand, Garnick (1970) and others have found the base multiplier to be stable over short time periods.[8]

Stability of the Other Multipliers

The dependency ratio and the other conversion factors applied to the economic base employment and population projections can also be unstable over time. For example, the number of dependents per employed person has traditionally been low in industries that employ a high proportion of women because many women are married to men who also work. This is changing with the increased incidence of single-parent households and the increased number of women working in previously all-male occupations. However, the proportion of females is still higher in the service sector and in some basic industries (e.g., textiles) than in others (e.g., construction and mining). As a result, the number of dependents per employed worker (and the dependency ratio) changes over time as a region's basic and nonbasic industries grow or decline by different rates.

The dependency ratio also changes over time due to changes in the regional unemployment rate and changes in the number of "independent nonworkers" supported by pensions, welfare payments, investments, and other non–job-related income. New or expanding communities generally have a small number of persons with non–job-related income. However, if a region's population matures or its employment base contracts, the number of independent nonworkers increases, causing the dependency ratio to decline (Blumenfeld 1955, 127–28; Andrews 1960, 143–46).

Similar changes can be expected for the conversion factors used to project future demand for residential, industrial, wholesale, and retail land. New residential areas rarely have the same housing mix and residential densities as the remainder of the community. Changing industrial technologies, distribution patterns, consumer tastes, and retail strategies generally mean that new manufacturing, wholesale, and retail facilities are often substantially different from existing ones.

Trending the Multipliers

The preceding discussion identifies a number of factors that may cause a region's base multiplier and other conversion factors to change over time. Recognizing this, Pfister (1976, 106) and others recommend that these multipliers should never be computed from observations for only one or two years. This is particularly true for employment multipliers, which are insensitive to short-run economic changes. Rather, basic employment estimates and base multipliers should be computed for a number of years and trended to project future multiplier values. This procedure not only smooths out erratic short-term fluctuations but also accounts for any underlying trends in the multiplier.

If significant trends are found in the base multipliers, the curve-fitting/extrapolation procedures described in Chapter 2 and Appendix A can be used to project the base multiplier in the projection year. For these purposes, the base multiplier values are treated as the dependent variable Y, and the estimation years are treated as the independent variable X. The projected multiplier value is then applied to the projected basic sector employment to predict the future total employment.

Multiplier values based on several observations are also preferable for short-term impact analyses because they are less susceptible to short-run economic fluctuations. Multiple observations can also be used to compute the dependency ratio and other conversion factors to reduce the effect of random fluctuations and account for any long-term changes in the region's growth patterns. The OBERS state or national population and employment projections can similarly be used to adjust the dependency ratio to account for long-term trends in the proportion of the population that is employed.

Current density standards for manufacturing and wholesale areas can also be modified to consider current development trends and community goals, objectives, and policies. Residential densities can also be modified to reflect local and national trends in average household size, vacancy rates, and other factors that determine the future relationship between residential population and residential acreage (Chapin and Kaiser 1979, 406–81).

ROLE OF THE BASIC SECTOR

The economic base technique is clearly the primary cause of local economic change for specialized economies such as a remote mining town dependent on a single income source that cannot easily be replaced.[9] If the mine's employment doubles, it is reasonable to assume that the local service sector employment will double as well. If the mine's employment declines, service employment will also decline. If the mine is closed, the village will likely disappear entirely. Attempts to promote the development of the local service sector will clearly have a negligible effect on the mine's employment or on the remainder of the local economy.

However, a large metropolitan area not only produces products for export, it also provides a wide range of goods and services for local residents. The larger and more diverse the community, the larger the proportion of nonbasic activity and the more its inhabitants "live by doing one another's washing." As a result, basic sector changes have a much smaller impact on large and diversified regional economies than they do on small specialized ones.

Local services such as transportation and communication networks, regional and local markets, and a skilled labor force also provide the environment that basic industries require for their continued existence. Thus, in the long term, nonbasic industries such as business and personal services and ancillary manufacturing often provide the real and lasting strength of the metropolitan community. If they continue to function effectively, the metropolis will always be able to substitute new basic industries for any that may be lost. For example, Boston has been transformed from a port city to a manufacturing center to a high technology mecca, largely because it has the local conditions needed to repeatedly attract new types of industry as others decline (Blumenfeld 1955, 130–31; also see Chinitz 1961).

In the short run, it is reasonable to assume that the basic sector does not substantially change and that changes in the local service industries do not alter the region's competitive position. As a result, the primacy of external demand for local economic change seems clear for time periods corresponding to normal business cycles (Thompson 1965, 30). When the time frame is extended, however, other factors can be expected to contribute to regional growth. Long-term economic growth is determined in large part by changes in technology, productivity, and consumer tastes, which are generally independent of external conditions. For example, the United States has grown tremendously with a small export base, and the earth as a whole has progressed steadily with no exports at all.[10]

Observation reveals that communities develop in a number of ways. An iron mine (totally basic) may open in Minnesota, stimulating the growth of an entire town complete with a complex of derivative local service industries. On the other hand, a farm service center in Iowa that provides efficient and pleasant local services (e.g., schools and shopping facilities) may attract a food processor or manufacturing plant (basic), which then would generate more local services. In a growth context, the question of the primacy of the basic sector is a chicken-and-egg problem that cannot be resolved at the level of gross generality (Thompson 1965, 30).

EVALUATION

The discussion in the preceding chapters has pointed out numerous theoretical and practical problems facing the economic base projection technique and its application.[11] These well-documented limitations have led many regional economists to reject the economic base technique as totally inappropriate for theoretical or applied use.[12] For example, most economists prefer the input-output technique, which improves on the economic base model by dividing the local economy into fifty or more sectors and by reporting how the inputs and outputs of each sector are distributed among the remaining sectors of the economy. This allows analysts to determine the direct, indirect, and induced effects of projected changes in one or more sectors for each sector of the economy. Interregional input-output models can also be prepared to study regional balance of payments and interregional trade flows—questions that cannot be examined within the economic base framework.[13]

However, the economic base continues to be used—and will be used for quite some time—because theoretically more appealing approaches such as input-output are expensive, are hard to understand and implement, and rarely yield significantly better results. This does not mean, of course, that the theoretical critiques of the economic base technique can be ignored.[14] Many of the critiques are perfectly appropriate for those economic base studies that are poorly conceived and conducted without recognizing the technique's underlying assumptions and limitations. Professional practice in the areas of economic projection and impact assessment is often woefully inadequate and justly deserves criticism.

More important, the critiques of the economic base technique provide positive suggestions for its improvement. The critiques of simple export-only models serve as reminders that other sources of exogenous demand such as state and federal government and sales to temporary residents must be included in the basic sector. The criticisms of the location quotient technique suggest that the technique should only be applied at a disaggregated level and must incorporate productivity, consumption, and national exports adjustments. The limitations of the constant-share and shift-share projection procedures indicate that neither approach can be applied mechanically without a careful evaluation of the projection results. The instability of the base multiplier similarly suggests that multiplier values should be computed for several years and trended for the future.

The limitations of the economic base technique also suggest that it is more appropriate for some applications than it is for others. The economic base framework is less appropriate for diversified metropolitan regions with large service sectors and significant interregional feedback effects than it is for small, isolated regions. It is also less applicable for long-term projections than for short-term impact analyses for which a stable economic structure can be assumed. As a result, the technique is particularly useful for short-term analyses of small regional economies for which the resources and data required by more sophisticated models are generally unavailable.

The economic base technique is especially attractive when compared with other simple projection techniques such as the curve-fitting/extrapolation procedure described in Part One. It readily uses available information such as annual employment data by industry to understand past trends and to determine the implications of alternative assumptions about the future. It also incorporates a model of local economic change that is admittedly simple but perfectly appropriate for many applications. As a result, if applied cautiously and appropriately in specific contexts, the economic base technique can provide a highly useful tool for examining past economic changes and projecting the future (Bendavid-Val 1983, 87; Thompson 1965, 30).

ENDNOTES

1. As pointed out in Chapter 11, this base multiplier is extremely high. Multipliers generally range from 1.0 to 2.2. The high value reflects the fact that the study area has a largely agricultural economy and that available county-level employment data do not adequately measure agricultural workers who largely serve external markets. As a result, the area's basic employment is underestimated, and the base multiplier is inflated.

2. The following discussion follows general practice and utilizes the "average" multiplier in Eq. (10.6) computed by dividing total employment by total basic employment. Merrifield (1987) suggests that "marginal" multipliers computed from changes in the total employment and total basic employment are more appropriate for impact assessment and short-term growth projections. Unfortunately these multipliers are much harder to implement in practice.

3. For a more complete discussion of these conversion procedures, see Chapin and Kaiser (1979, 410–78).

4. See, for example, Blumenfeld (1955, 126–27), Isard et al. (1960, 199–205), and Richardson (1978b, 11–14).

5. The discussion in this and the following section is based on Tiebout (1962, 58–61) and Martin and Miley (1983, 18–19). Also see North (1955).

6. This simple three-sector model can easily be converted into a long-run projection model by assuming that local investment is also a function of local income. It can also be expanded into a more complete seven-sector model that considers private exports, exports to the federal government, local consumption, local business investment, local housing investment, local government investment, and local government current operations. See Tiebout (1962, 27–43, 73–74).

7. The discussion in this section draws heavily on similar discussions in Martin and Miley (1983) and Tiebout (1962, 62–70). These references should be consulted for a more complete treatment of these issues.

8. Also see Martin and Miley (1983, 18).

9. The following discussion draws heavily on similar discussions in Blumenfeld (1955) and Thompson (1965, 29–30). Also see Hildebrand and Mace (1950).

10. The question of the timing of the impacts reflects a more fundamental

debate initiated by North (1955) and Tiebout (1956a) asking whether economic base is a theory of long-term growth or a short-run model of economic fluctuations. While the empirical data on impact timing are sparse and inconclusive, Gerking and Isserman (1981, 464) conclude that the use of economic base for short-run impact analysis is not contradicted by the available evidence. Also see Williamson (1975).

11. Also see Cullen (1984, 43–52).

12. See, for example, Blumenfeld (1955) and Richardson (1978b, 11–14). The latter concludes, "There is not much justification for its continuous use, even as a convenient shortcut."

13. See Miernyk (1965) for a nontechnical introduction to input-output analysis and Richardson (1985) for an extensive review of recent developments in this area.

14. The discussion in the following paragraphs draws heavily on Pfister (1976) and Williamson (1975).

Appendices

Appendix A

Curve-Fitting/Extrapolation Procedures

This appendix contains eleven complete examples illustrating computational procedures for fitting and extrapolating the six curves described in Chapter 2. All of the examples use a common data set—the population of Leon County, Florida, for 1940 through 1985. Criteria for selecting the best set of estimates and projections from these alternatives are described in Chapter 3.

LINEAR CURVE

Procedures for Odd Number of Observations

A number of computational procedures can be used to fit the linear curve to a set of observation data.[1] However, the procedures described here are particularly convenient because they assign index values, X, to the observations that eliminate several computational terms and greatly simplify the computations.

As Table A.1 illustrates, for an odd number of observations, the middle observation is assigned an index value of zero. Preceding observations are numbered from the middle in increasing negative order $(-1, -2,$ etc.), and later observations are numbered from the middle in increasing positive order $(1, 2,$ etc.). The sum of observed values, ΣY, and sum of products for the observed and index values, ΣXY, can then be computed. The following equations are used to compute the a and b parameters:

207

Table A.1

Linear Curve Computations for Odd Number of Observations

Year (1)	Observed Value[a] (Y) (2)	Index Value (X) (3)	Index Value Squared (X^2) (4)	Product of Observed and Index Values[a] (XY) (5)
1940	17.0	−4	16	−68.0
1945	23.0	−3	9	−69.0
1950	29.0	−2	4	−58.0
1955	35.0	−1	1	−35.0
1960	43.0	0	0	0.0
1965	52.0	1	1	52.0
1970	63.0	2	4	126.0
1975	77.0	3	9	231.0
1980	87.0	4	16	348.0
Sum	426.0	...	60	527.0

[a] These values are expressed in 1,000s.

$$a = \frac{\Sigma Y}{N} \tag{A.1}$$

$$b = \frac{\Sigma XY}{\Sigma X^2} \tag{A.2}$$

where

N = number of observations
ΣY = sum of observed values
ΣXY = sum of products of observed and index values
ΣX^2 = sum of squared index values

The sum of squared index values for an odd number of observations can be computed as follows:

$$\Sigma X^2 = \frac{N(N^2 - 1)}{12} \quad \text{for odd values of } N \tag{A.3}$$

For example, given the data in Table A.1, the *a* parameter can be computed by applying Eq. (A.1):

$$a = \frac{\Sigma Y}{N} = \frac{426.0}{9} = 47.33$$

The *b* parameter can similarly be computed with Eq. (A.2). The sum of the squared index values, ΣX^2, can be computed directly by squaring the index values and summing the values as shown in Table A.1. However, for a large number of observations it is more convenient to use Eq. (A.3). For this example,

$$\Sigma X^2 = \frac{N(N^2 - 1)}{12} = \frac{9(80)}{12} = 60$$

Therefore,

$$b = \frac{\Sigma XY}{\Sigma X^2} = \frac{527.0}{60.0} = 8.78$$

As a result, the linear curve that best fits the observed population data in Table A.1 has the following equation:

$$Y_C = 47.33 + 8.78X$$

As Table A.2 illustrates, linear estimates and projections can be computed by substituting the appropriate index values into this equation. For example, for 1960,

$$X = 0$$

and

$$Y_C = 47.33 + 8.78 \,(0) = 47.3$$

For 1990,

$$X = 6$$

and

$$Y_C = 47.33 + 8.78 \,(6) = 100.0$$

The estimation errors reported in Table A.2, column 5, indicate that the linear curve is clearly unsatisfactory for projecting the population of Leon County. The linear equation underestimates the population for the early and late observation years and overestimates the values for the middle observation years. Thus, as shown in Figure A.1, the observation data are not linear but are curved and concave upward. As a result, although the computed a and b parameters minimize the sum of squared errors between the observed values and linear estimates, the linear curve projections are clearly much lower than past trends suggest are appropriate for the future. Of course this does not indicate that the linear curve is inappropriate for extrapolation purposes; it only reveals that the linear curve is inappropriate for projecting the population of Leon County.

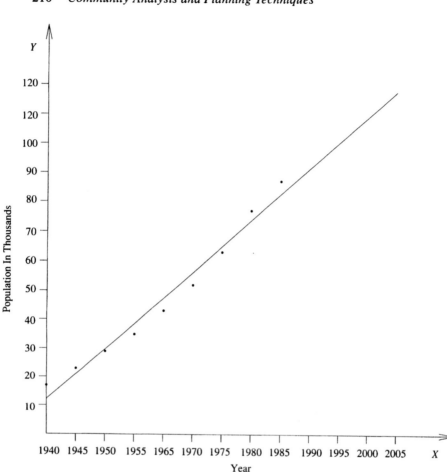

Figure A.1   Observed Population and Linear Estimates, 1940 to 1980

Source: Table A.2

Procedures for Even Number of Observations

The computational procedures for an odd number of observations can be applied to an even number of observations by modifying the procedures for assigning the index values and computing the sum of squared index values. These modifications are required because the previous procedures begin by assigning an index value to the middle observation value and the midpoint for an even number of observations falls between two observation values.

Table A.2

Linear Estimates and Projections for Odd Number of Observations

Curve Equation: $Y_C = 47.33 + 8.78X$

Year (1)	Observed Value[a] (Y) (2)	Index Value (X) (3)	Estimate/ Projection[a] (Y_C) (4)	Error of Estimate[a] $(Y - Y_C)$ (5)
1940	17.0	−4	12.2	+4.8
1945	23.0	−3	21.0	+2.0
1950	29.0	−2	29.8	−0.8
1955	35.0	−1	38.6	−3.6
1960	43.0	0	47.3	−4.3
1965	52.0	1	56.1	−4.1
1970	63.0	2	64.9	−1.9
1975	77.0	3	73.7	+3.3
1980	87.0	4	82.4	+4.6
1985	...	5	91.2	...
1990	...	6	100.0	...
1995	...	7	108.8	...
2000	...	8	117.6	...

[a] These values are expressed in 1,000s.

For example, given four observation years—1980, 1982, 1984, and 1986—the midpoint, 1983, falls between the two middle observations. These four observations can be transformed into an odd number by including intermediate points between the original observation years. That is, the inclusion of the three additional years—1981, 1983, and 1985—generates seven observation years with a midpoint of 1983.

As a result, the computational procedures for an odd number of observations can be applied to an even number of observations by inserting dummy observation points between the initial values. As shown in Table A.3, this is equivalent to assigning index values to the first half of the observations which are numbered from the middle with consecutive odd negative numbers (-1, -3, -5, etc.). Index values for the second half of the observations are similarly numbered from the middle with consecutive positive odd numbers (1, 3, 5, etc.). Index values are not required for the dummy observations.

When this is done, the equations for computing the a and b parameters are identical to those for an odd number of observations. The only change is in the formula for computing the sum of squared values of index X, as follows:

$$\Sigma X^2 = \frac{N(N^2 - 1)}{3} \qquad \text{for even values of } N \qquad \text{(A.4)}$$

Table A.3

Linear Curve Computations for Even Number of Observations

Year (1)	Observed Value[a] (Y) (2)	Index Value (X) (3)	Index Value Squared (X^2) (4)	Product of Observed and Index Value[a] (XY) (5)
1940	17.0	−9	81	−153.0
1945	23.0	−7	49	−161.0
1950	29.0	−5	25	−145.0
1955	35.0	−3	9	−105.0
1960	43.0	−1	1	−43.0
1965	52.0	1	1	52.0
1970	63.0	3	9	189.0
1975	77.0	5	25	385.0
1980	87.0	7	49	609.0
1985	100.0	9	81	900.0
Sum	526.0	...	330	1528.0

[a] These values are expressed in 1,000s.

As shown in Table A.3, the sum of observed values, ΣY, and the sum of products of observed and index values, ΣXY, must first be computed. The a parameter can then be computed by applying Eq. (A.1) as follows:

$$a = \frac{\Sigma Y}{N} = \frac{526.0}{10} = 52.60$$

The b parameter can be computed by applying Eq. (A.2). The sum of the squared index values can be computed directly by squaring the index values and summing these values or by using Eq. (A.4). For this example,

$$\Sigma X^2 = \frac{N(N^2 - 1)}{3} = \frac{10\,(99)}{3} = 330$$

Therefore,

$$b = \frac{\Sigma XY}{\Sigma X^2} = \frac{1528.0}{330.0} = 4.63$$

As a result, the linear curve that satisfies the least squares criterion has the following equation:

$$Y_C = 52.60 + 4.63X$$

As shown in Table A.4, appropriate index values can be substituted into this equation to compute the linear curve estimates and projections. For example, for 1960,

$$X = -1$$

and

$$Y_C = 52.60 + 4.63(-1) = 48.0$$

For 1990,

$$X = 11$$

and

$$Y_C = 52.60 + 4.63(11) = 103.5$$

GEOMETRIC CURVE

Procedures for Odd Number of Observations

As shown in Chapter 2, the geometric curve, $Y_C = ab^x$, can be transformed into the linear form, $\log Y_C = \log a + (\log b)X$, by

Table A.4

Linear Estimates and Projections for Even Number of Observations

Curve Equation: $Y_C = 52.60 + 4.63X$

Year	Observed Value[a] (Y)	Index Value (X)	Estimate/ Projection[a] (Y_C)
(1)	(2)	(3)	(4)
1940	17.0	-9	10.9
1945	23.0	-7	20.2
1950	29.0	-5	29.4
1955	35.0	-3	38.7
1960	43.0	-1	48.0
1965	52.0	1	57.2
1970	63.0	3	66.5
1975	77.0	5	75.8
1980	87.0	7	85.0
1985	100.0	9	94.3
1990	...	11	103.5
1995	...	13	112.8
2000	...	15	122.0

[a] These values are expressed in 1,000s.

Community Analysis and Planning Techniques

applying logarithms.[2] The computational equations for fitting a linear curve can then be used to compute the transformed geometric curve parameters log a and log b.

As shown in Table A.5, for an odd number of observations the middle observation is assigned an index value of zero. Preceding observations are numbered from the middle in increasing negative order (-1, -2, etc.). Later observations are numbered in increasing positive order (1, 2, etc.). The logarithms of the a and b parameters for the geometric curve can then be computed by applying the following equations:

$$\log a = \frac{\Sigma \log Y}{N} \tag{A.5}$$

$$\log b = \frac{\Sigma(X\log Y)}{\Sigma X^2} \tag{A.6}$$

$$\Sigma X^2 = \text{sum of squared index values} \tag{A.3}$$

$$= \frac{N(N^2 - 1)}{12} \quad \text{for odd values of } N$$

where

$$N = \text{number of observations}$$
$$\Sigma \log Y = \text{sum of logarithms of observed values}$$
$$\Sigma(X\log Y) = \text{sum of products of index and logarithms}$$

Table A.5

Geometric Curve Computations for Odd Number of Observations

Year (1)	Observed Value[a] (Y) (2)	Logarithm of Observed Value (log Y) (3)	Index Value (X) (4)	Product of Logarithm and Observed Value [X(log Y)] (5)
1940	17.0	1.2304	−4	−4.9218
1945	23.0	1.3617	−3	−4.0852
1950	29.0	1.4624	−2	−2.9248
1955	35.0	1.5441	−1	−1.5441
1960	43.0	1.6335	0	0.0000
1965	52.0	1.7160	1	1.7160
1970	63.0	1.7993	2	3.5987
1975	77.0	1.8865	3	5.6594
1980	87.0	1.9395	4	7.7581
Sum	...	14.5735	...	5.2564

[a] These values are expressed in 1,000s.

Given the population data in Table A.5, the geometric curve parameters can be derived by computing the sum of the logarithms of the observed values, $\Sigma\log Y$, and the sum of products of the index values and logarithms, $\Sigma X\log Y$. The logarithm of the a parameter can then be computed by applying Eq. (A.5):

$$\log a = \frac{\Sigma\log Y}{N} = \frac{14.5735}{9} = 1.6188$$

The logarithm of the b parameter can be computed by applying Eqs. (A.3) and (A.6):

$$\Sigma X^2 = \frac{N(N^2 - 1)}{12} = \frac{9(80)}{12} = 60$$

and

$$\log b = \frac{\Sigma(X\log Y)}{\Sigma X^2} = \frac{5.2564}{60} = 0.0882$$

The corresponding geometric estimates and projections can be computed in two ways. The first approach takes the antilogarithms of log a and log b to compute the geometric curve parameters a and b. That is,

$$a = \text{antilog (log } a) = \text{antilog (1.6188)} = 41.57$$
$$b = \text{antilog (log } b) = \text{antilog (0.0882)} = 1.225$$

These values can then be substituted into the geometric curve equation to derive the geometric curve equation. For this example,

$$Y_C = 41.57\,(1.225)^x$$

As shown in Table A.6, geometric estimates and projections can be obtained by substituting appropriate index values into the preceding equation. For example, for 1960,

$$X = 0$$

and

$$Y_C = 41.57(1.225)^0 = 41.6$$

For 1990,

$$X = 6$$

and

Table A.6

Geometric Estimates and Projections for Odd Number of Observations

Curve Equations: $Y_C = 41.57\,(1.225)^X$ and $\log Y_C = 1.6188 + 0.0882X$

Year	Observed Value[a] (Y)	Index Value (X)	Logarithm of Estimate/Projection (log Y_C)	Estimate/ Projection[a] (Y_C)
(1)	(2)	(3)	(4)	(5)
1940	17.0	−4	1.2660	18.5
1945	23.0	−3	1.3542	22.6
1950	29.0	−2	1.4424	27.7
1955	35.0	−1	1.5306	33.9
1960	43.0	0	1.6188	41.6
1965	52.0	1	1.7070	50.9
1970	63.0	2	1.7952	62.4
1975	77.0	3	1.8834	76.4
1980	87.0	4	1.9716	93.6
1985	...	5	2.0598	114.7
1990	...	6	2.1480	140.6
1995	...	7	2.2362	172.3
2000	...	8	2.3244	211.1

[a] These values are expressed in 1,000s.

$$Y_C = 41.57(1.225)^6 = 140.4$$

Geometric curve estimates and projections can also be obtained by substituting appropriate index values into the transformed geometric equation, solving for the value of log Y_C, and taking the antilogarithm of log Y_C. For example, for 1960,

$$X = 0$$

and

$$\log Y_C = 1.6188 + 0.0882(0) = 1.6188$$
$$Y_C = \text{antilog } (1.6188) = 41.6$$

For 1990,

$$X = 6$$

and

$$\log Y_C = 1.6188 + 0.0882(6) = 2.1480$$
$$Y_C = \text{antilog } (2.1480) = 140.6$$

The two procedures generate identical estimates and projections, as one would expect.

Procedures for Even Number of Observations

The computational procedures for an odd number of observations need only minor modification for an even number of observations. The only changes are in the procedures for assigning index values and for computing the sum of squared index values.

As with the linear curve, for an even number of observations, the values of the first half of the observations are numbered from the middle with consecutive negative odd numbers (-1, -3, etc.). The values of the second half of the observations are numbered from the middle with consecutive positive odd numbers (1, 3, etc.). The equations for the a and b parameters are identical to those for an odd number of observations. However, a different equation is used to compute the sum of squared index values, as follows:

$$\Sigma X^2 = \frac{N(N^2 - 1)}{3} \quad \text{for even values of } N \quad (A.4)$$

The procedures for computing the logarithms of the a and b parameters and the corresponding geometric curve estimates and projections are identical to those for an odd number of observations.

PARABOLIC CURVE

Procedures for Odd Number of Observations

As for the linear and geometric curves, the procedures for fitting the parabolic curve to an odd number of observations require that the middle observation be given an index value of zero, preceding observations be numbered from the middle in increasing negative order, and later observations be numbered from the middle in increasing positive order.[3]

The following equations can then be used to identify the parabolic curve parameters that satisfy the least squares criterion:

$$c = \frac{N\Sigma X^2 Y - \Sigma X^2 \Sigma Y}{N\Sigma X^4 - (\Sigma X^2)^2} \quad (A.7)$$

$$a = \frac{\Sigma Y - c\Sigma X^2}{N} \quad (A.8)$$

$$b = \frac{\Sigma X Y}{\Sigma X^2} \quad (A.9)$$

where

N = number of observations
ΣY = sum of observed values
ΣXY = sum of products of index and observed values
$\Sigma X^2 Y$ = sum of products of squared index and observed values

The sum of the squared index values, ΣX^2, can be computed using the following equation:

$$\Sigma X^2 = \frac{N(N^2 - 1)}{12} \qquad \text{for odd values of } N \qquad (A.3)$$

The sum of the fourth powers of the index values, ΣX^4, can be computed as follows:

$$\Sigma X^4 = \frac{3N^5 - 10N^3 + 7N}{240} \qquad \text{for odd values of } N \qquad (A.10)$$

For example, as shown in Table A.7, the sum of the observed values, ΣY, the sum of products of the index and observed values, ΣXY, and the sum of products of the observed and squared index values, $\Sigma X^2 Y$, must first be computed.

Table A.7

Parabolic Curve Computations for Odd Number of Observations

Year	Observed Value[a] (Y)	Index Value (X)	Index Value Squared (X^2)	Fourth Power of Index Value (X^4)	Product of Observed and Index Values[a] (XY)	Product of Observed and Squared Index Values[a] (X^2Y)
(1)	(2)	(3)	(4)	(5)	(6)	(7)
1940	17.0	−4	16	256	−68.0	272.0
1945	23.0	−3	9	81	−69.0	207.0
1950	29.0	−2	4	16	−58.0	116.0
1955	35.0	−1	1	1	−35.0	35.0
1960	43.0	0	0	0	0.0	0.0
1965	52.0	1	1	1	52.0	52.0
1970	63.0	2	4	16	126.0	252.0
1975	77.0	3	9	81	231.0	693.0
1980	87.0	4	16	256	348.0	1,392.0
Sum	426.0	...	60	708	527.0	3,019.0

[a] These values are expressed in 1,000s.

The sum of squares and fourth powers of the index values can be computed directly or by applying Eqs. (A.3) and (A.10). For this example,

$$\Sigma X^2 = \frac{N(N^2 - 1)}{12}$$

$$= \frac{9(80)}{12} = 60$$

$$\Sigma X^4 = \frac{3N^5 - 10N^3 + 7N}{240}$$

$$= \frac{3(9)^5 - 10(9)^3 + 7(9)}{240} = 708$$

The c parameter must first be computed by applying Eq. (A.7), as follows:

$$c = \frac{N\Sigma X^2 Y - \Sigma X^2 \Sigma Y}{N\Sigma X^4 - (\Sigma X^2)^2}$$

$$= \frac{9(3,019) - 60(426)}{9(708) - (60)^2} = 0.581$$

The b parameter can be computed by applying Eq. (A.9), as follows:

$$b = \frac{\Sigma XY}{\Sigma X^2}$$

$$= \frac{527}{60} = 8.78$$

The a parameter can then be computed by applying Eq. (A.8), as follows:

$$a = \frac{\Sigma Y - c\Sigma X^2}{N}$$

$$= \frac{426 - (0.581)(60)}{9} = 43.46$$

As a result, the equation for the parabolic curve that best fits these data is

$$Y_C = 43.46 + 8.78X + 0.581X^2$$

As shown in Table A.8, parabolic estimates and projections can be

Table A.8

Parabolic Estimates and Projections for Odd Number of Observations

Curve Equation: $Y_C = 43.46 + 8.78X + 0.581X^2$

Year (1)	Index Value (X) (2)	Estimate/ Projection[a] (Y_C) (3)
1940	−4	17.6
1945	−3	22.3
1950	−2	28.2
1955	−1	35.3
1960	0	43.5
1965	1	52.8
1970	2	63.3
1975	3	75.0
1980	4	87.9
1985	5	101.9
1990	6	117.1
1995	7	133.4
2000	8	150.9

[a] These values are expressed in 1,000s.

obtained by substituting appropriate index values into this equation. For example, for 1960,

$$X = 0$$

and

$$Y_C = 43.46 + 8.78(0) + 0.581(0)^2$$
$$= 43.4$$

For 1990,

$$X = 6$$

and

$$Y_C = 43.46 + 8.78(6) + 0.581(6)^2$$
$$= 117.1$$

Procedures for Even Number of Observations

As is true for the linear and geometric curves, the computational procedures for an odd number of observations need only minor modification for an even number of observations. The equations for the *a*, *b*, and *c* parameters are identical. The only changes are in the procedures for assigning index values and for computing the sum of squares and fourth powers of the index *X*.

For an even number of observations, the values of the first half of the observations are numbered from the middle with consecutive negative odd numbers (-1, -3, -5, etc.) and the values of the second half are numbered from the middle with consecutive positive odd numbers (1, 3, 5, etc.). The following equations are then used to compute the sum of the squares and fourth powers of the index values:

$$\Sigma X^2 = \frac{N(N^2 - 1)}{3} \qquad \text{for even values of } N \qquad \text{(A.4)}$$

and $\qquad\qquad\qquad\qquad\qquad\qquad\qquad\qquad\qquad\qquad\qquad\qquad$ (A.10)

$$\Sigma X^4 = \frac{3N^5 - 10N^3 + 7N}{15} \qquad \text{for even values of } N$$

The procedures for computing the *a*, *b*, and *c* parameters and corresponding parabolic estimates and projections for an even number of observations are identical to those for an odd number of observations.

MODIFIED EXPONENTIAL CURVE

Procedures for Assumed Growth Limits

As shown in Chapter 2, the modified exponential curve, $Y_c = c + ab^x$, can be transformed to the linear form by assuming an upper or lower growth limit and by applying logarithms. This allows the geometric curve-fitting procedures to be used to fit a modified exponential curve with an assumed growth limit, *c*.

Assumed Upper Growth Limit. For example, as shown in Figure 2.5, when the *a* parameter is negative and the *b* parameter is between zero and one, the modified exponential curve approaches an upper growth limit *c* for large positive values of *X*. In this case the modified exponential curve can be expressed as $Y_c = c - ab^x$ and the computational procedures for fitting a geometric curve can be used to fit a modified exponential curve, with the exception that $\log (c - Y)$ replaces the log *Y* term and $X \log (c - Y)$ replaces the $X \log Y$ term. That is, given an assumed upper limit *c*, the logarithms of the modified exponential curve parameters a and b can be computed by applying the following equations:

$$\log a = \frac{\Sigma \log (c - Y)}{N} \tag{A.11}$$

$$\log b = \frac{\Sigma [X \log (c - Y)]}{\Sigma X^2} \tag{A.12}$$

where

N = number of observations
$\Sigma \log (c - Y)$ = sum of logarithms of growth residuals
$\Sigma [X \log (c - Y)]$ = sum of products of index values and logarithms
ΣX^2 = sum of squared index values
$= \dfrac{N(N^2 - 1)}{12}$ for odd values of N

For example, Table A.9 illustrates the computational procedures for an odd number of observations and an assumed upper limit of 500. As for the first three extrapolation curves, the middle observation is assigned an index value of zero; preceding observations are numbered from the middle in consecutive negative order $(-1, -2,$ etc.); later observations are numbered in consecutive positive order $(1, 2,$ etc.).

Table A.9

Modified Exponential Curve Computations for Assumed Upper Limit

Year	Observed Value[a] (Y)	Upper Limit Minus Observed Value[a] (c − Y)	Logarithm of Upper Limit Minus Observed Value [log (c − Y)]	Index Value (X)	Product of Index Value and Logarithm [Xlog (c − Y)]
(1)	(2)	(3)	(4)	(5)	(6)
1940	17.0	483.0	2.6839	−4	−10.7358
1945	23.0	477.0	2.6785	−3	−8.0356
1950	29.0	471.0	2.6730	−2	−5.3460
1955	35.0	465.0	2.6675	−1	−2.6675
1960	43.0	457.0	2.6599	0	0.0000
1965	52.0	448.0	2.6513	1	2.6513
1970	63.0	437.0	2.6405	2	5.2810
1975	77.0	423.0	2.6263	3	7.8790
1980	87.0	413.0	2.6160	4	10.4638
Sum	...	...	23.8969	...	−0.5098

[a] These values are expressed in 1,000s.

The modified exponential curve parameters are derived by first subtracting the observed population values from the assumed upper limit to obtain the growth residuals listed in column 3 of Table A.9. For example, for an assumed upper growth limit of 500, the growth residual for 1940 is equal to $500.0 - 17.0$, or 483.00. The logarithms of these growth residuals are then computed and summed as shown in column 4. The products of the logarithms in column 4 and the index values in column 5 are then computed and summed as shown in column 6.

The logarithm of the a parameter is calculated by applying Eq. (A.11) as follows:

$$\log a = \frac{\Sigma \log (c - Y)}{N} = \frac{23.8969}{9} = 2.6552$$

The logarithm of the b parameter is computed by applying Eq. (A.12):

$$\log b = \frac{\Sigma [X \log (c - Y)]}{\Sigma X^2} = \frac{-0.5098}{60} = -0.0085$$

The a and b parameters can then be computed by taking the antilogarithms of $\log a$ and $\log b$. For this example,

$$a = \text{antilog } (\log a) = \text{antilog } (2.6552) = 452.1$$
$$b = \text{antilog } (\log b) = \text{antilog } (-0.0085) = 0.9806$$

As a result, the modified exponential curve with an assumed upper limit of 500 that best fits these data has the following equation:

$$Y_C = 500.00 - 452.1(0.9806)^x$$

As shown in Table A.10, modified exponential estimates and projections can be computed by substituting appropriate index values into the equation. For example, for 1960,

$$X = 0$$

and

$$Y_C = 500.0 - 452.1(0.9806)^0 = 47.9$$

For 1990,

$$X = 6$$

and

$$Y_C = 500.0 - 452.1(0.9806)^6 = 98.0$$

Table A.10

Modified Exponential Curve Estimates and Projections for Assumed Upper Limit

Curve Equation: $Y_C = 500.0 - 452.1(0.9806)^X$

Year (1)	Observed Value[a] (Y) (2)	Index Value (X) (3)	Estimate/ Projection[a] (Y_C) (4)	Error of Estimate[a] $(Y - Y_C)$ (5)
1940	17.0	−4	11.1	+5.9
1945	23.0	−3	20.6	+2.4
1950	29.0	−2	29.9	−0.9
1955	35.0	−1	39.0	−4.0
1960	43.0	0	47.9	−4.9
1965	52.0	1	56.7	−4.7
1970	63.0	2	65.3	−2.3
1975	77.0	3	73.7	+3.3
1980	87.0	4	82.0	+5.0
1985	...	5	90.1	...
1990	...	6	98.0	...
1995	...	7	105.8	...
2000	...	8	113.4	...

[a] These values are expressed in 1,000s.

The estimates and projections in Table A.10 are for the modified exponential equation with an assumed upper limit of 500 that best fits the observed population data. However, the estimation errors reported in column 5 indicate that this curve is unacceptable for these data. The curve underestimates population values for the early and late observation years and overestimates those for the middle years, because the observation data are concave upward as shown in Figure A.1 and the modified exponential curve is concave downward as shown in graph (a) of Figure 2.5. As a result, as is true for the linear curve, the modified exponential projections are much lower than past trends suggest.

Assumed Lower Growth Limit. As shown in Figure 2.5, when the *a* parameter is positive and the *b* parameter is between zero and one, the modified exponential curve approaches a lower limit *c* for large positive values of *X*. In these cases the modified exponential curve has the equation $Y_c = c + ab^x$. As a result, the computational procedures for fitting a modified exponential curve with an assumed lower growth limit are identical to the procedures for an assumed upper growth limit with the exception that log $(Y - c)$ replaces the log $(c - Y)$ term in all of the equations, as follows:

$$\log a = \frac{\Sigma \log (Y - c)}{N} \qquad (A.13)$$

$$\log b = \frac{\Sigma [X \log (Y - c)]}{\Sigma X^2} \qquad (A.14)$$

where the terms are defined as before. The procedures for computing the logarithms of the a and b parameters are identical to those for an assumed upper limit with the exception that the $c - Y$ terms in columns 3, 4, and 6 of Table A.9 are replaced by $Y - c$ terms. Modified exponential estimates and projections can then be computed by taking the antilogarithms of $\log a$ and $\log b$ and substituting these values and the appropriate index values into the modified exponential equation, $Y_C = c + ab^x$.

The procedures for an assumed upper or lower growth limit can be adopted for an even number of observations by using the appropriate procedures for assigning index values and computing the squared index values outlined for the linear, parabolic, and geometric curves.

Procedures for Computing Growth Limits

Completely different procedures are used to compute the growth limit, c, and the a and b parameters for the modified exponential curve that best fits a set of observation data.[4] Two conditions must be satisfied: (1) The total number of observations must be evenly divisible by three; the number of observations can be odd or even; and (2) the first observation must be assigned an index value of zero and later observations assigned consecutive positive values (1, 2, 3, etc.).[5]

The parameters of the modified exponential curve can then be determined by applying the following equations:

$$b^n = \frac{\Sigma_3 Y - \Sigma_2 Y}{\Sigma_2 Y - \Sigma_1 Y} \qquad (A.15)$$

$$a = (\Sigma_2 Y - \Sigma_1 Y) \left[\frac{b - 1}{(b^n - 1)^2} \right] \qquad (A.16)$$

$$c = \frac{1}{n} \left[\frac{(\Sigma_1 Y)(\Sigma_3 Y) - (\Sigma_2 Y)^2}{\Sigma_1 Y + \Sigma_3 Y - 2\Sigma_2 Y} \right] \qquad (A.17)$$

where

n = number of observations in each partial sum
$\Sigma_1 Y$ = partial sum of first third of observations
$\Sigma_2 Y$ = partial sum of second third of observations
$\Sigma_3 Y$ = partial sum of last third of observations

As shown in Table A.11, the observations must be assigned appropriate index values and the partial sums must be computed for each third of the observations. The number of observations in each partial sum, n, is equal to the total number of observations, N, divided by three. Thus, for this example,

$$n = \frac{N}{3} = \frac{9}{3} = 3$$

The value of b^n (in this case b^3) must first be computed by applying Eq. (A.15):

$$b^n = \frac{\Sigma_3 Y - \Sigma_2 Y}{\Sigma_2 Y - \Sigma_1 Y} = \frac{227.0 - 130.0}{130.0 - 69.0} = 1.590$$

Taking the nth root of this value yields the b parameter, which is, for this example,

$$b = (1.590)^{1/3} = 1.167$$

Table A.11

Modified Exponential Curve Computations for Computed Upper Limit

Year (1)	Index Value (X) (2)	Observed Value[a] (Y) (3)	Partial Sum of Observed Values[a] ($\Sigma_n Y$) (4)
1940	0	17.0	
1945	1	23.0	69.0
1950	2	29.0	
1955	3	35.0	
1960	4	43.0	130.0
1965	5	52.0	
1970	6	63.0	
1975	7	77.0	227.0
1980	8	87.0	

[a] These values are expressed in 1,000s.

The *a* parameter can then be computed by applying Eq. (A.16):

$$a = (\Sigma_2 Y - \Sigma_1 Y) \left[\frac{b - 1}{(b^n - 1)^2} \right]$$

$$= (130.0 - 69.0) \left[\frac{1.167 - 1.0}{(1.590 - 1.0)^2} \right]$$

$$= 29.25$$

The *c* parameter is computed by applying Eq. (A.17):

$$c = \frac{1}{n} \left[\frac{(\Sigma_1 Y)(\Sigma_3 Y) - (\Sigma_2 Y)^2}{\Sigma_1 Y + \Sigma_3 Y - 2\Sigma_2 Y} \right]$$

$$= \frac{1}{3} \left[\frac{(69.0)(227.0) - (130.0)^2}{69.0 + 227.0 - 2(130.0)} \right]$$

$$= -11.45$$

As a result, the equation for the modified exponential curve that best fits these data is

$$Y_C = -11.45 + 29.25(1.167)^x$$

The *a* parameter is positive and the *b* parameter is greater than one. As a result, the *c* parameter is the lower limit that the curve approaches for large negative values of *X*, that is, the curve corresponds to graph (d) in Figure 2.5. This is reasonable because the data are concave upward as shown in Figure A.1.

As shown in Table A.12, modified exponential curve estimates and projections can be obtained by substituting appropriate index values into this equation. For example, for 1940,

$$X = 0$$

and

$$Y_C = -11.45 + 29.25(1.167)^0 = 17.8$$

For 1990,

$$X = 10$$

and

$$Y_C = -11.45 + 29.25(1.167)^{10} = 125.6$$

Table A.12

**Modified Exponential Estimates and Projections
for Computed Upper Limit**

Curve Equation: $Y_C = -11.45 + 29.25(1.167)^X$

Year (1)	Index Value (X) (2)	Estimate/ Projection[a] (Y_C) (3)
1940	0	17.8
1945	1	22.7
1950	2	28.4
1955	3	35.0
1960	4	42.8
1965	5	51.9
1970	6	62.4
1975	7	74.8
1980	8	89.2
1985	9	106.0
1990	10	125.6
1995	11	148.5
2000	12	175.2

[a] These values are expressed in 1,000s.

GOMPERTZ CURVE

Procedures for Assumed Growth Limits

As shown in Chapter 2, the Gompertz curve, $Y_C = ca \exp(b^x)$, can be transformed to the modified exponential form, $\log Y_C = \log c + (\log a)b^x$, by applying logarithms. The transformed Gompertz curve can then be converted to the linear form by assuming an upper or lower growth limit and applying logarithms. This allows the linear curve-fitting procedures to be used to fit a Gompertz curve with an assumed growth limit, c.

Assumed Upper Growth Limit. As shown in Figure 2.7, when the logarithm of the a parameter is negative and the b parameter is between zero and one, the Gompertz curve approaches an upper limit, c, for large positive values of X. In these cases the transformed Gompertz curve is $Y_C = \log c - (\log a)b^x$ and the computational procedures for fitting a Gompertz curve are identical to the modified exponential curve procedures with the exception that $\log (\log a)$ replaces the $\log a$ term; $\log (\log c - \log Y)$ replaces the $\log (c - Y)$ term; and $X\log (\log c - \log Y)$ replaces the $X\log (c - Y)$ term.

As a result, given an assumed upper limit c, the logarithm of the logarithm of the a parameter and the logarithm of the b parameter can be computed by applying the following equations:

$$\log (\log a) = \frac{\Sigma[\log (\log c - \log Y]}{N} \qquad (A.18)$$

$$\log b = \frac{\Sigma[X\log (\log c - \log Y)]}{\Sigma X^2} \qquad (A.19)$$

where

$$N = \text{number of observations}$$
$$\Sigma\log (\log c - \log Y) = \text{sum of logarithms of logarithm differences}$$
$$\Sigma[X\log (\log c - \log Y)] = \text{sum of products of index values and logarithms of logarithm differences}$$

The sum of the squared index values, ΣX^2, can be obtained using Eq. (A.3) as follows:

$$\Sigma X^2 = \frac{N(N^2 - 1)}{12} \qquad \text{for odd values of } N \qquad (A.3)$$

For example, Table A.13 illustrates the computational procedures for an odd number of observations and an assumed upper limit of 500. As is true for the first three extrapolation curves, the middle observation is assigned an index value of zero; preceding observations are numbered from the middle in increasing negative order $(-1, -2, \text{etc.})$; and later observations are numbered in increasing positive order $(1, 2, \text{etc.})$.

The logarithm differences, $\log c - \log Y$, shown in column 4 are computed by subtracting the logarithm of the observed values from the logarithm of the upper growth limit. For example, for 1940, the logarithm of the assumed upper limit of 500, 2.6989, minus the logarithm of the observed value, 1.2304, is equal to the logarithm difference, 1.4685. The sum of the logarithms of these logarithm differences, $\Sigma\log (\log c - \log Y)$ (column 5), and the sum of products of the index and these values, $\Sigma[X\log (\log c - \log Y)]$ (column 7), are then computed. The logarithm of the logarithm of the a parameter is calculated by applying Eq. (A.18):

$$\log (\log a) = \frac{\Sigma[\log (\log c - \log Y)]}{N}$$

$$= \frac{0.2123}{9} = 0.0236$$

Table A.13

Gompertz Curve Computations for Assumed Upper Limit

Year	Observed Value[a] (Y)	Logarithm of Observed Value (log Y)	Logarithm Difference[b] (log c − log Y)	Log of Logarithm Difference[b] (log Y*)	Index Value (X)	Product[c] (Xlog Y*)
(1)	(2)	(3)	(4)	(5)	(6)	(7)
1940	17.0	1.2304	1.4685	0.1669	−4	−0.6675
1945	23.0	1.3617	1.3372	0.1262	−3	−0.3786
1950	29.0	1.4624	1.2366	0.0922	−2	−0.1844
1955	35.0	1.5441	1.1549	0.0625	−1	−0.0625
1960	43.0	1.6335	1.0655	0.0276	0	0.0000
1965	52.0	1.7160	0.9830	−0.0075	1	−0.0075
1970	63.0	1.7993	0.8996	−0.0459	2	−0.0919
1975	77.0	1.8865	0.8125	−0.0902	3	−0.2706
1980	87.0	1.9395	0.7595	−0.1195	4	−0.4780
Sum	...	...	...	0.2123	...	−2.1410

[a] These values are expressed in 1,000s.
[b] The term *logarithm difference* used here is the logarithm of the upper limit minus the logarithm of the observed value.
[c] The term *product* used here is the product of the index value and the logarithm of the logarithm difference (see note b).
* The expression Y^* equals $\log c - \log Y$, that is, the logarithm difference values listed in column 4 (see note b).

The logarithm of the b parameter is computed by applying Eq. (A. 19):

$$\log b = \frac{\Sigma[X\log(\log c - \log Y)]}{\Sigma X^2}$$

$$= \frac{-2.1410}{60} = -0.0357$$

The b parameter and the logarithm of the a parameter can then be computed by taking the antilogarithms of log b and log (log a). For this example,

$$\log a = \text{antilog } [\log(\log a)]$$
$$= \text{antilog } (0.0236) = 1.0558$$
$$b = \text{antilog } (\log b)$$
$$= \text{antilog } (-0.0357) = 0.9211$$

As a result, the transformed Gompertz curve, $\log Y_C = \log c - (\log a)b^x$, with an assumed upper limit of 500 that best fits these data has the following equation:

$$\log Y_C = 2.6989 - 1.0558(0.9221)^x$$

As shown in Table A.14, Gompertz estimates and projections can be derived by substituting appropriate index values into this equation and solving for the antilogarithm of log Y_C. For example, for 1960,

$$X = 0$$

and

$$\log Y_C = 2.6989 - 1.0558(0.9221)^0 = 1.6431$$
$$Y_C = \text{antilog } (1.6431) = 44.0$$

The estimation errors reported in column 6 of Table A.14 are reasonably small and do not reveal a consistent pattern similar to that observed for the modified exponential curve. This indicates that the curve estimates are concave upward like the observation data shown in Figure A.1 and that the Gompertz curve is a reasonable candidate for projecting these data.

Assumed Lower Growth Limit. As shown in Figure 2.7, when the logarithm of the *a* parameter is positive and the *b* parameter is between zero and one, the Gompertz curve approaches a lower limit *c* for large positive values of *X*. In these cases, the modified Gompertz curve takes the form $Y_C = \log c + (\log a)b^X$. As a result, the computational procedures for a Gompertz curve with an assumed lower growth limit

Table A.14

Gompertz Estimates and Projections for Assumed Upper Limit

Curve Equation: $\log Y_C = 2.6989 - 1.0558(0.9221)^X$

Year	Observed Value[a] (Y)	Index Value (X)	Logarithm of Estimate/Projection (log Y_C)	Estimate/ Projection[a] (Y_C)	Error of Estimate[a] ($Y - Y_C$)
(1)	(2)	(3)	(4)	(5)	(6)
1940	17.0	−4	1.2323	17.1	−0.1
1945	23.0	−3	1.3480	22.3	0.7
1950	29.0	−2	1.4546	28.5	0.5
1955	35.0	−1	1.5527	35.7	−0.7
1960	43.0	0	1.6431	44.0	−1.0
1965	52.0	1	1.7264	53.3	−1.3
1970	63.0	2	1.8031	63.6	−0.6
1975	77.0	3	1.8738	74.8	2.2
1980	87.0	4	1.9389	86.9	0.1
1985	...	5	1.9989	99.7	...
1990	...	6	2.0541	113.3	...
1995	...	7	2.1049	127.3	...
2000	...	8	2.1518	141.8	...

[a] These values are expressed in 1,000s.

are identical to the procedures for an assumed upper limit, with the exception that log (log Y − log c) replaces the log (log c − log Y) term in all of the equations. That is, for an assumed lower limit c,

$$\log (\log a) = \frac{\Sigma \log (\log Y - \log c)}{N} \tag{A.20}$$

$$\log b = \frac{\Sigma X \log (\log Y - \log c)}{\Sigma X^2} \tag{A.21}$$

where the terms are defined as they were for Eqs. (A.18) and (A.19). Gompertz curve estimates and projections can then be computed by (1) taking the antilogarithms of log (log a) and log b; (2) substituting these values and appropriate index values into the transformed Gompertz equation, log Y_c = log c + (log a)b^x; and (3) solving for the antilogarithm of log Y_c.

The procedures for an assumed upper or lower growth limit can be adopted for an even number of observations by using the appropriate procedures for assigning index values and computing the squared index values outlined for the linear, parabolic, and geometric curves.

Procedures for Computing Growth Limits

The procedures for identifying the growth limit, c, and the a and b parameters for the Gompertz curve that best fit a set of observation data are identical to those for the modified exponential curve, except that they incorporate the logarithms of the observed data.[6] As a result, the number of observations must be evenly divisible by three; the first observation must be assigned an index value of zero; and later observations must be numbered in increasing positive order. The Gompertz curve parameters can then be determined by applying the following equations:

$$b^n = \frac{\Sigma_3 \log Y - \Sigma_2 \log Y}{\Sigma_2 \log Y - \Sigma_1 \log Y} \tag{A.22}$$

$$\log a = (\Sigma_2 \log Y - \Sigma_1 \log Y) \left[\frac{b - 1}{(b^n - 1)^2} \right] \tag{A.23}$$

$$\log c = \frac{1}{n} \left[\frac{(\Sigma_1 \log Y)(\Sigma_3 \log Y) - (\Sigma_2 \log Y)^2}{\Sigma_1 \log Y + \Sigma_3 \log Y - 2\Sigma_2 \log Y} \right] \tag{A.24}$$

where

n = number of observations in each partial sum

$\Sigma_1 \log Y$ = partial sum of first third of logarithms of observed values

$\Sigma_2 \log Y$ = partial sum of second third of logarithms of observed values

$\Sigma_3 \log Y$ = partial sum of last third of logarithms of observed values

As shown in Table A.15, the observations must first be assigned appropriate index values. Next, the logarithms of the observations and partial sums of the logarithms, $\Sigma_n \log Y$, are computed for each third of the observations. The number of observations in each partial sum, n, is equal to the total number of observations divided by three, that is, three for this example. The value of b^n (in this case b^3) must first be computed by applying Eq. (A.22):

$$b^n = \frac{\Sigma_3 \log Y - \Sigma_2 \log Y}{\Sigma_2 \log Y - \Sigma_1 \log Y}$$

$$= \frac{5.6253 - 4.8936}{4.8936 - 4.0545} = 0.8720$$

Taking the nth root of this value yields the b parameter:

$$b = (0.8720)^{1/3} = 0.955$$

Table A.15

Gompertz Curve Computations for Computed Upper Limit

Year	Index Value (X)	Observed Value[a] (Y)	Logarithm of Observed Value (log Y)	Partial Sum of Logarithms [$\Sigma_n(\log Y)$]
(1)	(2)	(3)	(4)	(5)
1940	0	17.0	1.2304	
1945	1	23.0	1.3617	4.0545
1950	2	29.0	1.4624	
1955	3	35.0	1.5441	
1960	4	43.0	1.6335	4.8936
1965	5	52.0	1.7160	
1970	6	63.0	1.7993	
1975	7	77.0	1.8865	5.6253
1980	8	87.0	1.9395	

[a] These values are expressed in 1,000s.

The logarithm of the *a* parameter can be computed by applying Eq. (A. 23):

$$\log a = (\Sigma_2 \log Y - \Sigma_1 \log Y) \left[\frac{b-1}{(b^n - 1)^2} \right]$$

$$= (4.8936 - 4.0545) \left[\frac{0.955 - 1.0}{(0.872 - 1.0)^2} \right]$$

$$= -2.3047$$

The logarithm of the *c* parameter can be computed by applying Eq. (A. 24). That is,

$$\log c = \frac{1}{n} \left[\frac{(\Sigma_1 \log Y)(\Sigma_3 \log Y) - (\Sigma_2 \log Y)^2}{\Sigma_1 \log Y + \Sigma_3 \log Y - 2\Sigma_2 \log Y} \right]$$

$$= \frac{1}{3} \left[\frac{(4.0545)(5.6253) - (4.8936)^2}{4.0545 + 5.6253 - 2(4.8936)} \right]$$

$$= 3.5366$$

As a result, the transformed equation for the Gompertz curve that best fits the observed data is

$$\log Y_C = 3.5366 - 2.3047(0.955)^x$$

Since the logarithm of the *a* parameter is negative and the *b* parameter is less than one, the *c* parameter is equal to the upper limit of the Gompertz curve for large positive values of the *X* parameter. This asymptotic upper limit is equal to the antilogarithm of log *c*, that is, antilog (3.5366), or 3,476. Thus, since the original data are expressed in 1,000s, the calculated upper growth limit for the population of Leon County is 3,476,000.

As shown in Table A.16, Gompertz estimates and projections can be obtained by substituting appropriate index values into the transformed Gompertz curve equation, solving for log Y_C, and taking the antilogarithm of the result. For example, for 1940,

$$X = 0$$

and

$$\log Y_C = 3.5366 - 2.3047(0.955)^0 = 1.2319$$
$$Y_C = \text{antilog} (1.2319) = 17.1$$

Gompertz estimates and projections can also be obtained by taking

Table A.16

Gompertz Estimates and Projections for Computed Upper Limit

Curve Equation: $\log Y_C = 3.5366 - 2.3047(0.955)^X$

Year (1)	Index Value (X) (2)	Logarithm of Estimate/Projection ($\log Y_C$) (3)	Estimate/ Projection[a] (Y_C) (4)
1940	0	1.2319	17.1
1945	1	1.3348	21.6
1950	2	1.4330	27.1
1955	3	1.5269	33.6
1960	4	1.6166	41.4
1965	5	1.7023	50.4
1970	6	1.7841	60.8
1975	7	1.8623	72.8
1980	8	1.9370	86.5
1985	9	2.0084	102.0
1990	10	2.0766	119.3
1995	11	2.1418	138.6
2000	12	2.2040	160.0

[a] These values are expressed in 1,000s.

the antilogarithms of $\log a$ and $\log c$ to yield the Gompertz curve a and c parameters and substituting these values into the Gompertz curve equation. For this example,

$$a = \text{antilog} (-2.3047) = 0.00496$$
$$c = \text{antilog} (3.5366) = 3,440$$

Therefore, the equation for the Gompertz curve that best fits these data is

$$Y_C = 3,440 \times 0.00496 \exp [(0.955)^x]$$

Gompertz estimates and projections can be determined by substituting appropriate index values into this equation and solving for Y_C. For example, for 1950,

$$X = 2$$

and

$$Y_C = 3,440 \times 0.00496 \exp [(0.955)^2]$$
$$= 3,440 \times (0.00496)^{0.912}$$
$$= 27.1$$

LOGISTIC CURVE

Procedures for Assumed Growth Limits

As shown in Chapter 2, the logistic curve, $Y_c^{-1} = c + ab^x$, can be transformed to the linear form, $\log Y_c^{-1} = \log a + (\log b)X$, by assuming an upper or lower growth limit and applying logarithms. This allows the linear curve-fitting procedures to be used to fit a logistic curve with an assumed growth limit, $1/c$.

For example, as shown in Figure 2.8, when the b parameter is less than one, the logistic curve approaches an upper limit c for large positive values of X. The logistic curve for this situation can be expressed as $Y_c^{-1} = c + ab^x$, and the computational procedures for fitting a modified exponential curve with an assumed upper limit can be used for the logistic curve with the exception that $\log (Y^{-1} - c)$ replaces the $\log (c - Y)$ term, and $X\log (Y^{-1} - c)$ replaces the $X\log (c - Y)$ term. That is, given an assumed upper limit c, the logarithms of the logistic curve a and b parameters can be computed by applying the following equations:

$$\log a = \frac{\Sigma \log (Y^{-1} - c)}{N} \tag{A.25}$$

$$\log b = \frac{\Sigma [X\log (Y^{-1} - c)]}{\Sigma X^2} \tag{A.26}$$

where

$$N = \text{number of observations}$$
$$\Sigma \log (Y^{-1} - c) = \text{sum of logarithms of reciprocal differences}$$
$$\Sigma [X\log (Y^{-1} - c)] = \text{sum of products of index values and}$$
$$\text{logarithms of reciprocal differences}$$

The sum of the squared index values, ΣX^2, can be obtained as previously noted:

$$\Sigma X^2 = \frac{N(N^2 - 1)}{12} \quad \text{for odd values of } N \tag{A.3}$$

For example, Table A.17 illustrates the computational procedures for an odd number of observations and an assumed upper limit of 500. As is true for the first three extrapolation curves, the middle observation is assigned an index value of zero; preceding observations are numbered from the middle in increasing negative order (-1, -2, etc.); and

Table A.17

Logistic Curve Computations for Assumed Upper Limit

Year	Observed Value[a] (Y)	Reciprocal of Observed Value (Y^{-1})	Reciprocal Difference[b] $(Y^{-1}-c)$	Log of Reciprocal Difference[b] $(\log Y^*)$	Index Value (X)	Product[c] $(X\log Y^*)$
(1)	(2)	(3)	(4)	(5)	(6)	(7)
1940	17.0	0.0588	0.0568	−1.2455	−4	4.9819
1945	23.0	0.0435	0.0415	−1.3822	−3	4.1465
1950	29.0	0.0345	0.0325	−1.4883	−2	2.9767
1955	35.0	0.0286	0.0266	−1.5756	−1	1.5756
1960	43.0	0.0233	0.0213	−1.6725	0	0.0000
1965	52.0	0.0192	0.0172	−1.7637	1	−1.7637
1970	63.0	0.0159	0.0139	−1.8578	2	−3.7157
1975	77.0	0.0130	0.0110	−1.9591	3	−5.8774
1980	87.0	0.0115	0.0095	−2.0225	4	−8.0902
Sum	...	...	...	−14.9673	...	−5.7662

[a] These values are expressed in 1,000s.
[b] The term reciprocal difference used here is the reciprocal of the observed value minus the reciprocal of the upper limit.
[c] The term product here is the product of the index value and the logarithm of the reciprocal difference (see note b).
* The expression Y^* equals $Y^{-1}-c$, that is, the reciprocal difference values in column 4 (see note b).

later observations are numbered in increasing positive order (1, 2, etc.).

The reciprocal differences, $Y^{-1} - c$, shown in column 4 are computed by subtracting the reciprocal of the upper growth limit from the reciprocal of the observed values. For example, for 1940, the reciprocal of the observed value, 0.0588, minus the reciprocal of the assumed upper limit of 500, 0.0020, is equal to the reciprocal difference, 0.0568. The sum of the logarithms of these reciprocal differences, $\Sigma\log (Y^{-1} - c)$ *(column 5)*, and the sum of the products of the index and these values, $\Sigma X\log (Y^{-1} - c)$ *(column 7)*, are then computed. The logarithm of the a parameter is calculated by applying Eq. (A. 25):

$$\log a = \frac{\Sigma\log (Y^{-1} - c)}{N}$$

$$= \frac{-14.9673}{9} = -1.6630$$

The logarithm of the b parameter is computed by applying Eq. (A.26):

$$\log b = \frac{\Sigma[X\log (Y^{-1} - c)]}{\Sigma X^2}$$

$$= \frac{-5.7662}{60} = -0.0961$$

The a and b parameters can then be computed by taking the antilogarithms of log a and log b. For this example,

$$\begin{aligned} a &= \text{antilog (log } a) \\ &= \text{antilog } (-1.6630) = 0.0217 \\ b &= \text{antilog (log } b) \\ &= \text{antilog } (-0.0961) = 0.8015 \end{aligned}$$

As a result, the logistic curve, $Y_C^{-1} = c + ab^x$, with an assumed upper limit of 500 that best fits these data has the following equation:

$$Y_C^{-1} = 0.0020 + 0.0217(0.8015)^x$$

As shown in Table A.18, logistic estimates and projections can be derived by substituting appropriate index values into this equation and solving for the reciprocal of Y_C^{-1}. For example, for 1960,

$$X = 0$$

Table A.18

Logistic Estimates and Projections for Assumed Upper Limit

Curve Equation: $Y_C^{-1} = 0.0020 + 0.0217(0.8015)^X$

Year	Observed Value[a] (Y)	Index Value (X)	Reciprocal of Estimate/Projection (Y_C^{-1})	Estimate/ Projection[a] (Y_C)	Error of Estimate[a] $(Y - Y_C)$
(1)	(2)	(3)	(4)	(5)	(6)
1940	17.0	-4	0.0546	18.3	-1.3
1945	23.0	-3	0.0442	22.6	0.4
1950	29.0	-2	0.0358	27.9	1.1
1955	35.0	-1	0.0291	34.4	0.6
1960	43.0	0	0.0237	42.1	0.9
1965	52.0	1	0.0194	51.5	0.5
1970	63.0	2	0.0160	62.7	0.3
1975	77.0	3	0.0132	75.8	1.2
1980	87.0	4	0.0110	91.2	-4.2
1985	...	5	0.0092	108.9	...
1990	...	6	0.0078	128.9	...
1995	...	7	0.0066	151.2	...
2000	...	8	0.0057	175.5	...

[a] These values are expressed in 1,000s.

and

$$Y_c^{-1} = 0.0020 + 0.0217(0.8015)^0 = 0.0237$$

$$Y_c = \frac{1}{0.0237} = 42.1$$

These procedures can be adopted for an even number of observations by using the appropriate procedures for assigning index values and computing the squared index values outlined for the linear, parabolic, and geometric curves.

Procedures for Computing Growth Limits

The procedures for computing the logistic curve parameters are identical to those for the modified exponential curve, except that they incorporate the *reciprocals* of the observed values.[7] As a result, the total number of observations must be evenly divisible by three; the first observation must be assigned an index value of zero; and later observations must be numbered in positive increasing order. The logistic curve parameters can then be calculated by applying the following equations:

$$b^n = \frac{\Sigma_3 Y^{-1} - \Sigma_2 Y^{-1}}{\Sigma_2 Y^{-1} - \Sigma_1 Y^{-1}} \qquad (A.27)$$

$$a = (\Sigma_2 Y^{-1} - \Sigma_1 Y^{-1}) \left[\frac{b - 1}{(b^n - 1)^2} \right] \qquad (A.28)$$

$$c = \frac{1}{n} \left[\frac{(\Sigma_1 Y^{-1})(\Sigma_3 Y^{-1}) - (\Sigma_2 Y^{-1})^2}{\Sigma_1 Y^{-1} + \Sigma_3 Y^{-1} - 2\Sigma_2 Y^{-1}} \right] \qquad (A.29)$$

where

n = number of observations divided by three
$\Sigma_1 Y^{-1}$ = partial sum of first third of reciprocals
$\Sigma_2 Y^{-1}$ = partial sum of second third of reciprocals
$\Sigma_3 Y^{-1}$ = partial sum of last third of reciprocals

As shown in Table A.19, the observations must first be assigned appropriate index values. Then the reciprocals of the observations, Y^{-1}, and partial sums of the reciprocals, $\Sigma_n Y^{-1}$, must be determined for each third of the observations. The number of observations in each partial sum n is equal to the total number of observations divided by

Table A.19

Logistic Curve Computations for Computed Upper Limit

Year	Index Value (X)	Observed Value[a] (Y)	Reciprocal of Observed Value (Y^{-1})	Partial Sum of Reciprocals [\Sigma_n(Y^{-1})]
(1)	(2)	(3)	(4)	(5)
1940	0	17.0	0.0588	
1945	1	23.0	0.0435	0.1368
1950	2	29.0	0.0345	
1955	3	35.0	0.0286	
1960	4	43.0	0.0233	0.0711
1965	5	52.0	0.0192	
1970	6	63.0	0.0159	
1975	7	77.0	0.0130	0.0404
1980	8	87.0	0.0115	

[a] These values are expressed in 1,000s.

three, that is, three in this example. The value of b^n can be computed by applying Eq. (A. 27):

$$b^n = \frac{\Sigma_3 Y^{-1} - \Sigma_2 Y^{-1}}{\Sigma_2 Y^{-1} - \Sigma_1 Y^{-1}}$$

$$= \frac{0.0404 - 0.0711}{0.0711 - 0.01368} = 0.4672$$

Taking the nth root of this value yields the value for the b parameter. Since n is equal to three,

$$b = (0.4672)^{1/3} = 0.776$$

The a parameter can be calculated by applying Eq. (A.28):

$$a = (\Sigma_2 Y^{-1} - \Sigma_1 Y^{-1}) \left[\frac{b-1}{(b^n - 1)^2} \right]$$

$$= (0.0711 - 0.1368) \left[\frac{0.7760 - 1.0}{(0.4672 - 1.0)^2} \right]$$

$$= 0.0518$$

The c parameter can be computed by applying Eq. (A. 29):

$$c = \frac{1}{n}\left[\frac{\Sigma_1 Y^{-1})(\Sigma_3 Y^{-1}) - (\Sigma_2 Y^{-1})^2}{\Sigma_1 Y^{-1} + \Sigma_3 Y^{-1} - 2\Sigma_2 Y^{-1}}\right]$$

$$= \frac{1}{3}\left[\frac{(0.1368)(0.0404) - (0.0711)^2}{0.1368 + 0.0404 - 2(0.0711)}\right]$$

$$= 0.00448$$

As a result, the equation for the modified exponential curve that best fits the observed data is

$$Y_c^{-1} = 0.00448 + 0.0518(0.7762)^x$$

Since the a parameter is positive and the b parameter is less than one, the upper limit for large positive values of X is equal to the inverse of the c parameter, 1/0.00448, or 223.2, that is, 223,200, since the original values are expressed in thousands. The lower limit for large negative values of X is 0.

As shown in Table A.20, logistic estimates and projections can be obtained by substituting appropriate index values into this equation. For example, for 1940,

$$X = 0$$

Table A.20

Logistic Estimates and Projections for Computed Upper Limit

Curve Equation: $Y_C^{-1} = 0.00448 + 0.0518(0.776)^X$

Year	Index Value (X)	Reciprocal of Estimate/Projection (Y_C^{-1})	Estimate/ Projection[a] (Y_C)
(1)	(2)	(3)	(4)
1940	0	0.05628	17.8
1945	1	0.04468	22.4
1950	2	0.03567	28.0
1955	3	0.02869	34.9
1960	4	0.02326	43.0
1965	5	0.01906	52.5
1970	6	0.01579	63.3
1975	7	0.01326	75.4
1980	8	0.01129	88.6
1985	9	0.00977	102.4
1990	10	0.00858	116.5
1995	11	0.00766	130.5
2000	12	0.00695	143.9

[a] These values are expressed in 1,000s.

and

$$Y_{\bar{c}}^{1} = 0.00448 + 0.0518(0.776)^0 = 0.05628$$

$$Y_c = \frac{1}{0.05628} = 17.8$$

For 1990,

$$X = 10$$

and

$$Y_{\bar{c}}^{1} = 0.00448 + 0.0518(0.776)^{10} = 0.00858$$

$$Y_c = \frac{1}{0.00858} = 116.5$$

ENDNOTES

1. The procedures for computing the linear curve parameters *a* and *b* for an odd and an even number of observations are adopted from Croxton, Cowden, and Klein (1967, 235–43) and Stockton and Clark (1966, 356–59).

2. The procedures for identifying the geometric curve parameters for an odd and even number of observations are adopted from Croxton, Cowden, and Klein (1967, 256–60) and Stockton and Clark (1966, 367–70).

3. The procedures for identifying the parabolic curve parameters for an odd and even number of observations are adopted from Stockton and Clark (1966, 371–73) and Croxton, Cowden, and Klein (1967, 256–60).

4. The following procedures for identifying the modified exponential curve *a*, *b*, and *c* parameters are adapted from Croxton, Cowden, and Klein (1967, 719–20).

5. The following equations can only be used when the values for the partial sums of the observations are continuously increasing or decreasing, that is, if (1) the first partial sum, $\Sigma_1 Y$, is less (or greater) than the second partial sum, $\Sigma_2 Y$, and (2) the second partial sum is less (or greater) than the third partial sum, $\Sigma_3 Y$. If this is not the case, Eq. (A. 13) yields a negative value for b^n and undefined values for the *n*th root of b^n when *n* is odd. Similar restrictions apply to the equations for computing the Gompertz and logistic curve parameters for a computed growth limit.

6. The computational procedures for identifying the *a*, *b*, and *c* parameters for the Gompertz curve are adapted from Croxton, Cowden, and Klein (1967, 269–74).

7. The computational procedures for identifying the *a*, *b*, and *c* parameters for the logistic curve discussed in this section are suggested in Croxton, Cowden, and Klein (1967, 274).

Appendix B

Review of Logarithms

The *logarithm* of a number N is the number of times another number (the *base*) must be multiplied by itself to yield the initial value N. That is, the logarithm of a number N is equal to the exponent to which the base must be raised to yield the number N. For example, 100 is equal to 10×10, or 10^2. Thus, for a base of 10, the logarithm of 100 (log 100) is equal to 2.00. Because 1 is equal to 10^0, for a base of 10 the logarithm of 1 (log 1.0) is zero; logarithms for numbers between 1 and 10 are therefore between 0.0 and 1.0. Similarly, because one-tenth is equal to $\frac{1}{10}$ or 10^{-1}, for a base of 10 the logarithm of one-tenth, log 0.1, is -1.00.

The logarithm of a number N that uses a base of 10 is referred to as the *common logarithm,* or log N. The logarithm of a number N that uses a base of e (2.71828) is referred to as the *natural logarithm,* or ln N. Because the base for natural logarithms is smaller than the base for common logarithms, the natural logarithm of a number is approximately 2.303 times larger than its common logarithm. For example, log $100 = 2.00$, but ln $100 = 4.6052$.

The *antilogarithm* of a number N, antilog N or antiln N, is the inverse of the logarithm. That is, the antilogarithm of a number N is equal to the number obtained when a given base is raised to the power N. For example, for a base of 10, the antilogarithm of 2, antilog 2.0, is equal to $10^{2.0}$, or 100. For a base of e the antilogarithm of 2 (antiln 2.0) is equal to $2.78128^{2.0}$, or 7.389.

The following laws of logarithms can be applied to the logarithms of products, ratios, and exponents:

1. The logarithm of the product of two numbers is equal to the sum of their logarithms:

   $$\log (ab) = \log a + \log b$$

   For example,

   $$\log (10 \times 100) = \log (10) + \log (100)$$
   $$\log (1{,}000) = \log (10) + \log (100)$$
   $$3 = 2 + 1$$

2. The logarithm of the ratio of two numbers is equal to the difference between their logarithms:

   $$\log \left(\frac{a}{b}\right) = \log a - \log b$$

   For example,

   $$\log \left(\frac{1{,}000}{10}\right) = \log (1{,}000) - \log (10)$$
   $$\log (100) = \log (1{,}000) - \log (10)$$
   $$2 = 3 - 1$$

3. The logarithm of a number raised to (or reduced by) a power is equal to the logarithm of the number miltiplied by (or divided by) that power:

   $$\log (a^b) = b(\log a)$$
   $$\log (a^{\frac{1}{b}}) = \frac{\log a}{b}$$

   For example,

   $$\log (10^3) = 3 \times \log (10)$$
   $$\log (1{,}000) = 3 \times \log (10)$$
   $$3 = 3 \times 1$$

Appendix C

OBERS Industrial Groups and SIC Codes

Table C.1

OBERS Industrial Groups and Equivalent SIC Codes

Industries Projected for BEA Economic Areas, MSAs, and Other Substate Areas (1)	Industries Projected for States and the Nation (2)	OBERS Industrial Group[a] (g) (3)	1972 SIC Code[b] (4)
AGRICULTURAL PRODUCTION[c]	AGRICULTURAL PRODUCTION[d]	A,1	01,02
AGRICULTURAL SERVICES, FORESTRY, FISHERIES, AND OTHER	AGRICULTURAL SERVICES, FORESTRY, FISHERIES, AND OTHER	B,2	07–09
MINING	MINING	C	B
	Coal mining	3	11,12
	Crude petroleum and natural gas	4	13
	Metal mining	5	10
	Nonmetal mining, except fuels	6	14
CONSTRUCTION	CONSTRUCTION	D,7	C
MANUFACTURING	MANUFACTURING	E,F	D
Nondurable goods	Nondurable goods	E	20–23, 26–31
	Food and kindred products	8	20
	Tobacco products	9	21
	Textile mill products	10	22
	Apparel and fabricated textile products	11	23
	Paper and allied products	12	26
	Printing and publishing	13	27
	Chemicals and allied products	14	28
	Petroleum refining	15	29
	Rubber and miscellaneous plastics	16	30
	Leather and leather products	17	31
Durable goods	Durable Goods	F	24–25,32–39
	Lumber products, except furniture and fixtures	18	24
	Furniture and fixtures	19	25
	Stone, clay, and glass products	20	32
	Primary metals	21	33
	Fabricated metals	22	34
	Machinery, except electrical	23	35
	Electrical and electronic machinery	24	36
	Transportation equipment, except motor vehicles	25	37 (excluding 371)
	Motor vehicles and equipment	26	371
	Ordnance[d]	27	...
	Instruments	28	38
	Miscellaneous manufacturing	29	39

(Continued on next page)

Table C.1 *(Continued)*

OBERS Industrial Groups and Equivalent SIC Codes

Industries Projected for BEA Economic Areas, MSAs, and Other Substate Areas (1)	Industries Projected for States and the Nation (2)	OBERS Industrial Group[a] (g) (3)	1972 SIC Code[b] (4)
TRANSPORTATION, COMMUNICATION, AND PUBLIC UTILITIES	TRANSPORTATION,, COMMUNICATION, AND PUBLIC UTILITIES	G	E
	Railroad transportation	30	40
	Local and passenger transportation	31	41
	Motor freight and warehousing	32	42
	Water transportation	33	44
	Air transportation	34	45
	Pipeline transportation	35	46
	Transportation services	36	47
	Communication	37	48
	Electric, gas, and sanitary services	38	49
WHOLESALE TRADE	WHOLESALE TRADE	H,39	F
RETAIL TRADE	RETAIL TRADE	I,40	G
FINANCE, INSURANCE, AND REAL ESTATE	FINANCE, INSURANCE, AND REAL ESTATE	J	H
	BANKING	41	60
	Other credit and security agencies	42	61,62,67
	Insurance	43	63,64
	Real estate and combined offices	44	65,66
SERVICES	SERVICES	K	I
	Hotels and other lodging	45	70
	Personal and miscellaneous business and repair services	46	72,73,76
	Auto repair and services	47	75
	Motion pictures	48	76
	Amusement services, excluding motion pictures	49	79
	Medical and health services	50	80
	Private educational services	51	82
	Nonprofit organizations	52	83,84,86
	Private households	53	88
	Miscellaneous Professional services	54	81,89
GOVERNMENT	GOVERNMENT	...	...
Federal civilian	Federal civilian	L,55	...
Federal military	Federal military	M,56	...
State and local	State and local	N,57	...

[a] Employment and earnings are projected for States and the Nation for the 57 industrial groups identified by number. Employment and earnings are projected for BEA economic areas, MSAs, and other substate areas for the 14 industrial groups identified by letter.

[b] Historical data through 1974 are classified according to the 1967 SIC definitions; subsequent historical data and projections are classified according to the 1972 SIC definitions.

[c] Refers to U.S. residents employed by international organizations.

[d] The ordnance classification was discontinued in the 1972 SIC definitions. Data previously included in ordnance are now included in one or more of the following classes: Fabricated Metals (SIC 34), Electrical and Electronic Machinery (SIC 36), Transportation Equipment (SIC 37), and Instruments (SIC 38).

Source: U.S. Bureau of Economic Analysis (1985a, 107–108).

Bibliography

Andrews, Richard B. 1953. "Mechanics of the Urban Economic Base: Historical Development of the Base Concept." *Land Economics* 29: 161–67. (Reprinted in Ralph W. Pfouts, ed. 1960. *The Techniques of Urban Economic Analysis*. West Trenton, N.J.: Chandler-Davis.)

———. 1954a. "Mechanics of the Urban Economic Base: General Problems of Base Identification." *Land Economics* 30: 164–72. (Reprinted in Ralph W. Pfouts, ed. 1960. *The Techniques of Urban Economic Analysis*. West Trenton, N.J.: Chandler-Davis.)

———. 1954b. "Mechanics of the Urban Economic Base: The Problem of Base Area Delimitation." *Land Economics* 30: 309–19. (Reprinted in Ralph W. Pfouts, ed. 1960. *The Techniques of Urban Economic Analysis*. West Trenton, N.J.: Chandler-Davis.)

———. 1954c. "Mechanics of the Urban Economic Base: The Problem of Base Measurement." *Land Economics* 30: 52–60. (Reprinted in Ralph W. Pfouts, ed., *The Techniques of Urban Economic Analysis*. 1960. West Trenton, N.J.: Chandler-Davis.)

———. 1955. "Mechanics of the Urban Economic Base: The Concept of Base Ratios." *Land Economics* 31: 47–53. (Reprinted in Ralph W. Pfouts, ed. 1960. *The Techniques of Urban Economic Analysis*. West Trenton, N.J.: Chandler-Davis.)

Archer, B. H. 1976. "The Anatomy of a Multiplier." *Regional Studies* 10: 71–77.

Armstrong, J. Scott. 1978. *Long-range Forecasting: From Crystal Ball to Computer*. New York: John Wiley and Sons.

Beaumont, Paul M., and Andrew M. Isserman. 1987. "Comment." *Journal of the American Statistical Association* 82: 1004–1009.

Bendavid-Val, Avrom. 1983. *Regional and Local Economic Analysis for Practitioners*, rev. ed. New York: Praeger.

Blumenfeld, Hans. 1955. "The Economic Base of a Community." *Journal of the American Institute of Planners* 21: 114–32.

Bolton, Richard E. 1966. *Defense Purchases and Regional Growth*. Washington, D.C.: The Brookings Institution.

Bowles, Gladys K., Calvin L. Beale, and Everett S. Lee. 1975. *Net Migration of the Population, 1960–70 by Age, Sex, and Color*. Athens: University of Georgia.

Bowles, Gladys K., and James E. Tarver. 1965. *Net Migration of the Population, 1950–60 by Age, Sex, and Color*. Washington, D.C.: Government Printing Office.

Brodsky, Harold, and D. E. Sarfaty. 1977. "Measuring the Urban Economic Base in a Developing Country." *Land Economics* 53: 445–54.

Browing, Harley L. 1961. "Methods for Describing the Age-Sex Structure of Cities." In Jack Gibbs, ed., *Urban Research Methods*. Princeton, N.J.: Van Nostrand.

Brown, H. James. 1969. "Shift and Share Projections of Regional Economic Growth: An Empirical Test." *Journal of Regional Science* 9: 1–17.

Brownrigg, M. 1980. "Industrial Contraction and the Regional Multiplier Effect." *Town Planning Review* 51: 195–210.

Chapin, F. Stuart, and Edward J. Kaiser. 1979. *Urban Land Use Planning*, 3d ed. Champaign: University of Illinois Press.

Chinitz, Benjamin. 1961. "Contrasts in Agglomeration: New York and Pittsburgh." *American Economic Review, Papers and Proceedings* 51: 279–89.

Cox, Peter. 1976. *Demography*, 5th ed. Cambridge: Cambridge University Press.

Croxton, Frederick E., Dudley J. Cowden, and Sidney Klein. 1967. *Applied General Statistics*, 3d ed. Englewood Cliffs, N.J.: Prentice-Hall.

Cullen, Ian. 1984. *Applied Urban Analysis: A Critique and Synthesis*. London: Methuen and Co.

Daberkow, Stan G., and Leslie A. Whitener. 1986. *Agricultural Data Sources: An Update*. Agriculture Handbook No. 658. Washington, D.C.: U.S. Department of Agriculture.

Dickey, John W., and Thomas W. Watts. 1978. *Analytic Techniques in Urban and Regional Planning*. New York: McGraw-Hill.

Dunn, Edgar S., Jr. 1960. "A Statistical and Analytical Technique for Regional Science." *Papers, Regional Science Association* 6: 15–23.

Edwards, J. Arwell. 1976. "Industrial Structure and Regional Change: A Shift-

Share Analysis of the British Columbia Economy. *Regional Studies* 10: 307–17.

Emmerson, Richard R., R. Ramanathan, and Wolfgang Ramm. 1975. "On the Analysis of Regional Growth Patterns." *Journal of Regional Science* 15: 17–28.

Faber, Joseph F., and John C. Wilken. 1981. *Social Security Area Population Projections, 1981, Actuarial Study No. 85*. Washington, D.C.: Social Security Administration, Office of the Actuary.

Forward, Charles N. 1982. "The Importance of Nonemployment Sources of Income in Canadian Metropolitan Areas." *Professional Geographer* 34: 289–96.

Garnick, D. H. 1970. "Differential Regional Multiplier Models." *Journal of Regional Science* 10: 35–47.

Gerking, Shelby D., and Andrew M. Isserman. 1981. "Bifurcation and the Time Pattern of Impacts in the Economic Base Model." *Journal of Regional Science* 21: 451–67.

Gibson, Lay James, and Marshall A. Worden. 1981. "Estimating the Economic Base Multiplier: A Test of Alternative Procedures." *Economic Geography* 57: 146–59.

Gilles, James, and William Grigsby. 1960. "Classification Errors in the Base-Ratio Analysis." In Ralph W. Pfouts, ed., *The Techniques of Urban Economic Analysis*. West Trenton, N.J.: Chandler-Davis.

Greenberg, Michael R. 1972. "A Test of Alternative Models for Projecting County Industrial Production at the 2, 3, 4 Digit SIC Levels." *Regional and Urban Economics* 1: 397–418.

Greig, M. A. 1971. "The Regional Income and Employment Effects of a Pulp and Paper Mill." *Scottish Journal of Political Economy* 18: 31–48.

Greytak, David. 1969. "A Statistical Analysis of Regional Export Estimation Techniques." *Journal of Regional Science* 9: 387–95.

Hellman, Daryl A. 1976. "Shift and Share Models as Predictive Tools." *Growth and Change* 7: 3–8.

Hewings, Geoffrey J. D. 1976. "On the Accuracy of Alternative Models for Stepping Down Multi-County Employment Projections to Counties." *Economic Geography* 52: 206–17.

Hildebrand, George, and Arthur Mace, Jr. 1950. "The Employment Multiplier in an Expanding Industrial Market: Los Angeles County, 1940–47." *Review of Economics and Statistics* 32: 241–49.

Hirsch, Werner Z. 1973. *Urban Economic Analysis*. New York: McGraw-Hill.

Houston, David B. 1967. "The Shift and Share Analysis of Regional Growth: A Critique." *Southern Economic Journal* 33: 577–81.

Irwin, Richard. 1977. *Guide for Local Area Population Projections. Bureau of the Census Technical Paper 39.* Washington, D.C.: U.S. Government Printing Office.

Isard, Walter, et al. 1960. *Methods of Regional Analysis: An Introduction to Regional Science.* Cambridge, Mass.: MIT Press.

Isserman, Andrew M. 1977a. "The Accuracy of Population Projections for Sub-county Areas." *Journal of the American Institute of Planners* 43: 247–59.

———. 1977b. "A Bracketing Approach for Estimating Regional Economic Impact Multipliers." *Environment and Planning, A* 9: 1003–11.

———. 1977c. "The Location Quotient Approach to Estimating Regional Economic Impacts." *Journal of the American Institute of Planners* 43: 33–41.

———. 1980. "Estimating Export Activity in a Regional Economy: A Theoretical and Empirical Analysis of Alternative Models." *International Regional Science Review* 5: 155–84.

———. 1984. "Projection, Forecast, and Plan: On the Future of Population Forecasting." *Journal of the American Planning Association* 50: 208–21.

———. 1985. "Economic-Demographic Modeling with Endogenously Determined Birth and Migration Rates: Theory and Prospects." *Environment and Planning, B: Planning and Design* 17: 25–45.

Isserman, Andrew M., and Peter S. Fisher. 1984. "Population Forecasting and Local Economic Planning: The Limits on Community Control over Uncertainty." *Population Research and Policy Review* 3: 27–50.

Kansas City Federal Reserve Bank. 1952. *Monthly Review.* September: 1–7.

Keyfitz, Nathan. 1977. *Applied Mathematical Demography.* New York: John Wiley and Sons.

Klosterman, Richard E. 1985. "Arguments for and Against Planning." *Town Planning Review* 56: 5–20.

———. 1988. "The Politics of Computer-Aided Planning." *Town Planning Review* 58: 441–52.

———. 1989. *Community Analysis and Planning Programs User's Guide.* Akron: Center for Urban Studies, University of Akron.

Krueckeberg, Donald A., and Arthur L. Silvers. 1973. *Urban Planning Analysis: Methods and Models.* New York: John Wiley and Sons.

Lane, Theodore. 1966. "The Urban Base Multiplier: An Evaluation of the State of the Art." *Land Economics* 42: 339–47.

Lausen, J. R. 1971. "Venezuela: An Industrial Shift-Share Analysis: 1941–1961." *Regional and Urban Economics* 1: 153–220.

Lee, Everett S., and Harold F. Goldsmith. 1982. *Population Estimates: Methods for Small Area Analysis.* Beverly Hills, Calif.: Sage Publications.

Leven, Charles. 1961. "Regional Income and Products Accounts: Construction and Applications." In *Design of Regional Accounts,* edited by Warner Hochwald. Baltimore: Johns Hopkins University Press.

Lever, William F. 1981. "The Inner-City Employment Problem in Great Britain Since 1952: A Shift-Share Approach." In *Industrial Location and Regional Systems: Spatial Organization in the Economic Sector,* edited by John Rees, Geoffrey J. D. Hewings, and Howard A. Stafford. New York: J. F. Bergin.

Levine, Ned. 1985. "Planner's Notebook: The Construction of a Population Analysis Program Using a Microcomputer Spreadsheet." *Journal of the American Planning Association* 51: 496–511.

Light, Paul C. 1985. "Social Security and the Politics of Assumptions." *Public Administration Review* 45: 359–62.

McEvoy, James, III, and Thomas Dietz. 1977. *Handbook for Environmental Planning: The Social Consequences of Environmental Change.* New York: John Wiley.

Martin, Randolf C., and Harry W. Miley, Jr. 1983. "The Stability of Economic Base Multipliers: Some Empirical Evidence." *Review of Regional Studies* 13: 18–27.

Mathur, V. K., and H. S. Rosen. 1974. "Regional Employment Multipliers: A New Approach." *Land Economics* 50: 93–96.

Merrifield, John. 1987. "A Neoclassical Anatomy of the Economic Base Multiplier." *Journal of Regional Science* 27: 283–94.

Miernyk, William H. 1965. *The Elements of Input-Output.* New York: Random House.

Moore, Craig L. 1975. "A New Look at the Minimum Requirements Approach to Regional Economic Analysis." *Economic Geography* 51: 350–56.

Moore, Craig L., and Marilyn Jacobsen. 1984. "Minimum Requirements and Regional Economics, 1980." *Economic Geography* 60: 217–24.

Mulligan, Gordon F., and Lay James Gibson. 1984. "Regression Estimates of Economic Base Multipliers for Small Communities." *Economic Geography* 60: 225–37.

National Center for Health Statistics. 1966. *U.S. Decennial Life Tables for 1959–61.* Rockville, Md.: U.S. Department of Health, Education and Welfare.

———. 1975a. *U.S. Decennial Life Tables for 1969–71. Volume I, No. 3. Methodology of the National and State Life Tables for the United States: 1969–71.* Rockville, Md.: U.S. Department of Health, Education and Welfare.

————. 1975b. *U.S. Decennial Life Tables for 1969–71. Volume II, Number 36, State Life Tables: Ohio.* Rockville, Md.: U.S. Department of Health, Education and Welfare.

————. 1986. *U.S. Decennial Life Tables for 1979–81. Volume II. State Life Tables. Number 36, Ohio.* Rockville, Md.: U.S. Department of Health, Education and Welfare.

National Research Council. 1980. *Estimating Population and Income for Small Areas.* Washington, D.C.: National Academy Press.

Newman, James R. 1956. *The World of Mathematics.* Volume 3. New York: Simon and Schuster.

Norcliffe, G. B. 1983. "Using Location Quotients to Estimate the Economic Base and Trade Flows." *Regional Studies* 17: 161–68.

North, Douglas C. 1955. "Location Theory and Regional Economic Growth." *Journal of Political Economy* 63: 243–58.

Oakland, William H., et al. 1971. "The Economic Implications of Area-Oriented Anti-Poverty Programs." *Journal of Regional Science* 11: 1–13.

Ohio Bureau of Employment Services. 1979. *Workers Covered Under Ohio Unemployment Compensation Law by Industrial Group:* (RS 203.1). Columbus, Ohio: Ohio Bureau of Employment Services.

Ohio Bureau of Employment Services. 1986. *Workers Covered Under Ohio Unemployment Compensation Law by Industrial Group:* (RS 203.1). Columbus, Ohio: Ohio Bureau of Employment Services.

Ohio Department of Health, Division of Vital Statistics. 1972. *Report of Vital Statistics for Ohio, 1970.* Columbus, Ohio: Ohio Department of Health.

————. 1982. *Report of Vital Statistics for Ohio, 1980.* Columbus, Ohio: Ohio Department of Health.

Oppenheim, Norbert. 1980. *Applied Models in Urban and Regional Analysis.* Englewood Cliffs, N.J.: Prentice-Hall.

Park, Se-Hark. 1970. "Least Squares Estimate of the Regional Employment Multiplier: An Appraisal." *Journal of Regional Science* 10: 365–74.

Perloff, Harvey S., et al. 1960. *Regions, Resources and Economic Growth.* Lincoln: University of Nebraska Press.

Pfister, R. L. 1976. "On Improving Export Base Studies." *Regional Science Perspectives* 6: 104–16.

Pfouts, Ralph W., ed. 1960. *The Techniques of Urban Economic Analysis.* West Trenton, N.J.: Chandler-Davis.

Pittenger, Donald B. 1976. *Projecting State and Local Populations.* Cambridge, Mass.: Ballinger.

————. 1977. "Population Forecasting Standards: Some Considerations Concerning Their Necessity and Content." *Demography* 14: 363–68.

————. 1980. "Some Problems in Forecasting Population for Government Planning Purposes." *The American Statistician* 34: 135–39.

Pleeter, Saul, ed. 1980. *Economic Impact Analysis: Methodology and Applications.* Boston, Mass.: Martinus Nijhoff Publishers.

Pratt, Richard T. 1968. "An Appraisal of the Minimum-Requirements Technique." *Economic Geography* 44: 117–24.

Reilly, William J. 1931. *The Law of Retail Gravitation.* New York: G.P. Putnam's Sons.

Richardson, Harry W. 1978a. *Regional and Urban Economics.* New York: Penguin.

————. 1978b. "The State of Regional Economics: A Survey." *International Regional Science Review* 3: 1–48.

————. 1985. "Input-Output and Economic Base Multipliers: Looking Backward and Forward." *Journal of Regional Science* 25: 607–62.

Rosen, H. S., and V. K. Mathur. 1973. "An Econometric Technique Versus Traditional Techniques for Obtaining Regional Employment Multipliers: A Comparative Study." *Environment and Planning* 5: 273–82.

Smith, Stanley K. 1986. "Accounting for Migration in Cohort-Component Projections of State and Local Populations." *Demography* 23: 127–35.

————. 1987a. "Rejoinder." *Journal of the American Statistical Association* 82: 1009–12.

————. 1987b. "Tests of Forecast Accuracy and Bias for County Population Projections." *Journal of the American Statistical Association* 82: 991–1003.

Stevens, Benjamin H., and Craig L. Moore. 1980. "A Critical Review of the Literature on Shift-Share as a Forecasting Technique." *Journal of Regional Science* 20: 419–35.

Stockton, John R., and Charles E. Clark. 1966. *Introduction to Business and Economic Statistics.* Cincinnati: Southwestern Publishing Co.

Terry, Edwin F. 1965. "Linear Estimates of the Export Employment Multiplier." *Journal of Regional Science* 6: 17–34.

Thompson, Wilbur. 1965. *A Preface to Urban Economics.* Baltimore: Johns Hopkins University Press.

Tiebout, Charles M. 1956a. "Exports and Regional Growth." *Journal of Political Economy* 64: 160–64.

————. 1956b. "The Urban Economic Base Reconsidered." *Land Economics* 31: 95–99. (Reprinted in Ralph W. Pfouts, ed. 1960. *The Techniques of Urban Economic Analysis.* West Trenton, N.J.: Chandler-Davis.)

————. 1962. *The Community Economic Base Study.* Committee for Economic Development Supplementary Paper No. 16. New York: Committee for Economic Development.

Ullman, Edward L., and Michael H. Dacey. 1960. "The Minimum Requirements Approach to the Urban Economic Base." *Papers and Proceedings, Regional Science Association* 6: 175–94.

Ullman, Edward L., Michael H. Dacey, and Harold Brodsky. 1969. *The Economic Base of American Cities: Profiles for the 101 Metropolitan Areas over 250,000 Population Based on Minimum Requirements for 1960.* Seattle: University of Washington Press.

———. 1971. *The Economic Base of American Cities*, rev. ed. Seattle: University of Washington Press.

U.S. Bureau of the Census. 1973. *1970 Census of the Population. Volume I, Chapter B, General Population Characteristics, Part 37: Ohio* (PC70(1)-B37). Washington, D.C.: U.S. Government Printing Office.

———. 1975. *The Methods and Materials of Demography*, by Henry S. Shryock, Jacob S. Siegel, and Associates. Third Printing (Rev.) Washington, D.C.: U.S. Government Printing Office.

———. 1977. *Current Population Reports* (Series P-25, No. 701), "Gross Migration by County: 1965 to 1970." Washington, D.C.: U.S. Government Printing Office.

———. 1978. *Current Population Reports* (Series P-25, No. 739), "Estimates of the Population of Counties and Metropolitan Areas: July 1, 1975 and 1976." Washington, D.C.: U.S. Government Printing Office.

———. 1979. *Current Population Reports* (Series P-25, No. 796), "Illustrative Projections of State Populations by Age, Sex and Race: 1975 to 2080." Washington, D.C.: U.S. Government Printing Office.

———. 1981. *1978 Census of Agriculture. Volume I, Geographic Area Series, Part 35: Ohio* (AC78-A-35). Washington, D.C. U.S. Government Printing Office.

———. 1982. *1980 Census of Population. Volume I, Chapter B, General Population Characteristics, Part 37: Ohio* (PC80-1-B37). Washington, D.C.: U.S. Government Printing Office.

———. 1983. *1980 Census of Population. Volume I, Chapter D, Detailed Population Characteristics* (PC80-1-D). Washington, D.C.: U.S. Government Printing Office.

———. 1984a. *Current Population Reports* (Series P-25, No. 952), "Projections of the Population of the United States, by Age, Sex and Race: 1983 to 2080." Washington, D.C.: U.S. Government Printing Office.

———. 1984b. *Gross Migration for Counties: 1975 to 1980* (PC80-S1-17). Washington, D.C.: U.S. Government Printing Office.

———. 1984c. *1982 Census of Agriculture. Volume I, Geographic Area Series, Part 35: Ohio* (AC82-A-35). Washington, D.C.: U.S. Government Printing Office.

————. 1984d. *1982 Census of Agriculture. Volume I, Geographic Area Series, Part 51: United States* (AC82-A-51). Washington, D.C.: U.S. Government Printing Office.

————. 1984e. *1982 Census of Construction Industries: Geographic Area Series; East North Central States* (CC82-A-3). Washington, D.C.: U.S. Government Printing Office.

————. 1984f. *1982 Census of Construction Industries: Industry Series: U.S. Summary* (CC82-I-28). Washington, D.C.: U.S. Government Printing Office.

————. 1985a. *1982 Census of Manufactures: Geographic Area Studies: Ohio* (MC82-A-36). Washington, D.C.: U.S. Government Printing Office.

————. 1985b. *1982 Census of Mineral Industries: Geographic Area Series: East North Central States* (MIC82-A-3). Washington, D.C.: U.S. Government Printing Office.

————. 1985c. *1982 Census of Mineral Industries: Subject Series; General Summary* (MIC82-S-1). Washington, D.C.: U.S. Government Printing Office.

————. 1986a. *Current Population Reports* (Series P-26, No. 84-ENC-SC), "East North Central 1984 Population and 1983 Per Capita Income Estimates for Counties and Incorporated Places." Washington, D.C.: U.S. Government Printing Office.

————. 1986b. *Current Population Reports* (Series P-26, No. 85-52-C), "Provisional Estimates of the Population Counties, July 1, 1985." Washington, D.C.: U.S. Government Printing Office.

————. 1986c. *1982 Census of Manufactures: Subject Series; General Summary* (MC82-S-1, Part 1). Washington, D.C.: U.S. Government Printing Office.

U.S. Bureau of Economic Analysis. 1985a. *1985 OBERS, BEA Regional Projections. Volume I, State Projections to 2035.* Washington, D.C.: U.S. Government Printing Office.

————. 1985b. *1985 OBERS, BEA Regional Projections. Volume II, Metropolitan Statistical Area Projections to 2035.* Washington, D.C.: U.S. Government Printing Office.

————. 1986. *Local Area Personal Income, 1979–84. Volume IV, Great Lakes Region.* Washington, D.C.: U.S. Government Printing Office.

U.S. Bureau of Labor Statistics. 1987. *Employment and Wages: Annual Averages, 1983.* Washington, D.C.: U.S. Government Printing Office.

U.S. International Trade Administration. 1986. *Contribution of Exports to U.S. Employment.* Washington, D.C.: U.S. Government Printing Office.

U.S. Office of Management and Budget. 1987. *Standard Industrial Classification Manual, 1987.* Washington, D.C.: U.S. Government Printing Office.

Community Analysis and Planning Techniques

Williamson, Robert B. 1975. "Regional Growth: Predictive Power of the Export Base Theory." *Growth and Change* 6: 3–10.

Zimmerman, Rae. 1975. "A Variant on the Shift and Share Projection Formulation." *Journal of Regional Science* 15: 29–38.

Index

resident births, definition of, 81
residual net migration estimation
   methods, 91

second-degree curve, 17
sex ratio at birth (*SR*), 84–85
shift-share approach,
   application of, 175–82
   evaluation of, 184–86
special populations, 104
standard deviation, 39–40
standard industrial classification
   (SIC) system, 122–23
stationary population, definition of,
   69
study area (economic base), 117–19

survival rates,
   adjusting, 70
   application of, 55–59, 75–77
   estimating, one-year cohorts, 71–
   73
   estimating, multiple-year cohorts, 73–75
   projecting, 77–78
   survival-rate net migration
   estimation method, 91

value added per employee, ratio of
   (*v,*), 135–36, 156–57
variables, definition of, 9
vital statistics net migration estimation method, 91